HANDBOOK OF
STATISTICAL METHODS IN MANUFACTURING

HANDBOOK OF
STATISTICAL METHODS IN MANUFACTURING

RICHARD BARRETT CLEMENTS

PRENTICE HALL
Englewood Cliffs, New Jersey 07632

Prentice-Hall International (UK) Limited, *London*
Prentice-Hall of Australia Pty. Limited, *Sydney*
Prentice-Hall Canada Inc., *Toronto*
Prentice-Hall Hispanoamericana, S.A., *Mexico*
Prentice-Hall of India Private Limited, *New Delhi*
Prentice-Hall of Japan, Inc., *Tokyo*
Simon & Schuster Asia Pte. Ltd., *Singapore*
Editora Prentice-Hall do Brasil, Ltda., *Rio de Janeiro*

Taguchi Method™ © by American Supplier Institute, Dearborn MI

10   9   8   7   6   5   4   3

Library of Congress Cataloging-in-Publication Data

Clements, Richard Barrett
  Handbook of statistical methods in manufacturing / by Richard
Barrett Clements.
    p.   cm.
  Includes bibliographical references and index.
  ISBN 0-13-372947-8
  1. Production management—Statistical methods. 2. Quality
control—Statistical methods.   I. Title.
TS155.C54 1991   90-7966
658.5—dc20   CIP

ISBN 0-13-372947-8

PRENTICE HALL
BUSINESS & PROFESSIONAL DIVISION
A division of Simon & Schuster
Englewood Cliffs, New Jersey 07632

Printed in the United States of America

Dedicated to
the uncles:
Bill and Dick

CONTENTS

What This Book Will Do for You

Handbook of Statistical Methods in Manufacturing is written for you, the manufacturing professional who wants to use statistical methods effectively, yet does not want to become a statistician.

The manufacturing environment has undergone several dramatic changes recently. The manufacturing engineer is a perfect example of these changes. Twenty years ago, a typical manufacturing engineer had worked with the shop floor equipment and used common sense to solve manufacturing problems. Today, manufacturing engineers are required to have a diverse background in several technical fields to complement their common sense. They may be helping to plan the production schedule one day, and conducting experiments to optimize the manufacturability of a new product the next day.

This massive increase in the complexity of manufacturing means that a single person cannot hope to retain all of the technical knowledge necessary for the job. Therefore, you need a comprehensive library of technical procedures available as the need arises.

This book is one such reference. In almost every aspect of manufacturing there is the need to use statistical reasoning. The recent revival of statistical process control (SPC) is a typical example of how statistical tools are becoming a dominant force in the planning, building, and execution of a manufacturing process. We will discuss SPC in detail in chapter 4. Other technologies, such as just-in-time, quality function deployment, experimental design, and CAD/CAM, all rely in part on the use of statistics. By learning and using new techniques, you help make your company a world-class manufacturer.

You will learn the following specific skills by reading this book:

- You will adopt a common-sense approach to the basic calculations used for statistical reasoning.
- You will learn how to think statistically.
- You will be able to estimate the actual cost of a manufacturing project given a small sample cost data.
- You will be able to estimate the conformance to tolerance for future parts that you manufacture provided with the data from a few production parts.
- You will be able to identify which statistical control chart to apply to a particular manufacturing process.
- You will be able to establish statistical process control for a manufacturing process following a simple six-step process.
- You will be able to calculate Cp and Cpk ratios to describe the capability of your manufacturing processes.
- You will learn how to select the most efficient sample size for the inspection of manufactured parts.

- You will perform a failure mode and effects analysis (FMEA) on one of your company's products.
- You will define the reliability of your machinery and products.
- You will use reliability information to better schedule your preventive maintenance.
- You will learn specific statistical tools that can be used in the implementation of a just-in-time method of production and delivery.
- You will be able to perform a "two-cube experiment" that will test three manufacturing factors at two levels each and thus provide you with valuable design information.
- You will see how the parameters of your production process can be optimized using experimental designs through an exploration of Taguchi's principle of robust designs.
- You will be able to summarize the quality of an entire shipment in just a few minutes given a sample of parts supplied by a vendor company.
- You will learn a simple system for auditing the quality of a system at a vendor's location.
- You will be able to design surveys or focus groups to obtain more information about your customer's needs.
- You will be able to identify safety problems within the factory and in the use of your products using hazard analysis and fault-tree analysis.
- You will be able to organize teams of workers to examine and improve your current manufacturing system using the six-step problem-solving process.
- You will be able to evaluate objectively all possible results of your decisions when faced with a decision where the outcome is uncertain.
- You will learn guidelines on how to make a professional presentation of data to management once you have conducted some statistical studies.
- You will learn the critical issues involved in assuring that the purchase of statistical software is cost-effective.

Most manufacturing professionals have shied away from learning or using statistical tools because of the commonly held belief that they involve complex mathematical calculation. This book demonstrates the fallacy of that belief. Statistics are treated as a form of communication and as a method of examining a situation where little is known to gain usable knowledge.

How this Book Should Be Used

Think of this book as a cookbook. Each statistical method is presented as a recipe. Follow the recipe and you will reap the benefits of statistical analysis.

Completing the formulas should be simple for anyone with at least a high school background in algebra. The definition of each variable is presented with each formula along with a discussion of how the values were obtained. Simple replacement of the variables in the formulas with obtained values will start each calculation. There are no tricks involved, such as having to know some of the laws of statistical theorems. Statistical calculations are meant to be practical tools for professionals, and this book is written in that spirit.

An inexpensive scientific calculator can complete all of the formulas in this book. Such a calculator should be able to raise a number to any power, calculate logarithms, and hold at least one number in memory. It is a further advantage if the calculator can generate random digits. In addition, the serious manufacturing professional should investigate the purchase of computer software that can calculate statistical formulas. Between these extremes, a person with a microcomputer using a good electronic spreadsheet, such as Lotus 1-2-3 or Excel, can duplicate the formulas in this book with little trouble.

Each chapter includes a discussion of when a particular method should be used. Consult this to confirm that the statistical method you have chosen fits a particular application within your company. Each chapter also includes a few cautions and warnings to prevent you from collecting bad data or making an erroneous conclusion.

After each method is introduced, examples are given of its possible application. This should help you to confirm the appropriateness of a method and guide you toward adapting the method to a special situation. For example, chapter 2, "Estimating Production Time and Manufacturing Costs Using Statistical Samples" can easily be used to measure office productivity.

Each statistical method and its related formulas are presented in a step-by-step fashion. The calculation of an average in Chapter 1 is a good example.

There are two pieces of information that must be known to describe any group of data. One is the variation, described later. The other is the average, which describes the arithmetic center of the data points. The statistical name for this type of average is the *mean*. We calculate it with the formula

$$\bar{x} = \frac{\Sigma x}{n}$$

where

$\bar{x}$ = mean
Σx = sum of all the number
n = number of numbers

Example: A production planner is counting the number of skids that are loaded at the end of a powder fill line every hour. After five hours, he has counted the following number of completed skids: 23, 25, 22, 29, and 26. What is the average number of skids filled every hour?

We would solve by adding up the five numbers and dividing by 5.

$$\frac{23 + 25 + 22 + 29 + 26}{5} = 25$$

The result is a mean of 25 skids per hour.

> *Caution:* Although this calculation gives us the average number of skids filled every hour, it reveals nothing about the variation in skid counts. You should calculate a measure of variation whenever an average is calculated. Only with both of these pieces of information can you accurately describe a situation with statistics.

This book is a guide to statistical reasoning. It frees you from having to remember dozens of statistical formulas and rules. Instead, when statistics are called for, you can use this book without fear or hesitation. Thus, you are freed to concentrate more on the problem at hand. After all, statistics should always be seen as one tool among many for solving problems or realizing opportunities.

CHAPTER 1

Making Statistical Problem Solving Easier by Understanding Basic Statistical Techniques

It is interesting to note how many so-called statistical problems in manufacturing are really a failure in communication. In some cases, the people that made decisions were not informed of the numbers involved. In other situations, the focus of a problem-solving effort was lost because no one established a simple measure of performance. Therefore, this book will look at statistical methods as both a tool for problem-solving and as a means of communication.

The problem-solving aspect of statistical methods will be obvious in the repeated examples of using numeric information to describe and perform common manufacturing tasks. The communication aspect will be much more subtle, but always present. The first goal with any statistical task is to make everyone involved aware of the facts. Background information and the use of statistical techniques to portray the magnitude of the situation will be a common first step.

How to Think Statistically

Before using any of the methods described in this book, it is important that you understand the basic nature and use of statistical methods. To do this, you must think statistically: be able to visualize what is occurring in a situation by examining a few numbers that summarize the statistics involved. For example, the average age of students at a local community college is 36 years. You perceive a school made up of only older students. However, the next statistic you read says that 60% of the student body is under the age of 21. Now you see that a large group of older people returning to college has altered the normal composition of young students. Your mind has "seen" an entire college student body by looking at just a few numbers.

Statistics are a form of language. They describe the reality around us through the use of numbers. When used expertly, statistics blend in with our day-to-day language. In contrast, mathematics is a philosophy that both forms and describes realities separate from our own. Math has its own language that very few people understand completely. Thus, the most important rule to remember about statistics is not to confuse their use with the way mathematics are used. The following example illustrates this point.

The equation for a straight line eloquently describes a reality that exists on paper in the language of mathematics. For example, consider the expression,

$$Y = a + bX$$

When discussing the relationship of two statistics, the proper method would be to express your conclusions as a sentence, such as, "I find that the average performance of these two machines differs significantly." Thus, a mathematical expression is improper for the informal situations where statistics are frequently employed.

The preceding example exposes the second nature of statistics: They must be used. Statistical techniques were not developed for an academic pastime. Instead, they are the product of people who wanted to solve real-world problems. For example, many statistical methods developed from the need to make an accurate census of a population. Modern experimental statistics were the results of seeking a faster method for conducting agricultural research. Therefore, the practitioner should always put statistical methods to profitable and practical use.

Statistics should never be used by themselves. Many of the examples in this book may give you the impression that a thorough analysis will solve all problems, but the reality is different. Although the analysis of a situation will provide many answers, the application of the information requires the cooperation of people. Therefore, the practitioner of statistics will often find that marshalling political forces to implement a solution is more problematic than finding the answer.

An example of this situation is the case of the plastic injection molding company that wanted to know why many of its parts were too small in diameter to meet customer expectations. A plastics engineer's examination of the operation revealed that the size of the molds were, on average, two-thousandths of an inch too small for the type of part being produced. The mold had been cut to produce the correct outside diameter, but the shrinkage rate of the plastic resin used was not considered. Most of the work on this particular statistical study actually involved trying to tell top management something they did not want to know; namely that their molds had to be recut, and at great cost. It is in a situation such as this that the user of statistical methods discovers that statistics are indeed just a tool to probe the unknown. Applying statistical knowledge to correct real-world situations requires a host of other skills, including diplomacy in a politically sensitive situation.

The methods described in this book are not presented to make you a statistician. My intention is to give you the ability to use statistical methods intelligently and effectively. If you are a plant manager, you will become a plant manager with strong statistical skills. Practical statistical methods are intended to complement other skills. Only the inexperienced practitioner of statistics allows statistical reasoning to overcome all other forms of thinking.

How to Solve Any Statistical Problem

No matter what statistical problem arises in the manufacturing environment, there are three steps to take as part of seeking a solution:

1. Simplify,
2. Summarize, and
3. Visualize.

In later chapters, you will see these three steps repeated for many problems. The intention is to break down each problem into easily understood elements. In fact, one way to look at the role of the statistician is as a person who reduces a confusing array of information into an easier to understand summary. For example, examining every mortgage written in the United States would overwhelm any one, but reporting that the average mortgage is $95,000 gives you a summary that can be easily compared to specific situations to gain insight.

Step 1: Simplify the problem

A common phrase in both statistics and mathematics is that all problems look complex until they are examined. This is especially true in manufacturing. The continuous demands of the work schedule and quality requirements of today's manufacturing plant rarely allow an individual time to examine a problem.

Therefore, to simplify a problem, two actions are suggested. The first is to examine the actual situation. The method of the statistical summary presented in this chapter and some of the methods in later chapters will encourage you to describe a situation in accurate numbers. Sometimes the mere act of expressing the problem will lead to a solution.

An interesting example of this situation occurred one day in a manufacturing plant that was having periodic problems with one particular machine. A stream of reports to the production engineer showed that every now and then the quality of the parts made by this machine would deteriorate suddenly. As a step toward simplification, the engineer asked the machine operators to note anything unusual happening on the days the machine failed.

Upon examination of these reports, the engineer noticed the comment "high humidity." A walk down to the production area on a rainy day revealed the problem. A leak in the roof was forming a puddle around the machine's control box—the same control box that had a sign reading "high voltage." Therefore, a seemingly complex problem was actually simple to fix. When a puddle formed around the control box, no one dared adjust the machine for fear of electrocution. A simple patching of the roof solved the production problem.

The second action is to remove from a situation all elements that are not immediately necessary. It is important to study the most basic component of a situation when using statistical methods. For example, if the production capacity of a process is too low, the practitioner of statistics studies the basic causes, such as individual machine rates, quality levels, and process capability. Extraneous factors, such as worker morale, pay scales, and management personalities, are excluded. Similarly, the data collected will often involve numbers with many digits. This can create a confusing page of long numbers. Therefore, it is acceptable for a practitioner to simplify data, as long as the simplification is noted and accounted for in future calculations.

Let us examine a specific example. A grinding machine shop is producing precision bearings to a specification of a few millionths of an inch. A measurement of the diameter of five bearings may produce the following readings:

$$0.025001$$
$$0.025003$$
$$0.025000$$
$$0.025001$$
$$0.025002$$

It is easy to imagine that a report with over 100 of these numbers would present an imposing sight. Therefore, you would want to simplify these numbers to make them easier for everyone to understand. This can be done by subtracting 0.0250000 from each number and then multiplying by 1,000,000. This is the same as reporting only the last significant digit,

$$1$$
$$3$$
$$0$$
$$1$$
$$2 \qquad\qquad 0.025 + 0.00000x$$

The data is now easier to read and work with.

When you have coded data to make it simpler, be sure to decode it when you are done. The note at the right in the preceding example is the decoding footnote. It tells you to translate the numbers into millionths and then to add

0.025. For example, the average of these five numbers is 1.4. This would be translated into millionths and added to 0.025. The resulting answer is 0.0250014.

Step 2: Summarize the Problem

The statistical summary is part of almost every statistical procedure and is the focus of most of this chapter. The purpose of the summary is to portray a large numeric database with a few numbers. The summary describes the current situation and is vital for making comparisons between situations or adjustments to a manufacturing process.

For example, a design engineer may wish to change a bottle's shape to make it more resistant to breakage. This effort will be futile unless the engineer already has a good idea of the current strength of the bottle. Without this knowledge, the engineer will be uncertain whether an improvement in strength came from the new design or was by random chance.

Another reason why a practitioner of statistics must summarize many situations is to make the situation clearly understood for all involved. As mentioned earlier, once people understand a problem or task completely, it is easier to mobilize their cooperation. In addition, a summary gives the practitioner a specific goal. If a process creates too much variation in delivery times, then the control of delivery times is a primary goal. When the goal is clear, improvement is easier to achieve.

Step 3: Visualize the Problem

One aspect of statistics that is often overlooked is the visual nature of the analysis. Many of the more complex techniques, as well as all of the simple methods, can be reported visually—usually as a chart or graph. Therefore, this book will frequently advocate summarizing results as an illustration. Such illustrations help you and your audience to better understand the situation by visualizing the information.

For example, some people are aware that a high correlation coefficient means that two factors are strongly associated. However, anyone can understand the association better if they see a scattergram of the data points showing that dots line up into a linear pattern.

Another advantage of using illustrations is that you can conceive of mathematical models to fit to your data. An example is to plot the effect of adjusting a control on a machine against the final yield. A computer is needed to search for the correct curve to fit the response of the machine, but the hand and eye can quickly sketch that same curve on a piece of paper (see chapters 8, 9, and 10 to obtain more information on forecasting and experimental design).

Reviewing the Basics of Statistical Reasoning

Now that we have discussed the nature and basic techniques of using statistical reasoning, let us review how they are used in practice.

Whenever you encounter a situation that seems to require statistical techniques, you should ask the following questions:

1. How can I simplify the number of factors being studied and the data being collected?
2. How should the information I gather be summarized?
3. How can I visually present the results for better audience understanding?

These three questions are the basis of the rest of this chapter.

How to Write a Statistical Report

Any large collection of numbers can be summarized quickly and easily by reporting the following characteristics:

1. the average;
2. the amount of variation;
3. the pattern the data forms.

How to Calculate an Average

An average is also called a *central tendency*. It reports where the "center" of a collection of data is located. However, there are several ways to define the center.

The five numbers in the following chart will be used to explain how to calculate central tendency and degrees of variation. In manufacturing, it is more likely that 30 or more numbers are being used, such as the case of gathering 30 pieces of production for a simple quality capability study. Only five numbers are used here to enable you to concentrate on the concepts being presented.

Let us suppose that you are studying the rate of absenteeism among the press operators at a factory. When an operator does not show up for work, time and money are lost trying to locate a replacement. The figures for this week show the following:

	Number Absent
Monday	3
Tuesday	5
Wednesday	7
Thursday	6
Friday	9

The first piece of information required is the central tendency of the data. There are several types of measures, but we will concentrate on the three types that apply to most manufacturing situations: the mean, the median, and the geometric average.

The Mean

The mean is also called an arithmetic average. It is the type of average that most people think of and use for averaging. The formula is

$$\bar{x} = \frac{\Sigma x}{n}$$

where n = number of numbers

Σx = total of the numbers

$\bar{x}$ = mean

The numbers are added up and then divided by the number of numbers. In the preceding example, the total number of absent operators during the week was 30. When we divide this by the five days of the week, we get a mean of 6.

$$3 + 5 + 7 + 6 + 9 = 30$$

$$\frac{30}{5} = 6$$

The mean represents the mathematically balanced average of the data. If we took a ruler that was 12 inches long, we could balance it at the 6-inch mark. If we then place 1-ounce weights at the 3-, 5-, 6-, 7-, and 9-inch locations, the ruler would continue to balance. The average of 6 represents a balance point for the set of data under study.

In 90% to 95% of the situations involving averages, the mean will work just fine. However, there will be situations where another type of average is required.

The Median

The median is the next most commonly used way to measure central tendency. It is used whenever there are extremes in data. A good application for the median would be the reporting of the average salary within the plant. The bulk of the work force would be below $50,000 a year. However, one or two people may make over a $100,000 annually. These extreme salaries would "throw off" a mean. A mean would sift its balance toward the extreme. Thus, the mean salary could be higher than a typical salary.

The median is the calculation of a typical value of a group of data. It is an average that is unaffected by a few extreme numbers. To calculate a median, you must first put the data into ascending order. In our case, we would sort absentee numbers from the lowest to the highest.

$$
\begin{array}{l}
3 \\
5 \\
6 \quad \leftarrow\text{Median} \\
7 \\
9
\end{array}
$$

To find the median, you select the value that has one-half of the data below it and one-half of the data above it. In our example, that value is 6. Two data points are less than or equal to its value, and two are greater than or equal to its value.

When an even number of data points has been collected, the median will fall between two numbers. When this occurs, the median is found by adding the two numbers together and dividing by 2. Suppose that we had collected 100 numbers and sorted them into ascending order. We would find the median between the fiftieth and fifty-first numbers. If those two numbers were 59 and 63 respectively, the median is calculated as

$$\frac{59 + 63}{2} = 61$$

Thus, the median would be 61. Although no actual value in our set of numbers was 61, this is still reported as the median, or typical value.

The Mode

The mode is the most frequently occurring number. In our example, each number occurs only once, so we have no mode. However, in larger collections of data, a single number may occur more frequently than others. In most cases, this number will occur near the center of the data distribution. Thus, the mode is considered another measure of central tendency.

The Geometric Average

Rates of change have to be averaged differently than other numbers. A typical situation in manufacturing is reporting the average amount of change in a process. For example, each month a productivity report shows the following percent increases in output:

3%
5%
6%
7%
9%

These are the same numbers used in previous averaging examples. The formula for a geometric mean is

$$\sqrt[n]{p_1 \times p_2 \times p_3 \ldots \times p_n}$$

You multiply together a series of nonnegative numbers and take the nth root of the product. The n is the number of numbers used. In our example, the results are

$$\sqrt[n]{3 \times 5 \times 6 \times 7 \times 9} = 5.633\%$$

The answer represents the average percent increase. Notice how it is different than a conventional mean of 6 for these same numbers. The geometric average is averaging change and is unaffected by extreme cases; thus it does not seek a mathematical balance.

In the preceding example, we had to find the fifth root of the product. This is easy to accomplish on a hand-held calculator with the "x of y" function. This key on a calculator requires you to enter the product, press the key, enter the power you want to raise the number to, and then press the equal sign key for an answer. To take a root, you invert the power. In our example, we would enter 1/5th, or 0.20, as the power. This is the same as taking the fifth root of a number. If we wanted the tenth root of a number, we would enter 0.10 to represent the 1/10th value.

Although the geometric mean has limited applications because it is restricted to positive numbers and rates of change, it still serves an important role in manufacturing. Many production reports issued today include percents of increase as mean averages. A geometric mean will tend to give a more accurate picture of the average rate of change as opposed to the conventional mean.

How to Calculate Measures of Variation

Although averages are perhaps the most frequently reported statistics in business reports and the media, by themselves they are practically meaningless. An average tells us only where the center of a data set exists. The critical second piece of information is how much variation there is in the data.

An example illustrates the importance of this information. You may read in the newspaper one day that the average washing machine lasts 10 years. Unfortunately, you know that your company's product usually fails after 8 years. On the surface, this looks like bad news, but we do not know how much variation occurred in the sample that created the 10-year average. If the variation ranged from 1 year to 20, we would not worry as much as finding out that the variation was from 8 to 12 years. The latter case shows your company to be nearly the worst performer. The former case leaves you comfortably in the middle.

There are three common methods for calculating variation: a range, variance, and the standard deviation.

Calculating the Range

A range is the distance between the highest and the lowest number in a data set. Let us return to the numbers used in the averaging examples.

$$
\begin{array}{lll}
3 & & \\
5 & \text{High} = 9 & \\
6 & & 9 - 3 = 6 \\
7 & \text{Low} = 3 & \\
9 & &
\end{array}
$$

The range of the five numbers is 6. Therefore, we can say that these numbers have a mean of 6 and a range of 6. It is important that any average reported is immediately followed with a measure of variation. The two must always go together to give a complete summary of a set of data.

The range represents a measure of variation that is easy to calculate and quick to interpret. However, it is of limited use. Although it tells how far to the extremes a data set reaches, it does not tell about the density of the data points or the variation of the population from which they were drawn. Still, if the range is obviously too large for a particular application, further analysis is unnecessary.

In the preceding example, we examined the amount of absenteeism the plant has been experiencing. If we now take these results to the personnel department, we may find that the range of 6 is too large for making predictions about how many people to have on standby to fill in for missing workers.

Another problem involved with a range is that it only reports the amount of variation in a sample. It says nothing about the population from which it was drawn. The following measures of variation solve that problem.

Calculating a Variance

A range is of limited utility because it fails to give a clear picture of the amount of variation occurring within a set of data. A better approach would be to find some average amount of variation. The variance and standard deviation do just that. Both formulas are based on taking the deviation of each measurement from the mean and averaging the results.

To accomplish this, both formulas must square the deviations to avoid a pitfall; that is, if we averaged the deviations from a mean the total would always be zero. For example, our data had an average of 6.

$$3 - 6 = -3$$
$$5 - 6 = -1$$
$$6 - 6 = 0$$
$$7 - 6 = 1$$
$$9 - 6 = 3$$

$$Total = 0$$

Because a mean balances the data equally around the average, the sum of all deviations has to be zero by definition. To escape this problem the variance codes the data to remove negative signs by squaring each of the deviations.

Deviation	Deviation Squared
3 - 6 = -3	9
5 - 6 = -1	1
6 - 6 = 0	0
7 - 6 = 1	1
9 - 6 = 3	9
	Total = 20

$$V = \frac{\text{Total Deviation Squared}}{(n - 1)}$$

where V = Variance

n = the number of numbers

so

$$V = \frac{20}{5 - 1} = 5$$

The variance is calculated by dividing the total of squared deviations by one less than the number of numbers used. This $n - 1$ is called the degrees of freedom for this equation.

As part of the calculation for a mean, we always divide by the number of numbers. This changes when we make an estimation of variation. Let us take a moment and explain why this is so.

The new divisor is called the degrees of freedom. Mathematically it represents a slight correction in the estimate because we are using an average in our formula to calculate the variance. That is, whenever an estimate is made, we lose a degree of the freedom we had with the information.

An interesting example shows how this happens. Take five empty glasses and set them in a row on a table. Now pick up a pitcher of water and choose which glass you want to fill first. For the first glass you will have complete freedom of choice. In fact, this freedom of choice lasts through the second and third glass you choose to fill. However, once you fill the fourth glass you will lose your freedom of choice. Only one glass is left empty and you must choose to fill it next. Thus, five glasses give you four degrees of freedom—one less than the number of objects.

An Easier Formula for Variance. The preceding formula for variance is easy to calculate as long as too many numbers are not involved. The effort of subtracting and squaring dozens of numbers requires the use of a simpler formula, as follows

$$V = \frac{\Sigma x^2 - \frac{(\Sigma x)^2}{n}}{n-1}$$

where $(\Sigma x)^2$ = square of the total of all measurements

Σx = sum of measurements

Σx^2 = sum of each squared measurement

n = number of numbers

V = variance

The variance is a measure of the magnitude of variation. The higher this number, the more variation is present in the data. However, the results are coded and not directly applicable to the original data and its average. For example, using the data from our absentee example, we find

Number Absent	Numbers Squared	
3	9	
5	25	
6	36	
7	49	
9	81	
30	200	Totals

Applying these totals to the formula, we obtain

$$V = \frac{200 - \frac{(30)^2}{5}}{5 - 1} = 5$$

The answer of 5 is the same as calculated earlier. Thus, we could say that the data has an average of 6 and a variance of 5. However, this does not provide a clear picture of the variation. In our example, the variance is five squared people. Since there is no such thing as a "squared person," the direct utility of the variance is limited. The variance is more widely used in experimental work and in the powerful Analysis of Variance (ANOVA) discussed in chapter 9.

Calculating the Standard Deviation

The standard deviation is a decoding of the variance by taking the square root of its results. This brings the information the variance contains back to the level of the original data and makes the standard deviation the most powerful measure of variation available. This power lies in the fact that a standard deviation does not report variation in the sample, it estimates total variation in the population from which the sample was drawn.

This is done by a combination of calculating the standard deviation and knowing its relationship to the normal curve. We will begin by examining how a standard deviation is calculated.

In a manufacturing environment, the following formula is used for calculating standard deviations from sample information (see chapter 2 for information on proper sampling techniques). There is another formula for calculating the standard deviation when all of the data in a population has been measured. However, in a manufacturing situation it is economically impossible to measure an entire population of objects, thus only the sample formula is presented.

$$s = \sqrt{\frac{\Sigma x^2 - \frac{(\Sigma x)^2}{n}}{n - 1}}$$

Notice how this is merely the foregoing variance formula under the square root function. Taking the results of the foregoing variance calculation, we can find the standard deviation for our example data.

$$s = \sqrt{5} = 2.236$$

The standard deviation of 2.236 represents a standardized unit of variation for the data. The higher this number, the more variation there is in the data. Because this unit of variation is standardized, it allows us to make direct comparisons between sets of data. Many of the techniques in this book rely heavily on the calculation of a standard deviation. In addition, the standard deviation allows us to make estimates of how much variation exists in a population and where the variation occurs. For example, 6 times the standard deviation represents a very accurate estimate of the variation of the population the sample was drawn from.

How to Describe a Pattern of Variation

There are three key pieces of information in any statistical summary: the average, the variation, and the pattern the data forms. The data pattern is found by creating a frequency distribution and a histogram.

Creating a Frequency Distribution

A frequency distribution is formed by sorting our raw data into distinct and equal categories. A category is a specific range of numbers, for example, we could divide our data into groups of five units. The range of numbers we have is from a low of 1 to a high of 48. Thus, we could divide the data into 10 categories of 5 from 0 to 50.

0 to 4
5 to 9
10 to 14
15 to 19
20 to 24
25 to 29
30 to 34
35 to 39
40 to 44
45 to 49

Note how each category is exactly five numbers in size and that no two categories can share the same number.

We can now sort our data into these categories by taking each number and determining in which category it belongs. For example, the first number on our list of parts rejected in every sample of 1,000 is 33. It belongs in the category "30 to 34." Therefore, we place a tally mark after this category to indicate that one of our numbers belongs there. We continue to tally the numbers until we obtain the following distribution of numbers.

Categories	Tally	Count
0 to 4	/	1
5 to 9	/	1
10 to 14	////	4
15 to 19	//	2
20 to 24	/	1
25 to 29	/////	5
30 to 34	////	4
35 to 39	/	1
40 to 44		0
45 to 49	/	1
	Total	20

This summary of the data is called a frequency distribution because it describes how many numbers occur in each category.

If you tip the foregoing distribution on its side you can begin to see the distribution of the numbers. In this case, the numbers are scattered with various frequencies over the entire range. There is a slight clustering near the center, or average, of the distribution. The histogram in Figure 1-1 also shows this pattern.

This "picture" of the data will become vital in many forms of statistical analysis discussed later. For now it is a strong visual presentation of the data collected. The center of the data, its variation, and how it is distributed are becoming visible. To make the picture complete, a histogram is drawn.

Creating a Histogram

The histogram is a visual translation of the frequency distribution. It is a simple bar chart of the frequency of numbers in each of the categories. The categories are marked off along the horizontal axis and the frequencies along the vertical axis. Bars are drawn to show the frequency of numbers per category (see Figure 1-1).

The histogram is a more accurate presentation of the data distribution because it is drawn to scale. The "picture" of the data distribution is the final major piece in a statistical summary. It is always included with an average and a measure of variation.

The average and range of the data is apparent in a histogram. If the data clusters near the center of the histogram, the average can be spotted visually. The beginning and end of the bars mark out the range. The mode is the highest bar on the chart. In short, a lot of statistical information can be presented

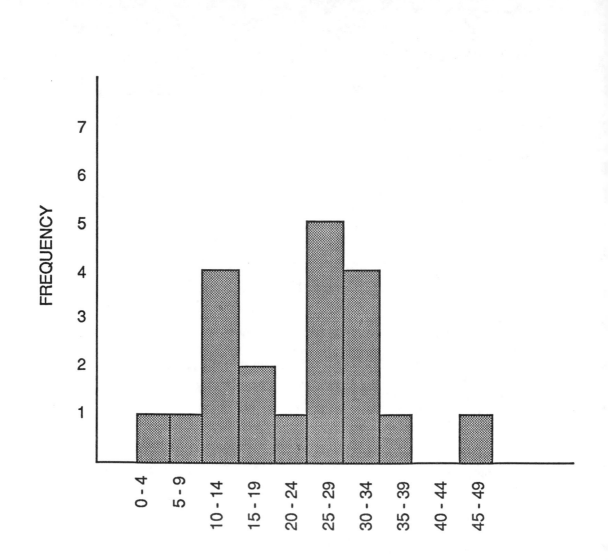

Figure 1-1: A histogram created from a frequency distribution.

with a histogram. In addition, an audience needs little statistical knowledge to divine the same information. Thus, the histogram is a powerful statistical tool.

Finding the Normal Distribution. The real power of a histogram lies in obtaining a particular distribution of the data. Figure 1-2 shows what is called a normal distribution of data. But what makes this particular pattern normal?

The distribution of the numbers is affected by two situations. The first is the random errors that occur in nature. A measuring gauge always has some amount of error in its accuracy. However, these errors tend to balance out, that is, readings larger than the size of a part occur as frequently as readings under the actual size of a part. In contrast, consistent errors will bias the distribution. These errors are called assignable causes because they can be traced to a specific source. For example, if a measurement gauge is improperly calibrated, it might always create a reading under the actual size of a part. The consistency of this error disturbs the normal distribution of error.

When a sample has been randomly sampled and the natural causes of variation are left undisturbed by assignable causes, a distinct pattern called the normal curve is usually created by a histogram. For example, a process that is running to its best ability will have part size errors occurring in a distribution that closely matches the normal curve. Most pieces will be near an ideal size, but a few are either much larger or smaller. Also, when we find a normal curve, we have found a situation that is operating close to its natural state.

Most of the statistics presented in this book assume that a normal distribution of the data is present. A second important aspect of the normal curve is that if the normal curve is not present, then the estimates of average and variation, as well as many other tests, give inaccurate results. Therefore, the histogram is presented in a statistical summary so that you can evaluate the validity of your conclusions.

The normal curve is the model that makes the standard deviation so powerful. Look again at Figure 1-2. Standard deviation cut the curve into 6 pieces. This will happen with any normal curve; 99.7% of its area will always be within plus and minus three standard deviations from the average. (Note: Some people refer to the standard deviation by its Greek symbol sigma; thus they say that plus and minus three sigmas mark out this same range.)

This relationship between the standard deviation and normal curve is unique because 99.73% of the area under the curve represents the variation in the population, not the sample. Returning to the example we calculated previously, 20 numbers have an average of 23.1 and a standard deviation of 11.62. We can add and then subtract three times the standard deviation from the average and determine the actual variation within our population of assembly mistakes.

The Curve of Normal Distribution
and the Area Under the Curve

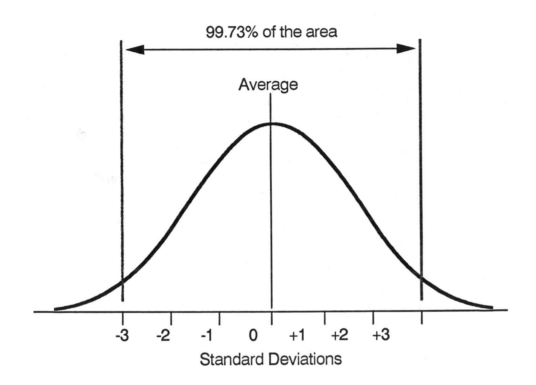

Figure 1-2: The relationship of the normal curve and standard deviations.

$$11.62 \times 3 = 34.86$$

thus

$$23.1 + 34.86 = \ 57.96 \text{ mistakes}$$

$$23.1 - 34.86 = \ \text{less than zero mistakes}$$

Examining this information tells us that this process is capable of making an average of about 23 mistakes out of every 1,000 assemblies. This is the most likely number of mistakes. However, the actual count of mistakes can vary from as few as zero mistakes to as many as 58 mistakes. Because the normal curve accounts for 99.7% of the possibilities between plus and minus three standard deviations, there is almost no chance of more than 58 mistakes being made in any one group of 1,000 parts.

Clearly, information such as this is powerful for production planning and quality assurance. It can also be used for making estimates and evaluating risk. These applications will be presented later in this book. The important point to remember right now is that the normal distribution is what to look for in any data distribution.

Detecting Non-Normal Distributions. In most cases a normal distribution is detected in a statistical summary. However, manufacturing will frequently detect nonnormal distributions. Figure 1-3 shows what a few of these distributions may look like on a histogram.

When a nonnormal distribution is found, steps must be taken to correct the situation. A nonnormal distribution indicates that an assignable cause is systematically interfering with the situation under study. A common example is a machine that is constantly being adjusted without justification. This is the "nervous tweaking" of the machine by an operator. Such actions will frequently cause a skewness in the data distribution. To correct this situation, a statistician will inform the production staff that the machine must run unadjusted while information is being gathered. If adjustments are necessary, they are noted in the final summary.

If a nonnormal distribution cannot be corrected through simple countermeasures, then you can code the data to simulate normality. The probability plotting paper presented in chapter 3 is one of the easiest methods for quickly estimating the correct variation and average for nonnormally distributed data. If you ignored the nonnormal distribution and used the standard formulas for variation and average, your results could be misleading.

Nonnormal distributions can also be evidence of specific actions having occurred in the population sampled. For example, a bimodal distribution is evidence of two activities occurring within a population, such as two filler heads on a machine filling tubes of product to two different amounts. This property of the nonnormal distributions is fully explored in chapter 12.

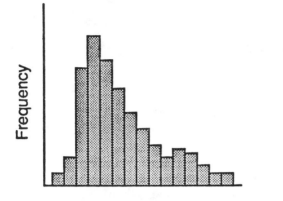

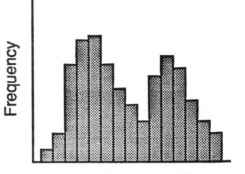

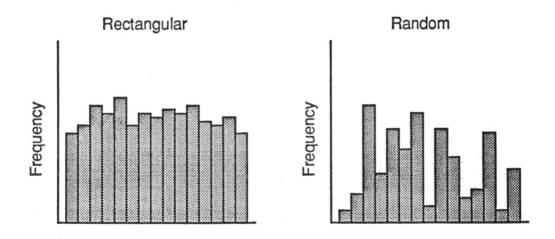

Figure 1-3: Nonnormal distributions.

More Ways to Summarize Information

Data is often collected that is not just a sample from a population. Instead, sales information, rates of change, time-sensitive data, and so on is collected. The common feature is that the normal distribution curve is not important. Instead, other distribution models are important. The summary of this type of data can best be presented visually.

Summarizing Time-Sensitive Data Using a Line Chart

To show the change over time for a set of data, a line chart is recommended. Consider the example of production output figures by month for an entire year. The audience for such information would be looking for trends, seasonal patterns, and any sign of increased performance. Merely listing the figures in columns will not reveal the required interpretations. Instead, you should plot the information on a chart (see Figure 1-4).

In addition to the chart, time-related information can be complemented with a geometric average. The geometric average will report the average amount of change over the reported period of time. For example, our production figures went from 120,000 units in January to 135,000 in December. To calculate the average percent change per month we use the following formula

$$\left[\sqrt[n-1]{\frac{Ending\ Value}{Beginning\ Value}}\right] - 1$$

where n = the number of time periods

Since there are 12 months in a year, we will take the eleventh root of the end-of-the-year figure divided by the beginning-of-the-year figure, or

$$\left[\sqrt[11]{\frac{135,000}{120,000}}\right] - 1 = 0.0108$$

The results are 0.0108. If we multiply this by 100 we will obtain a percentage of 1.08%. In other words, this production line had an average increase of about 1% per month in output.

Showing Rates of Change Using a Cumulative Chart

Another situation apart from a normal distribution is the tracking of projects over time. Reporting how much of the project is completed every day is raw data without a defined distribution. The correct way to portray this information is to create a cumulative line chart.

Consider the example of a project to build a new manufacturing cell in your company. The original estimates stated that 10,000 labor hours would

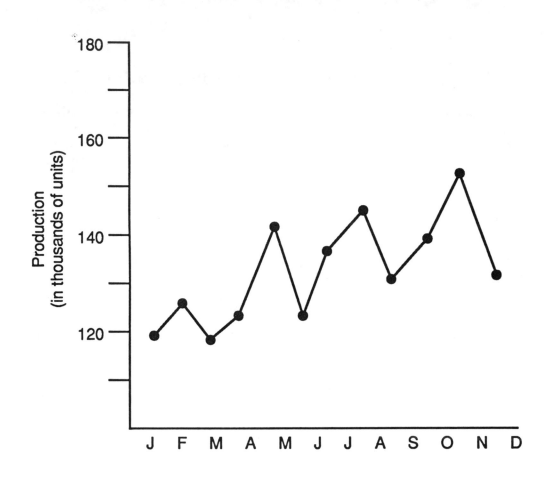

Figure 1-4: A production chart as an example of a line chart.

be required to complete the project, and the finishing date should be April 1. In this case, we will assume that the work will be spread fairly evenly over the life of the project. On our chart we would draw a straight line from zero to 10,000 hours. Across the bottom would be the time from now until April 1. Then actual accumulated involvement times would be plotted across the chart (see Figure 1-5). As the chart progresses, you and others can monitor actual time versus planned time on the project. At the end of the project, you can evaluate the successful use of labor by seeing if the predicted pattern of involvement was closely matched in reality and whether the project was completed on time.

Making Direct Comparisons Using a Bidirectional Bar Chart

Sales and profit figures are easily summarized using a bidirectional bar chart. Such a chart can show both gains and losses. Consider the example of a company president who wants to know the amount of income generated by each department in manufacturing. A bidirectional bar chart can quickly rank and present each department in order of their profitability (see Figure 1-6).

The center line of the chart represents no profit or loss. Bars drawn to the right represent profits, and bars drawn to the left represent loss. By ranking each group according to the magnitude of profit, a clear picture of profit performance emerges.

Portraying Proportions Using a Pie Chart

Budget information is best presented using the pie chart (see Figure 1-7). The pie chart works well whenever there is a fixed resource that is divided among many parties. Budgets are an excellent example. There is only so much money to be used in operations. Which departments get how much money is quickly summarized on a pie chart.

The only difficulty in creating a pie chart (when software is unavailable) is translating percentages into an arc on a circle. The formula to do this is

$$\text{percentage} \times 360 = \text{arc in degrees}$$

For example, a 25% piece of the pie is one-quarter of the full circle. This is confirmed by our formula.

$$0.25 \times 360 = 90 \text{ degrees}$$

In other words, you would draw an arc of 90 degrees to mark out 25% of a pie chart.

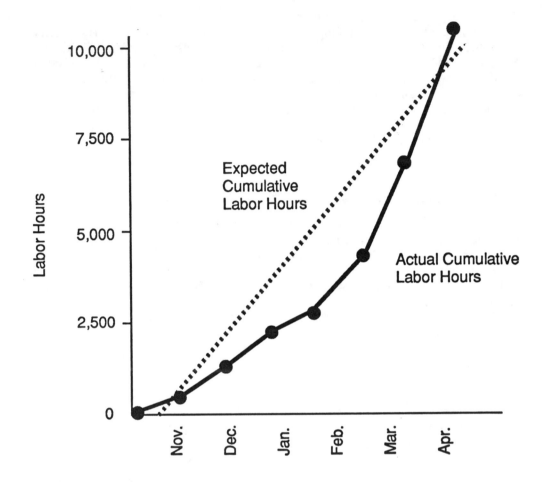

Figure 1-5: An example of a cumulative chart tracking a project.

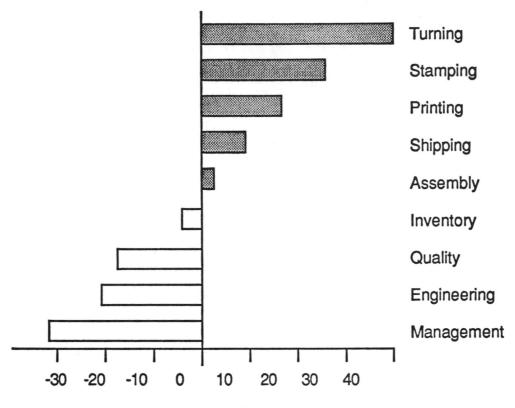

Turning

Stamping

Printing

Shipping

Assembly

Inventory

Quality

Engineering

Management

-30 -20 -10 0 10 20 30 40

Profit or Loss (in millions)

Figure 1-6: A bidirectional bar chart showing both profits and losses.

Budget (by Expenses)

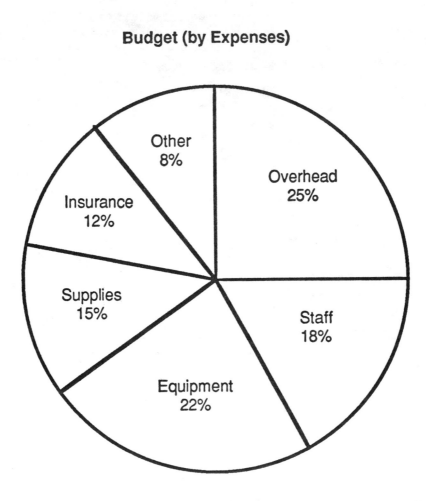

Figure 1-7: An example of a pie chart.

Conclusion

When numeric information is gathered, a statistical summary of the information is needed to make the raw data more understandable. Many of the techniques that are presented later in this book require or imply that a statistical summary be conducted first. Experimentation is an excellent example. We can only learn if a new method tested in an experiment is successful by comparing its effect to the existing normal conditions before the test. Without the vital information provided by a statistical summary, we will not know if a detected improvement is real or a fluke.

CHAPTER 2

Estimating Production Time and Manufacturing Costs Using Statistical Samples

One of the most powerful aspects of statistics is its ability to probe the unknown. Consider the example of 10,000 production pieces being evaluated for their conformance to print specifications. Wouldn't an examination of every part give us the best answer to how well the parts conform? Yes, it would, but it would not be the most efficient method.

Examining a large population of parts requires time, money and personnel. These are usually in short supply in a manufacturing company. Furthermore, most situations do not require a definitive answer. Instead, a good estimate taken from a sample of parts will usually be effective at portraying the quality of the parts within a population. Therefore, by taking a sample and estimating the parameters of the population, we are usually using the most efficient means available.

It is possible to make a good estimate from only a few representative members of a population. Sampling done well has a strong ability to reflect accurately the characteristics of a larger population. In situations where testing is destructive or the cost of inspection is high, a small sample is obviously cost-effective.

In this chapter we will examine how a sample is taken, how to form estimates based on the sample data, and how to pick a sample size to maximize the efficiency of your estimates.

The Basic Principles of Sampling

The first step in sampling is to identify the population involved. A population is defined as all of the members under study. For example, all of the products produced by your company in a single day can be considered a population. Likewise, every time movement by an employee, every penny in the accounting budget, every word in a proposal, and every product returned to your company are all examples of populations.

The specific characteristics of a population are called parameters. For example, the central tendency of a population is called the mu (μ), a Greek letter. The amount of variation in a population is represented by the lowercase sigma (σ). These values are fixed and generally unknown.

The characteristics of a sample are called statistics. For example, we will use x-bar ($\bar{x}$) to represent a mean and s to represent a sample standard deviation.

The central idea behind estimations is to make statements about the population parameters based on data gathered using sample statistics. Thus, if you want a best guess of the overall quality of a production run, you would sample the parts and use the information to make your statements. However, the first step in the process of estimating is to take a good sample. There are basically two ways to sample, randomly and nonrandomly.

HOW TO TAKE A RANDOM SAMPLE

A random sample means that each member of the population has an equal chance of being chosen.

To draw a random sample you will need a sequence of random numbers. These can be obtained from hand-held calculators with a random function, some computer programs, and by using the RND command in the BASIC programming language. For example, the following random numbers were generated using a statistical software package.

.4404

.3330

.1598

.3036

.4114

.1408

.1412

.1250

.5752

.1575

A series of numbers, such as these, are then multiplied to fit the sample size you wish to obtain. For example, if you wanted to draw a sample of 10 parts from a production run of 100 parts, you would read the last two digits of each number. That would tell you to sample parts number 4, 30, 98, 36, 14, 8, 12, 50, 52, and 75. That would be your random sample.

How to Draw a Small Random Sample from a Large Number of Production Parts

If you needed to draw a sample of 10 parts from 800, you would multiply each random fraction by 800. For example, the first sample would be calculated as

$$.4404 \times 800 = 352.32$$

You would round this number off to 352 and select the 352nd part. You repeat this process until 10 unique numbers are selected. If you repeat a previously obtained value, delete the answer and try the calculation again.

In some cases, merely randomizing your sample will not be adequate. This is especially true in situations where distinct groups exist within a population. In those situations you need to stratify your sampling. In other words, you divide your sampling plan into smaller groups proportional to how your population is stratified. Each of these subgroups is then randomly sampled. This preserves the representativeness that is so important in sampling.

How to Take a Stratified Random Sample to Measure Worker Satisfaction

Consider the example of sampling worker satisfaction. Assume that you have developed a short survey to sample each employee's level of satisfaction. You notice that 80% of the employees are earning under $25,000 a year. Therefore, you may want to stratify your sample to assure that each level of income is equally represented in the sample. For example, the percentage of workers may be distributed across the following income levels.

Income	Percent
0-15,000	15
15,000-25,000	65
25,000-50,000	15
50,000+	5

In this example, you would randomly select 15% of your sample from the first group, 65% from the second group, and so on. Each group's samples are drawn randomly, but steps are taken to assure equal representation.

Another method of keeping a sample representative is to sample systematically. For example, you may wish to audit the purchase orders by randomly sampling 5% of the orders for examination. If the purchase orders are filed by date, a strict random sample might leave large gaps in the dates examined. Therefore, you would randomly sample each month's orders.

HOW TO TAKE A NONRANDOM SAMPLE

Nonrandom methods of sampling are also widely used in industry and can obtain valuable information. However, when a nonrandom sample is drawn, the ability to measure the reliability of the sample is lost. In some situations, this is not a problem, but in the majority of applications this loss is unacceptable.

A nonrandom sample involves a person making the direct selection of the members of a population to be tested. Panel tests and many opinion surveys rely on volunteers for their information. The fact that the sample is comprised only of people that would volunteer for a survey makes the sample nonrandom. At the same time, when carefully supervised and confirmed, such survey methods have proven to be remarkably accurate.

In the production area it may be necessary to estimate the capability of a machine. As a preliminary study, you might take the first 30 pieces produced for a new part number. These 30 pieces are your sample. This nonrandom approach saves time and effort as opposed to a random sample taken over a longer period of time. However, you have sacrificed the ability to evaluate the performance of the machine over time.

How to Improve Your Statement About a Population Parameter by Obtaining a Point Estimate

Once data is collected through sampling, estimations can be formed. There are two types of estimates: the point estimate and the interval estimate. The point estimate is the single value used to estimate a parameter of the population. For example, if you sampled 10% of the employee records and found an average age of 33 years, then 33 years of age is the best estimate of the average age of all employees.

An interval estimate would state a range where the actual parameter of the population is likely to exists. We will examine how these interval estimates are calculated later in this chapter.

How to Calculate a Point Estimate for the Average Cost of Scrap

The following example illustrates how a point estimate can be calculated. Assume that you are trying to estimate the average cost to scrap one fully assembled unit of production. To find the cost, the accountant needs to add together the following information:

1. the cost to produce the unit;
2. the cost to sort out one defective unit;
3. the cost to document and scrap the unit;
4. the loss to productivity because a good part was not made.

This list of costs will vary by situation and the philosophy of the accounting system used by a company. We will assume that 30 defective units were randomly selected from production runs of varying sizes and that the costs were calculated for each unit. The resulting data is

$99.60	96.70	91.40
100.30	99.90	92.30
99.80	102.00	96.00
100.30	90.30	94.50
100.40	96.50	93.10
98.60	97.00	90.00
101.40	93.10	92.90
99.90	101.30	96.00
98.40	92.70	96.80
97.80	92.00	97.00

Total = $2,898.00

The best point estimate for a sample is to calculate the mean. In this case, the mean is $96.60 ($2,898.00/30 = $96.60). In other words, the most likely cost for scrapping any unit is $96.60.

A sample average is the best guess of the true average of a population. A randomly drawn sample from an unknown population will tend to mimic the population from which it is drawn. Thus, the central tendency of the sample will tend to estimate the central tendency of the population.

To increase the accuracy of an estimate you would need to increase the sample size. However, this presents you with a dilemma. As you increase the sample size, you also increase the time and costs associated with sampling. Thus, your efficiency is decreasing. Therefore, you must strike a balance between the accuracy you desire and the realities of the situation. After we review how to create an estimate, we will examine the method used to pick an efficient sample size.

How to Improve Your Statement About a Population Parameter Using an Interval Estimate

With a point estimate you specify a single value as your estimate. Chances are slight that your single value estimate is actually the value of the population parameter. To improve your statement about the population parameter, you could state a range where the actual parameter most likely lies. This stating of a range of possible variables is called an *interval estimate*. For example, we might say that the average size of a population of parts is between 12.00 and 12.05 inches in total length.

Our key assumption in making an interval estimate is that the original population data forms a normal curve. When this is true, the sample data will mimic the normal curve. Thus, you could use the area under a normal curve to describe the probability of a population average occurring within a specific range.

The range that we state the population parameter is within is called the *confidence interval*. The points at each end of the range are called *confidence limits*. The amount of confidence we have in an interval estimate is called the *degree of confidence*. For example, using the data from the preceding scrap cost example we can state a range of values around the average scrap cost of $96.60 where we have 95% confidence the true population average exists.

This is possible because the variation in averages with repeated samples have their own measure of variation, called the *standard error*. The standard error can be estimated with a single sample. The sample size must be 30 or higher for the following formula to produce an accurate estimate.

$$S_{\bar{x}} = \frac{\sigma}{\sqrt{n}}$$

where $S_{\bar{x}}$ = standard error of an average
        n = sample size
        σ = population standard deviation

Returning to our example data on the cost to scrap a single unit, we will assume the standard deviation of the population to be $3.59434, or $3.59. To calculate the standard error of the estimate

$$S_{\bar{x}} = \frac{\$3.59434}{\sqrt{30}} = \$0.6562337$$

Thus, the standard error is 0.656. This figure is then used in the confidence limit formula to create the interval estimate for the population mean. To create the confidence interval, we need to find the area under the curve that corresponds to our degree of confidence. For example, if we wish to find the value for 0.95 degrees of confidence (95%), we would look up the Z-value on a table of area under the normal curve (see Appendix A). To make this process easier, the most commonly used values are presented in Table 2-1.

The formula for the confidence interval is

$$C.I._{0.95} = \bar{x} \pm Z \cdot \left(\frac{s}{\sqrt{n}}\right)$$

where $\bar{x}$ = sample average
        Z = Z-value from the table or Appendix A
        $\frac{s}{\sqrt{n}}$ = standard error

In our example, we are searching for the 95% confidence limits on the estimate. To find these we must multiply the standard error by 1.96. The constant of 1.96 is obtained by looking up the 95% area under the curve limits on Table 2.1.

Table 2.1 Commonly Used Z-values for Interval Estimates

Confidence	Limiting Constant
90%	1.645
95%	1.960
98%	2.326
99%	2.576
99.9%	3.291

Inserting the 1.960 constant into the confidence formula results in the following calculations.

$$C.I._{0.95} = \$96.60 \pm 1.96 \left(\frac{3.59434}{\sqrt{30}} \right)$$

$$= \$95.31 \text{ and } \$97.89$$

The high figure of $97.89 represents the top confidence limit of the interval estimate we are forming. The $95.31 figure represents the lower confidence limit of the same interval. Thus, this series of calculations has given us two numbers to describe our interval estimate. Specifically, we would say that we have 95% confidence that the true population average cost for scrapping a single unit is between $95.31 and $97.89.

The information created is of great value to you. Not only can you report that the most likely cost of scrapping a unit of production is $96.60, you can also report that the actual average cost may go as high as $97.89 per unit or as low as $95.31. Thus, a best-case/worst-case estimate is available. In addition, you can describe the risk involved in using this information. With 95% confidence, your figures include a 5% risk of being wrong. In most management decisions, a 5% risk is seen as acceptable.

What to Do When You Have to Estimate Using a Small Sample or the Population Standard Deviation Is Unknown

Up to this point, we have assumed that a sample size of thirty had been taken. In our scrap cost example, thirty pieces of information were sampled. However, there will be many instances where a small sample will have to be used. Statisticians call any sample of less than thirty pieces "small" because the mimicking of the normal distribution is unlikely to happen with fewer bits of data.

For samples under 30 units, another statistical technique is employed called *small sample statistics*. To illustrate the effective use of a small sample, we will again look at scrap costs, but this time only 10 pieces of information will be sampled.

Cost
$96.70
99.90
102.00
90.30
96.50
97.00
93.10
101.30
92.70
92.00

Total = $961.50
Average = $96.15
Standard Deviation = $4.06

Estimating the Cost of Scrap Using Small Sample Statistics

When small samples are drawn from a population, small sample statistics have to be employed. Any sample with fewer than 30 members is considered a small sample. The point estimate remains the sample average, but the constant used in the confidence interval formula is different. In a small sample situation, you replace Z-values from a normal curve with *t*-values from a *t*-distribution curve.

The *t*-distribution curve is actually a family of curves. Each resembles the normal curve. Data points cluster near the average and have symmetry. However, the curves become wider and flatter as the sample size decreases. Thus, a *t*-distribution widens interval estimations due to the lesser amount of information in a small sample.

To find the correct *t*-value to insert into the following confidence limit formula, you must first calculate how many degrees of freedom are available in the sample data. In the case of making an interval estimate, there is one less degree of freedom than the sample size ($df = n - 1$).

$$C.I. = \bar{x} \pm t \cdot \left(\frac{S}{\sqrt{n}} \right)$$

To find the correct *t*-value we refer to Appendix B. Across the top of the table are the confidence levels. The confidence levels depend on whether you are estimating the area under one tail of the distribution, or both tails of the distribution. Because an interval estimate is made both above and below the sample average, a two-tail model is used. Therefore, the confidence level for an interval estimate should be read from the two-tail row.

We now select the 95% confidence level. This is the second column of *t*-values. We next go down this column to the row representing the nine degrees of freedom for our sample (*df* = 10 − 1). The value we find is 2.262. This is inserted into the confidence limit formula.

$$C.I._{0.95} = \$96.15 \pm 2.262 \left(\frac{4.06}{\sqrt{10}} \right)$$

$$= \$99.05 \text{ and } \$93.25$$

The resulting interval estimate is from $99.05 to $93.25. Notice how this is slightly larger than the original estimate made using the values from a normal curve. Also, note how the average of $96.15 is very close to the 30 piece sample average of $96.60.

Using Both Point and Interval Estimates in a Time-motion Study

Consider a second example of a small sample and calculate both a point and interval estimate of the population's mean at the 90% confidence level.

Assume that a time-motion study is examining a random sample of workers for the time it takes them to complete a complex assembly. The following information is reported in minutes.

$$
\begin{array}{r}
41.2 \\
56.7 \\
46.8 \\
56.1 \\
58.2 \\
21.8 \\
78.2 \\
47.5 \\
18.5 \\
6.9 \\
\end{array}
$$

Total = 431.9

A close examination of these numbers reveals a wide variation. Obviously, the time-study person would be curious about the 6.9-minute completion time and what method this individual is using. After accounting for this outlier the central consideration in this study is the average assembly time to plan for the average worker.

The first step is to form the point estimate by calculating a sample average. In this case we divide the total by the sample size (431.9/10 = 43.19) to obtain a point estimate of 43.19 minutes. This is the most likely time to complete the task for an average worker. However, the average experience on the factory floor could be considerably different. The interval estimate can assess both the amount of possible variation between the plan and actual experience, as well as the risk in the estimate.

The standard deviation for the sample data is 21.65 minutes. Plugging that information into the standard error formula results in an answer of 7.22 minutes.

$$S_{\bar{x}} = \frac{21.65}{\sqrt{10-1}} = 7.22$$

The t-value for our interval estimate is found in the 90% confidence column at nine degrees of freedom. That value is 1.833. Now we have all of the numbers needed to complete the interval estimate.

$$C.I._{0.90} = 43.19 \pm 1.833 \cdot \frac{21.65}{\sqrt{10-1}}$$

$$= 56.42 \text{ and } 29.96$$

Thus, the actual average time for completion could range anywhere from 56.42 minutes down to 29.96 minutes. This is a range of 25 minutes, and there is still a 10% chance for error. A production planner or time-motion person would realize that the quick sample of 10 workers has revealed that there is too much variation, and countermeasures have to be taken. One possibility would be to train the test subjects on a standard method of assembly and sample their times again.

How to Make an Estimation Statement about Variation in a Population

In some manufacturing situations it will be necessary to sample a large population and estimate the amount of variation. For example, quality and engineering requirements may demand that production pieces be consistent with tolerance ranges. Audit procedures may require that the variations in sampled pieces from one process be compared to the pieces from a similar process operated by a vendor.

In cases such as these it is possible to make both point and interval estimates of the amounts of variation. For example, the sample standard deviation is assumed to represent the standard deviation of the population from which it was drawn. Returning to our data from the time-motion study, we found a standard deviation of 21.65 minutes. We would then assume that the general population of all workers would also have a standard deviation in their times of 21.65 minutes.

To obtain an interval estimate of these time variations, we use the variance as a unit of measurement and the chi-square distribution as a model. The variance is merely the square of the standard deviation. In our example data, the square of 21.65 minutes would be 468.7225. This reflects the magnitude of variation.

The chi-square distribution is a heavily skewed distribution representing how variances distribute themselves when repeated samples are taken. (The skewness makes sense when we recall that a variance has a difficult time reaching zero, but can easily obtain large numbers.) To find the correct chi-square value, we use a procedure similar to that for the t-values. Appendix C contains the chi-square values for small and large samples.

The first step is to choose the level of confidence for the interval estimate. Assume a confidence level of 95%. Since this leaves a total of 5% in two separate tails of the distribution, we divide the error in half and add it to the 95%. This results in 97.5% to describe the limit of one tail of the distribution and 2.5% to mark the other limit. The values for these two number are found in Appendix C at the ninth degree of freedom row ($df = n - 1$). The two values are 19.02 and 2.70. These are inserted into the interval estimate formula for variance.

$$\frac{n \cdot s^2}{\chi^2_{\frac{\alpha}{2}}} < \sigma^2 < \frac{n \cdot s^2}{\chi^2_{1-\frac{\alpha}{2}}} = \frac{10 \cdot 21.65^2}{19.02} < \sigma^2 < \frac{10 \cdot 21.65^2}{2.70}$$

where $\chi^2_{\frac{\alpha}{2}}$ = chi-square of the right tail

$\chi^2_{1-\frac{\alpha}{2}}$ = chi-square of the left tail

The resulting interval estimate tells us that the population variance has a 95% chance of occurring between 246.44 and 1,736.01. The square roots of these variances would tell us that the standard deviation for the population of time-motions could be between 15.7 and 41.7 minutes.

This information is helpful for comparing variations or for comparing a single variation against a standard, such as tolerance. As we shall see in chapters 9 and 10 on experimentation, this is the basis for the analysis of variance, which also represents one of the most powerful tools of analysis in manufacturing engineering.

How to Make Estimation Statements
When Working with Proportions

Proportions are the decimal representation of percentages. In other words, a proportion of 0.60 is 60%. The decimal version is used in calculation for both ease and clarity.

Suppose that out of a work force of 500 employees, 25 were absent today. What proportion of the work force is absent? To find out, we would divide the number absent by the total number of employees.

$$\frac{25}{500} = 0.05$$

The proportion absent is 0.05. To convert this to a percentage, we would multiply by 100.

$$0.05 \times 100 = 5\%$$

In other words, there is a 5% absenteeism.

There are many circumstances in manufacturing where proportional data is gathered. A few of the many examples would include such data as percent of sales, percent scrap, ratio of supervisors to hourly workers, and absenteeism.

To make point and interval estimates, a new set of statistics is used. The point estimate is created by adding up all of the cases of a specific event and dividing it by the total number of all events. The following example simplifies this definition.

Estimating the Accuracy of Pick Orders in the Inventory Area

Suppose that an inventory clerk tracked the number of pick orders that resulted in an error in stock placement. These figures were gathered daily and compared to the total number of pick orders sampled and audited each day.

	Number of Orders	Orders with Errors
	120	7
	150	19
	200	8
	180	6
	130	11
Total	780	51

To obtain a point estimate of the proportion of errors occurring in the population of pick orders we would divide the total errors found by the total number of orders audited.

$$\frac{51}{780} = 0.0654$$

This is 6.54% of the orders. To obtain an interval estimate we would use the following formula.

$$C.I._{0.95} = p \pm Z \cdot \sqrt{\frac{p(1-p)}{n}}$$

where p = proportion of errors
$1 - p$ = proportion correct
n = total of samples sizes
Z = value from area under curve table (Appendix A, or Table 2-1)

Thus, we can determine the 95% confidence range of where the actual population proportion lies by using the constant 1.96 for Z. The proportion of correct orders is found by $1 - p$, or $1 - 0.0654 = 0.9346$. Inserting these numbers into the equation,

$$C.I._{0.95} = 0.0654 \pm 1.96 \sqrt{\frac{0.0654 \times 0.9346}{780}} = 0.0827 \text{ and } 0.0480$$

The results tell us that we have 95% confidence that the population proportion lies somewhere between 0.0827 and 0.0480. As percentages, this would be between about 8.3% and 4.8%. Thus, we find that a sample of order picks taken on any normal day could find between 4.8% and 8.3% of the orders in error. Information such as this would indeed be valuable to an inventory department interested in first measuring, and then improving the performance of their stocking accuracy. If a daily audit found more than 8.3% of the orders in error, corrective action would be required. If fewer than 4.8% were found, then an improvement has been detected and it should be exploited.

Evaluating the Cost-Effectiveness of Estimations and Sample Sizes

Estimations rely on sampling a large population to probe its unknown characteristics. As we have seen in the preceding discussion, and has been demonstrated repeatedly in practice, a small sample can effectively measure a larger population. Because the principles of sampling and estimation work so well in practice, they represent large cost reductions over the alternative of measuring every member in a population. As we shall see in chapter 5 on quality assurance, sampling and estimation make it possible to assess the quality of a population of parts that would cost a small fortune to sort and examine.

Another savings represented by estimating is the increase in work effectiveness. The planners, supervisors, technicians, and engineers that have to sample to obtain information can select the level of confidence they can have in their results. This leads directly to selecting the smallest and most cost-efficient sample size to obtain the information needed (see chapter 5).

Finally, there are many tasks to perform in manufacturing that cannot be measured completely. Take the example of time studies. The idea is to study the time and motion components of a task and design more efficient work methods. If all times and motions used to complete a production run were measured, you would have an accurate set of useless information because the task is over. Only by sampling at the beginning of a task can you make estimates for later improvements.

How to Select the Proper Sample Size for an Estimate

To select the proper sample size, you must make a few decisions. The first is how much error you can tolerate in your final estimate. Specifically, how far can your point estimates and interval estimate be from the actual parameter values? The next decision is how to estimate the standard deviation of the population. This can usually be done using a small pilot sample of the population. The final decision is how much confidence you will be using in your estimates. The following example illustrates the process of selecting the proper sample size.

How to Select the Proper Sample Size for Measurements of a Steel Shaft

You are auditing the quality of a steel shaft. A critical dimension is the outside diameter of the shaft at the location where a piston rod is connected. The blueprint specifications call for an outside diameter of 1.000 inches.

You decide that you can tolerate an error in the estimate up to 0.001 inches. In your estimates, you want to be 95% confident in the results. A small sample of parts obtained a standard deviation of 0.002 inches. You decide to use this as an estimate of the population's standard deviation. The formula to complete is

$$n = \left(\frac{Z \cdot s}{E} \right)^2$$

where s = estimate of the population's standard deviation
n = sample size calculated
E = tolerable error
Z = the Z-value for your confidence factor

Using the information in this example, you calculate the needed sample size as follows:

$$n = \left(\frac{1.96 \times 0.002}{0.001} \right)^2 = 15.37$$

Rounding this number up to the next highest whole number ensures the proper sample size is selected. In this case, we need to sample 16 shafts to get the information we need for our estimate.

This method of sample-size determination should be used whenever possible. However, when the necessary data for performing the calculation is hard to obtain, you can still use the "minimum of 30" rule of thumb mentioned earlier in this chapter.

How to Determine the Proper Sample Size When Proportions Are Used

You have been assigned the task of measuring the overall scrap rate for a particular department. You suggest to your boss that instead of paying a full-time inspector to review every part made, a sample can be drawn by a part-time inspector. This should save money for the company. However, your boss tells you that the estimates from the sample should be accurate within plus or minus 2%.

An investigation of the past scrap reports shows that the department has averaged 15% scrap rates. You still want to use the 95% confidence figure. Thus, the formula to use is

$$n = p \, (1 - p) \left[\frac{Z}{E} \right]^2$$

where, p = historic percentage
E = tolerable error
Z = Z-value for your confidence factor

Filling in the formula using the available data,

$$n = 0.15 \, (0.85) \left[\frac{1.96}{0.02} \right]^2 = 1{,}224.51$$

Thus, you need to draw a sample of 1,225 parts each day to obtain an estimate of scrap that meets the aforementioned criteria.

Conclusion

The principles of estimation will resurface in the remaining chapters. Experiments, studies, and investigations all rely on accurate estimates. Therefore, you should take care to learn how to sample properly and calculate estimates quickly.

CHAPTER 3

Evaluating the Quality Potential of a Process by Conducting Statistical Studies

Manufacturing is a series of production processes. Consider the example of a 35-mm camera. Several different machining processes produce the gears, springs, lenses, electronics, and other parts of the camera. One of the last processes of production is the assembly of the parts. If any piece is of low quality, then the assembled camera will not work properly. But how can a company determine the quality of each part before it is assembled? How do they know which dimensions and other characteristics are important? How can they prevent problems, while also saving money?

The first step in finding answers to all of these questions is a process capability study.

How to Perform a Process Capability Study to Determine the Inherent Variation in a Process

Continuing with the camera example, each part of a camera has many dimensions, but only one or two of these dimensions on each part are critical to the successful operation of the finished product. These are called the *critical characteristics* of the parts. By studying the average size and the amount of inherent variation in these critical characteristics, you can accurately predict the quality of future production runs, evaluate the cost of quality for the process, and adjust a process for optimal quality. And, if all of these actions are done with the overall strategy of production in mind, you can save considerable money.

To understand how a process capability study is conducted, it is necessary to examine a few definitions with subtle differences. These differences will determine the type of capability study you need to perform.

A process capability study is really a prediction of process adequacy. This prediction is not formed by directly studying the variation in the process, but by examining the variation the process creates in the product.

What a capability study does is to randomly sample production parts from a specific process and statistically examine the variation between, and sometimes within, parts. This data is your estimate of process variation. This amount of inherent process variation is compared to the corresponding specifications. For example, if a milling machine must produce parts to within 0.010 inches of optimal dimensions and we find that a particular milling machine creates parts to within 0.001 inches, we would say that this process is very capable. Thus, the central question in a capability study is whether a process can exceed tolerances for a specified dimension.

There are two basic types of capability studies. The first is called a *process performance study*. It measures capability while many sources of variation are present, such as different operators, different lots of materials being used, settings on the machine adjusted as needed, and so on. This type of capability study measures the full range of inherent variation the process will probably experience during normal production runs. This inherent variation is described by a range of six standard deviations after statistical control is achieved.

The second type of capability study is the *machine capability study*. It measures the variation in the process after all assignable causes are eliminated from the process. An *assignable* cause is a nonrandom, identifiable source of variation, such as the use of an incorrect tool, quality differences in raw material, and unnecessary changes in machine settings.

The Benefits of Conducting a Capability Study

Too often in manufacturing it is believed that once a tolerance is set for a part, the tolerance will somehow keep the products within conformance. A world-class manufacturer does not rely on engineering to control the size of parts. Instead it studies the performance of its production processes to assure that quality targets will be met. This desire to "know what's happening during production" by using capability studies results in several benefits.

1. The capability studies highlight which processes are able to meet engineering requirements and which are not capable. This allows the top management of the company to target specific production areas for improvement.

2. By predicting the process's inherent variation, you can be assured of holding a tolerance in advance of the production run.

3. The capability study will find sources of potential quality problems so that you can implement countermeasures to prevent the problem.

4. You can use the data from a capability study to schedule parts with tight tolerances to capable machines.

5. If the capability samples are studied over time, effects such as tool wear can be discovered and quantified to permit predictable and efficient machine adjustments.

6. Occasionally, a capability study will reveal a machine that is in need of repair.

7. You can use a capability study to evaluate new machinery before purchase.

8. You can also use capability study data to establish control limits on SPC charts.

When to Use a Capability Study

Capability studies require at a minimum several hours of personnel time. Therefore, a capability study should be used where and when it is needed most. You should resist the temptation to study everything. For example, if your shop has 16 screw machines, then study them first as a group to see if machine-to-machine variation is a problem.

Use the following guidelines to determine when to conduct a capability study.

1. Under the quality requirements of a modern manufacturing plant, a capability study is required for any new process or product. Usually a process performance study is conducted after statistical control has been demonstrated for 30 days.

2. A capability study is used to evaluate the potential of a new machine before it is purchased. Today, several machine suppliers allow potential customers to run 30 pieces of actual production parts on a new machine. Then the customer can evaluate whether the machine will meet the tolerances called for by their engineers.

3. For existing processes under statistical control, capability studies are conducted on a schedule by the priority of the process. The schedule is usually based on the following three-level priority system:

Level 1: Customer quality requirement demands data collection at the process.

Level 2: No customer demand, but strong internal demand for information from the process.

Level 3: No external or internal demand, but process information could be useful.

4. Often a capability study will be conducted on a process before experimentation. An industrial experiment requires that normal behavior of a process under study be documented before the experimenter begins to manipulate controlling factors. Therefore, when experimenting, it is not unusual to study the characteristic part or process that originally escaped the standard capability tests.

How to Conduct a Process Variation Study—A Demonstration of the Basic Steps Used in Any Process Capability Study

For illustrative purposes, suppose that what we are sampling is a fan motor cover made by a plastic injection molding process. A critical characteristic of this part during the molding process is its weight. The ideal cover should contain 175 grams of plastic resin. If too much resin is injected, it will force its way out of the mold and cause flashing. This is costly and time consuming to remove. On the other hand, if too little resin is injected the piece will be incomplete and will have to be scrapped. This, too, is very expensive.

Therefore, the company is critically interested in whether this process can maintain resin weights close to the 175-gram requirement. Through testing and research, the plastic engineers have determined that to make a successful cover with no flashing the resin shot into the mold must be within 2 grams of the 175-gram target value. A variation study will evaluate whether this particular process can perform to these requirements, as well as predict the future performance of the process.

The first step is to establish statistical control of this process. Statistical control shows that the process is experiencing its inherent variation, without assignable causes of variation occurring.

The following general steps are used in a capability study:

1. Select the process to be studied.
2. Define and document the existing conditions during the study.
3. Select the operator for the machine. Use a single operator unless you can assure that multiple operators make no difference in process variation.
4. Use one batch of raw material for the study.
5. Test the measurement gauges for repeatability and reproducibility, and calibration.
6. Record sample data by the time it was sampled.
7. Calculate the capability of the process.

Step 1: Select the process to study.

In our example, the fan housing is selected.

Step 2: Define and document existing conditions.

It is vital to remember that a capability study only estimates inherent variation for the conditions during the time of the study. For example, if the molding machines are studied while black plastic parts are being formed, then the capability estimates only apply to black plastic. If the process switches to white resins, then a new capability study is required.

Existing conditions include factors such as the settings on the machine, materials used, operator present, special controls in use, environmental conditions, and other related conditions that could affect the variation of the process.

Step 3. Select the operators.

In this example, a single operator is used since there is little evidence that different operators affect the inherent variation of the process.

Step 4. Use one batch of raw material.

A hopper of black resin plastic is filled and used throughout the course of the study.

Step 5. Test the measurement gages.

The critical characteristic under study is the weight of the part. Therefore, the weight scale used is calibrated and tested for possible sources of error such as repeatability.

Step 6: Record the data by time.

For a normal process performance study, we would select 30 or more pieces from a preproduction run of up to 300 pieces. For the sake of clarity, this example will use only a 10-piece sample so that the calculations will be easier to follow. During an actual process performance study, use at least 30 pieces.

Each of the sampled pieces are weighed on a scale that is at least a decimal place more accurate than the tolerance requirements. The tolerance is in grams, so the scale we use must be capable of measuring at least in tenths of grams. In this case, we use a scale that measures to hundredths of a gram.

The weight of the part is recorded along with the time it was produced. This data can then be plotted along a time line to see if identifiable patterns appear. For example, if a trend of rising part weights appeared, you would have identified a nonrandom source of variation to eliminate.

In this example we obtain the following weights:

	Weight	Time
	174.70	8:00
	174.07	8:05
	175.27	8:10
	175.14	8:14
	175.06	8:19
	175.10	8:20
	176.08	8:21
	175.83	8:25
	173.84	8:27
	175.02	8:31
Total	1,750.11	

Step 7: Calculate the capability of the process.

There are many ways to express the capability of a process. In the following section we examine some of these.

How to Evaluate Process Capability Using Averages, Standard Deviation, Histograms, and Capability Ratios

The first step is to examine the data visually. This initial examination reveals that the 10 readings are within the tolerance of plus or minus 2 grams. However, this tells us nothing about the variation for the population of production parts this sample was drawn from. To discover the actual performance of this process, we must proceed with several simple statistical calculations.

A sample of parts from a population can be used to estimate the parameters of that population. For example, does this sample indicate that the process is on target at 175 grams? If it is, then the average for these 10 numbers should be near 175 grams. To find the sample average, we add all of the values and divide by the sample size.

$$\bar{x} = \frac{\sum_x}{n}$$

where $\sum_x$ = sum of the readings
n = number of pieces in the sample
$\bar{x}$ = mean

In our example, the total is 1,750.11 and we have a sample size of 10. Therefore, our average is 175.011. This is very close to the target value of 175 grams. We can assume that this production process is on target by performing a *t*-test. If the *t*-test finds that the average is too far away from its target, you would note that the process should be adjusted.

The next step is to examine the variation in the process. Specifically, we use the plus and minus three standard deviation spread as a definition of the variation we expect in the production process.

To find the standard deviation, we use the sample formula that was presented in chapter 1.

$$ s = \sqrt{\frac{\Sigma x^2 - \frac{(\Sigma x)^2}{n}}{n-1}} $$

where $\left(\Sigma_x\right)$ = sum of all readings

Σ_x^2 = sum of all readings squared

n = sample size
s = standard deviation

From our previous calculation of the average, we know that the sum of all the readings is equal to 1,750.11. We also know that the sample size is 10. The only extra piece of information we need to know is the square of each reading. This is easily obtained by placing all of our readings in a single row and then creating a second row of corresponding squares.

	Original Readings	Squares
	174.70	30,520.090
	174.07	30,300.364
	175.27	30,719.720
	175.14	30,674.019
	175.06	30,646.003
	175.10	30,660.010
	176.08	31,004.166
	175.83	30,916.188
	173.84	30,220.345
	175.02	30,632.000
Totals	1,750.11	306,292.760

Each number can be squared easily on any calculator or computer. However, you can also square numbers with a simple four-function hand-held calculator. Just enter the number, then press the "X" key and the "=" key in succession.

By entering the sum of the squares into the standard deviation formula,

$$s = \sqrt{\frac{306{,}292.76 - \frac{(1{,}750.11)^2}{10}}{10-1}}$$

we get an answer of 0.688. This represents a standard unit of variation in the process. Thinking back to the curve of normal distribution, we know that three standard deviations above and below the average marks out a zone where we can expect 99.7% of all production to land. In industrial practice, this plus and minus three standard deviation is the most common definition of the inherent variation in a process. A few companies use plus and minus four standard deviations.

The average and the standard deviation give you a rough idea of the process performance. This information can be used to calculate precise ratios of capability. However, we are assuming that a normal distribution exists within our data. Therefore, your next step would be to confirm the normality of the data.

A histogram is drawn for the process performance samples to check for a normal distribution. If normalcy of the data is not obtained because skewed data is a characteristic of the process, such as measuring roundness, then proceed to the section on probability plotting and complete your capability study.

Using the data from the fan cover weights, we can create the histogram shown in Figure 3-1. Because only 10 pieces were used in this study it is not unusual to get an indistinct distribution as in our histogram. However, Figure 3-1 has a fairly normal distribution. Our first clue is the lack of a skewness apparent in the histogram. Most of the data seems clustered near zero. To confirm that the data is not skewed, we can calculate a coefficient of skewness.

$$S_k = \frac{3(\bar{x} - med)}{s}$$

where, $\bar{x}$ = mean average
  med = median average
  s = standard deviation
  S_k = coefficient of skewness

We already have calculated the mean as being 175.011. The standard deviation is calculated as 0.688. To find the median, we have to sort the ten readings in order and find the central value.

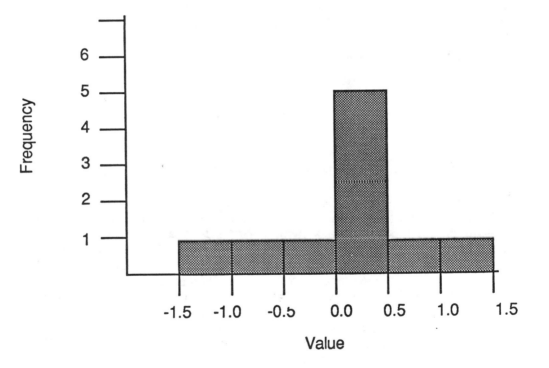

0.0 = 175 grams

Value Range	Count
-1.5 to -1.0	1
-1.0 to -0.5	1
-0.5 to 0.0	1
0.0 to 0.5	5
0.5 to 1.0	1
1.0 to 1.5	1

Figure 3-1: Frequency distribution and histogram.

173.84
174.07
174.70
175.02
175.06
                ←Median
175.10
175.14
175.27
175.83
176.08

Naturally, this task is made much easier when proper computer software is available. In this case, we would obtain a value of 175.08 as being the midway point between the fifth and sixth reading. The resulting formula would be

$$Skewness = \frac{3 \cdot (175.011 - 175.080)}{0.688}$$

or

$$Skewness = -0.30$$

If a skewness coefficient is between –1.0 and +1.0, then the corresponding distribution is considered to be normal. In our example, the coefficient is near the ideal of 0.00; therefore this distribution is assumed to be normal.

To visualize the inherent variation, begin by drawing a scale of measurements with the target value for the plastic resin in the middle, as shown in Figure 3-2. Now place on the scale a mark for the average and then determine how far the process variation will spread from the average. Three times the standard deviation is 2.064. Our sample average is 175.011. To this figure we add and subtract 2.064 to obtain a process variation range of 177.075 grams to 172.947 grams (roughly the tolerance spread of 177 to 173 grams).

By creating Figure 3-3 you can see the inherent process variation versus the tolerance range. You can see if the variation stays within the tolerance spread and whether the process is centered on the optimal target specification. This picture is what you try to visualize in your head when reading a capability study. Again, this is part of thinking statistically.

How to Rate a Process for Capability Using the Capability Ratio (*Cr*)

At this point, we have all of the information necessary to make informed judgments about the process performance. Managers, customers, and vendors will want the process performance reported in a single, easy-to-interpret number. In addition, this number must be from a standardized formula and set of criteria to enable comparisons between competing processes.

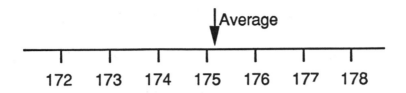

Figure 3-2.

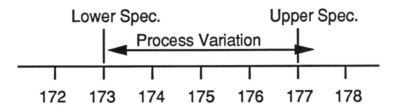

Figure 3-3.

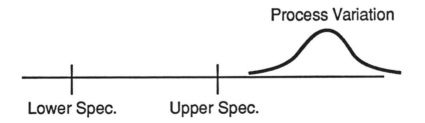

Figure 3-4.

The *Cr* ratio is a measure of how much of the tolerance range laid down in the specification is "used up" by the process variation. A *Cr* ratio is calculated by taking the process variation (6 x standard deviation) and dividing by the tolerance spread.

$$Cr = \frac{6 \times \text{standard deviation}}{\text{tolerance spread}}$$

In our plastic resin example, six times the standard deviation is 4.128, and the tolerance spread was 4 grams (plus and minus 2 grams from 175). Dividing these gives us a *Cr* ratio of 1.032.

If we would rather think of this figure as a percentage of tolerance "used up" by the process variation, we merely multiply our results by 100.

$$Cr\% = 1.032 \times 100 = 103.2\%$$

A *Cr* ratio of 103.2% is unacceptable in the manufacturing world. Any figure over 100% represents a process that is certain to produce products outside of tolerance. In fact, the current industrial standard says that all processes should have a *Cr* ratio of 75% or less for bilateral tolerances and 88% or less for unilateral tolerances. However, a good *Cr* ratio does not mean that the process performance is adequate. The process could be far enough off target to create large amounts of scrap. A process performance study is only looking for the capability of achieving the tolerances, and not at whether the tolerances are being met.

Overview of the Example

The plastic resin weights we measured for our capability study were broken down into an average, a standard deviation, and a histogram. With these three pieces of information we were able to compare the actual performance of the plastic injection process with the specifications for weight. This comparison created the *Cr* ratio. This ratio told us quickly that the process performance was not capable.

An Important Final Step: Taking Action
to Promote Continuous Improvement

The information provided by a capability study can be used in several different ways. Perhaps the estimated scrap rates from several similar machines are compared to determine the production schedule that will result in the minimum operating costs. A common use for the capability ratios is to list them in order of magnitude so that incapable processes are assigned continuous improvement teams first. Capability studies can also be used to evaluate the quality of purchased material. Supplied parts of low quality will alert a production control group to issue cautions for the use of the material.

Whatever the capability study is being used for, it is important that the information it provides be used to take some form of action to adjust a process, improve a design, change a method, or even to justify doing nothing.

An Example of Conducting a Machine Capability Study to Assure the Quality of a Mounting Bracket

In contrast to a process capability study, a machine capability study deliberately controls sources of variation. Such a study will give you an estimate of the maximum potential of a process. Thus, you will be able to estimate whether expensive countermeasures will be required during production.

Let us begin with the case of a metal stamping company. One of their primary products is a metal bracket that goes into the assembly of a bus seat. Critical to the function of this bracket is the location of two holes. The holes must be 3 inches apart for the bracket to assemble easily to the bus seat. Specifications call for a location to within 0.050 inches.

The manufacturing engineer at this company decides to conduct a capability study at the stamping presses. Each press takes an already formed bracket and stamps the two critical holes. A previous process performance study found a *Cr* ratio of 0.50. The histogram was normally distributed.

Since the bracket will be produced for many years and the assembly of the unit is critical by customer definition, the engineer decides to conduct a machine capability study. Following the steps outlined earlier in this chapter, the engineer takes the following actions.

First he selects the worst performing machine in the group, press 3. This press is assigned a control chart to monitor the location of the holes. The operator is instructed to document assignable causes of variation. The engineer hopes that by discovering assignable causes on the worse performing machine, the improvements can be applied to more capable presses to further their performance. Also, the machine capability study defines the "best possible" performance of the machine.

The engineer carefully defines the conditions for this study as being the stamping of the mounting bracket with as many sources of variation as possible under control. In this case, he will use one operator, one coil of steel, and not allow any machine adjustments. It is important to remember that with a process potential study you strictly control assignable causes during the study.

In addition, the caliper normally used to measure the locations of holes is tested and found to be too imprecise for the study. Therefore, the engineer will measure the sample pieces using a coordinate measuring machine.

Before the data can be collected for the study, 30 days of statistical control must be demonstrated. Therefore, the engineer will wait until the control chart on the press indicates statistical control. This wait will not be wasted time, however.

How to Identify Assignable Causes of Process Variation—Using a Time Study and a Process Log

The engineer will be actively studying the process to help the operator identify and control assignable causes. The engineer will collect a few sample pieces each hour for days at a time. The results of this data will be compared to a carefully kept process log book. The log book will record any changes made to the process, such as a new coil of steel being mounted or the shimming of a die.

This collection of data is called a time study because the sample averages are plotted across a time line. The changes in the pattern of sample averages are compared to the process log to see if any of the changes in averages are associated with specific alterations of the process. For example, the engineer may discover that when a new roll of steel is mounted, the average location of the holes changes. This could indicate that changing thicknesses in a new roll of steel affects the dimensions of the part. This would then be tested to see if roll thickness is an assignable cause of variation.

SPC (statistical process control) is continued until the statistical control of the process is demonstrated on the control chart. Chapter 4 discusses statistical control in detail.

Once statistical control has been demonstrated, the engineer collects 100 or more sample parts. This sample is created by collecting a few parts at regular intervals until at least 100 data points are created.

As in the process performance study, an average and standard deviation should be calculated and a histogram used to evaluate normalcy in the data. In this example, we will assume that the 100-piece sample obtained the following:

> Average = 3.010 inches
> Standard Deviation = 0.005 inches
> Tolerance = 3.000 +/- 0.050 inches

We will also assume that the histogram demonstrated a normal distribution.

Scoring the Machine Capability Using the *Cp* Ratio and the *Cpk* Index

The *Cp* ratio is actually the inverted version of the *Cr* ratio. The formula looks like this:

$$Cp = \frac{\text{tolerance spread}}{6 \times \text{standard deviation}}$$

With the *Cr* ratio the idea is the get the number as low as possible. However, the opposite is true for the *Cp* ratio: You want to get as high a number as possible. If we insert the numbers from our bracket example, we get a *Cp* ratio of 3.33.

$$Cp = \frac{0.100}{6 \times 0.005} = 3.33$$

The minimum requirement for a *Cp* ratio is 1.33. Higher figures are even better. We can see where the 1.33 figure comes from by taking the inversion of 75% required of the *Cr* ratio (1/0.75 = 1.33). The reason lies in the weakness of the *Cr* and *Cp* ratios and the strength of the *Cpk* ratio. What the *Cr* and *Cp* ratios are telling us is only the potential of a process. They express how much of the tolerance range could be "used up" by the process variation. They do not tell us whether the process variation is anywhere near the tolerances. In Figure 3-4, the process variation has a *Cr* ratio of 0.75, but all of the production pieces are outside of tolerance.

Therefore, an ideal capability ratio would use one number to tell us whether the process is capable of meeting tolerances, and whether the process is centered around the optimal dimension (target value). The *Cpk* ratio does exactly that.

Before we can calculate the *Cpk* ratio, we must refer back to the capability data. The *Cpk* ratio is really two formulas. Which formula to use is based on whether your process average is closer to the upper specification limit or the lower specification limit. For a process average closer to the upper specification,

$$\frac{US - \bar{x}}{3 \times s} = Cpk$$

For a process average closer to the lower specification,

$$\frac{\bar{x} - LS}{3 \times s} = Cpk$$

where s = standard deviation
       LS = lower specification
       US = upper specification

Note how the top line is reversed depending on your selection. Mathematically, this will create a negative answer if the process average is found to be outside of the tolerance range. In such a situation, over half of the production would be out of specification. Therefore, a negative *Cpk* index is one indication of an inadequate process.

In our example, the process average is closer to the upper specification. Thus, we use the first formula and fill in the corresponding values. When calculated, we get a *Cpk* ratio of 2.667. The ideal is to get a *Cpk* ratio of

1.33 or higher, just as with a *Cp* ratio. Our *Cpk* ratio of 2.667 is telling us that the process is more than meeting capability requirements.

A *Cpk* ratio can fail either by having too much variation in the process, a process average too far from the target value, or both. A quick check of the situation in our example reveals that the process average is close to the target value with very little variation. This is a machine with strong potential.

Case Study 1: Deciding Whether to Make or Buy a Product: Using a Capability Study

A common practice in industry today is to submit every new production run to a process capability study. Typically, any new product that will be produced to stock is tested for capability. Consider the example of an electronics company that will make 700 power bridges for an original equipment manufacturer (OEM). The OEM is the customer of this firm and has specified that the power bridges must produce 15 volts DC (plus or minus a quarter volt).

A logical step for the electronics firm would be to produce the first 30 bridges, test them, and estimate how many will meet specifications during production. If too many are not meeting specifications, then the company is facing what is called a *make-or-buy decision*. If too many bridges will end up as scrap, the company may spend so much money building extra bridges that it will realize no profit. If this occurs, it may be wiser to let a more capable subcontractor do the work.

In this example, the electronics firm found that they had a process average of 15 volts, a standard deviation of 0.15 volts, and the data was normally distributed. Let us go through a few calculations that will lead to the make-or-buy decision. Assume that each bridge produced out of specification will cost $5.00 to scrap and that the company has bid the job to make $1,000 profit on 700 bridges.

First, we calculate the *Cpk* ratio so that we have an overall picture of the process capability. The specification is 15 volts, plus or minus 0.25 volts. The process average is right at the target value, so either *Cpk* formula can be used since the answers will be the same.

$$Cpk = \frac{15.25 - 15.00}{3 \times 0.15} = 0.56$$

The resulting *Cpk* of 0.56 tells us that this process is not capable. The process average and the target value both agree, the data is normally distributed, and there is very little chance that adjustments to this process will improve the situation because control charts on this process have shown statistical control with many assignable causes prevented.

The next step is to calculate the economic damage from the incapability. We begin by estimating the number of bridges per 100 that would be out of specification. This is done with the Z-scores.

Z-scores represent the area under a normal curve from the mean to a point on the curve. (See Appendix A for these values.) For example, the area under the curve from the mean to three standard deviations to the right is 0.49865. Thus, the chance of a part being within this range is 0.49865, or 49.865% probability. By converting actual readings from the power bridge into standard Z-scores, you can calculate the probability of a part being out of specifications.

$$Z = \frac{x - \mu}{\sigma}$$

where μ = population mean
σ = population standard deviation
x = score of interest

The distance from our process mean to the tolerance limits is 0.25 volts. Our standard deviation is 0.15 volts. Thus, the tolerance limit is 1.67 standard deviations above and below the average.

$$Z = \frac{15.25 - 15.00}{0.15} = 1.67$$

From Appendix A we find that this represents 45.25% in each direction for a total of 90.5%. Thus, the probability of a part being in specification is 90.5%. That leaves 9.5%, or 9.5 out of every 100 bridges, out of specifications.

To fill the order, the company would have to build 774 units, so that after 9.5% are scrapped they have 700 units left. To scrap a bridge costs $5 each. For 74 bridges, this represents a cost of $370. Thus, the scrap costs of this process will decrease profits by at least $370. However, this is not the entire picture.

If the company has to build an additional 74 bridges to counteract the scrap rate, then it also has to spread the cost of constructing these bridges into its manufacturing process. If management knew that it costs $10 to build each bridge, then the additional production cost is $740 more. Added to the $370 scrap cost, the potential profit of $1,000 is lost.

It is at this point that the company's management engages in a make-or-buy decision. If they make the bridges under the current conditions, chances are that they will lose a little money. A bid by a subcontractor might ensure usable bridges with a small profit, but the company will have lost full control over the bridge production process. On the other hand, if the scrap rates were cut by, say half, the electronics firm would enjoy a good profit from this job. However, the process is already under statistical control so the assignable causes that are easy to find and correct are already eliminated.

As you can see, the capability study provided the essential information for management to make an intelligent decision. Combined with simple cost accounting figures, management has the complete picture. They know the most likely outcomes of their decisions.

Case Study 2: Using a Capability Study to Help Develop a New Product: Testing pH Factor for a New Perfume

Chapter 9 discusses statistical methods used in experimentation and emphasizes the review of existing knowledge before an experiment is considered. The capability study represents one of the primary sources of that knowledge.

Consider the example of a cosmetic company mixing batches of a perfume. Like many examples from the chemical industry, this example involves batch production. Once chemicals are mixed together, they tend to have the same quality. A chemist may be able to make minor adjustments to the batch, but in the end, you have the quality of the finished mixture.

Suppose that pH is critical to the customer satisfaction of this perfume. Too much or too little pH is known to cause skin complaints from users. Therefore, the company wishes to experiment with the formula and mixing instructions to find a combination that will best prevent the variation in pH.

The first step in this experiment would be to determine the existing variation in pH. Capability studies would supply this information. By taking the pH readings from at least the last 30 batches, a company could estimate variation using the sample standard deviation. In this example, we will assume that the standard deviation of pH was found to be 0.5 pH. This means that the pH could vary by plus or minus three standard deviations on either side of the average, or 1.5 pH. This represents a dramatic swing in pH's.

Any experimental results would be compared directly to this amount of variation. For example, if the experiment reduced the expected pH variation to only 0.1 pH, then the results would be seen as a great success.

There is no specification present in this problem. One is not needed when variation reduction is the goal. A simple before-and-after comparison of standard deviations is all that is initially needed. The experimental tests will determine whether the change was significant.

In addition, the risk of having a wild pH swing can be evaluated. By using the methods described in the section on estimation, management can estimate the zone where there is a 95% chance that an actual pH in a particular batch could occur.

Case Study 3: Determining the Capability of Several Spindles on a Single Machine Using a Capability Study

In this example a metal fabrication company is using six-spindle, automatic screw machines to produce pistons for a small hydraulic system. The outside diameter of the piston must be 1.00 inches, plus or minus 0.005 inches.

The six-spindle machine presents a problem: Is it best to study the machine as a process or each spindle as a separate process? The answer is to study each of the spindles separately to determine if each distribution comes from the same population. If all six spindles are shown to be from a single population, then the entire machine can be treated as a single process.

A process performance study is a good first choice for a machine that has not been studied before. The small sample sizes involved reduce the time required to perform the study. In addition, if you find that the spindles are all capable when assignable causes are not being controlled, then the actual potential of the machine will only benefit from SPC.

A single, representative machine is selected from the gang of screw machines. A single operator is chosen to operate the machine during the study. You have decided to perform a process performance study on each of the six spindles to see if they can meet specifications.

Using six rods of steel selected from the same batch, you load the machine and prepare for the study. You instruct the operator to note any adjustments made to the machine during this 180-part run. You anticipate tool wear to be a small factor. The measurement gauges have been recently calibrated and tested for repeatability error.

The machine operator should collect 30 pieces from each spindle. You and the operator are curious whether the six spindles create parts of equal averages and variation. The initial test of this question will be done visually. Histograms are made of each 30-piece sample from each spindle. The six histograms are examined for a normal curve. They appear normal, so you proceed with making *Cp* calculations.

Following are the averages and standard deviations calculated for each spindle.

Machine 234		
Spindle	Average	Standard Deviation
1	1.000	0.0010
2	0.999	0.0015
3	1.002	0.0012
4	1.001	0.0010
5	1.000	0.0010
6	0.999	0.0012

Before proceeding with calculations, it is always a good idea to examine the data visually. Such an examination reveals that the averages for the six spindles are close to the target value of 1.000 inches. Spindle 3 seems to be the farthest off target. The standard deviations of the six spindles are in close agreement, except for spindle 2. Chapter 9 reviews a method of data analysis called ANOVA that could determine whether the variations within spindles and between spindles are similar.

In short, nothing in the initial examination of the data raises a red flag in your mind.

Our next step is to calculate Cp ratios for each of the spindles. For example, spindle 1 has a standard deviation of 0.001.

$$\text{Spindle 1} \quad Cp = \frac{0.010}{6 \times 0.0010} = 1.67$$

Spindle	C_p
1	1.67
2	1.11
3	1.39
4	1.67
5	1.67
6	1.39

Another visual examination shows that every spindle except 2 can achieve a performance of 1.33 or higher. If the process was adjusted so that each spindle cut to a 1.000-inch average, the variation in spindle 2 would still be too high.

At this point, you could calculate how much scrap will result if no further adjustments are made to the machine. However, in the spirit of continuous improvement, you recommend the implementation of SPC for each of the spindles. Once the assignable causes of variation in the spindles, especially spindle 2, are found and eliminated, statistical control will be achieved. Only at that point should you conduct a process potential study to confirm that the machine spindles are capable. Then the entire machine is treated as a single process.

Case Study 4: How to Use Probability Plotting Paper to Determine the Capability of a Lathing Process

Probability plotting paper has many uses, such as capability studies, tests of normality, estimates with nonnormal data, and reliability testing. To use the paper, you plot the accumulated frequency of data from your histogram and plot the accumulated percentages on a logarithmic graph. If the data points form a straight line, the distribution of the data is considered normal.

There are many instances where you will want to confirm that a sample has data that is normally distributed. We have just examined several examples where normal distributions indicate that a process is operating to the best of its ability. Using probability plotting paper, you can perform this task quickly and easily.

In addition, this same plotting paper can identify specific nonnormal distribution and produce an adjusted capability report. Therefore, probability plotting paper represents an easy alternative to high-order statistics when coping with normal and nonnormal distributions of data in your capability study.

Take a moment to examine Figure 3-5. Note how the horizontal lines on the plotting paper are spread into a logarithmic order. When a normal distribution is plotted across this paper it will form a straight line. Naturally, samples sizes of 30 or more are required for probability plotting analysis.

The following example illustrates the use of probability plotting paper during a capability study.

Assume that you are the process engineer for a lathe department. Your assignment today is to check on the capability of lathe 34 for turning a crankshaft. A sample of 40 crankshafts creates the following frequency distribution.

Size	Coded Size	Frequency
1.049	49	0
1.050	50	2
1.051	51	5
1.052	52	8
1.053	53	10
1.054	54	9
1.055	55	4
1.056	56	2
1.057	57	0
	Total	40

The frequency distribution you create should go one unit before and beyond your range of data. This will facilitate the calculation of the plotting points later.

Step 1: Find the estimated accumulated frequency (EAF) for each frequency distribution category. Each EAF is calculated by adding the accumulated frequency to the frequency in the same category, and then adding the next category's frequency. Although this sounds difficult, it is easy if you use the following visual method.

Code Size	Frequency	EAF
49	0 ← — + — 0	
	+ ↓	
50	2 = →2	
	+ ↓	
51	5 = →9	
	+ ↓	
52	8 — → =	

After some practice, it becomes second nature to add the numbers in the loops formed by the arrows.

The rest of the EAFs are calculated using the aforementioned method. The last EAF should equal twice the sample size. This verifies that you have calculated the EAFs correctly. For our example, the correct EAFs are as follows.

Coded Size	Frequency	EAF
49	0	0
50	2	2
51	5	9
52	8	22
53	10	40
54	9	59
55	4	72
56	2	78
57	0	80

Step 2: You use the foregoing EAFs to calculate the plotting points for the probability paper by dividing each EAF by twice the sample size and then multiplying by 100. This creates an approximate accumulated percentage. The formula is

$$\frac{\text{EAF}}{2n} \times 100 = \text{plotting point}$$

For the first EAF the answer would be zero, since the EAF is zero. However, the calculation for the second EAF would be

$$\frac{2}{80} \times 100 = 2.5\%$$

The plotting point for the third EAF is

$$\frac{9}{80} \times 100 = 11.25\%$$

Probability Plotting Paper

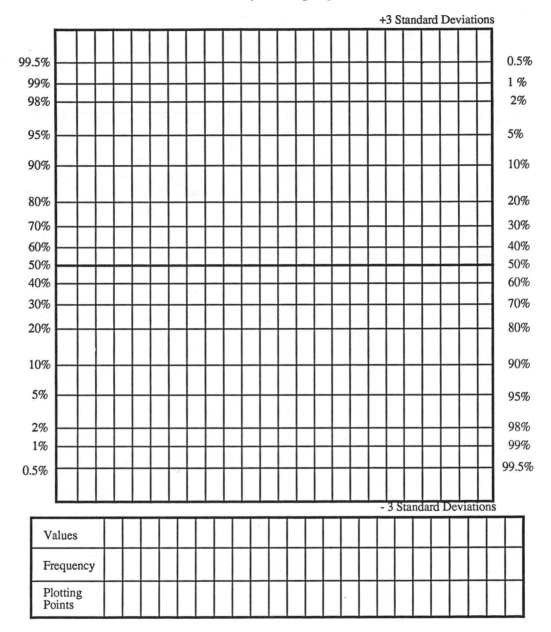

Figure 3-5: Capability plotting paper.

Step 3: These calculations are repeated for each EAF. The results are plotted onto the probability plotting paper. Figure 3-6 shows the results for our example.

Step 4: The first interpretation of any probability plotting chart is to check for the plottings forming a straight line across the page. A straight line indicates a normal distribution. A curving line indicates skewness in the data. A line with a distinct *S* shape indicates a bimodal distribution or rectangular distribution.

Any of the nonnormal plots might indicate that assignable causes are still present in the process. These should be corrected and the capability study repeated.

Step 5: You can continue to interpret the probability plot by drawing two vertical lines where the tolerance limits correspond to the measurement scale on the chart. The point where the plotting line crosses these tolerance limits is an estimate of the percentage of pieces that will be produced beyond the limit.

To find this percentage, follow the horizontal line from the point of intersection to the edge of the chart. There are percentages printed along the edge that indicate the amount of production beyond this point.

The top and bottom of the chart represent the plus and minus three standard deviation limits for the population. Whether or not the distribution is normal, where the plotting crosses the top and bottom of the chart corresponds to the variation that can be expected in the process. The limits of variation are found by taking the points where the plottings cross the top and bottom of the chart and following the vertical lines to the measurement scale at the bottom of the chart.

Figure 3-7 shows how this is done for a skewed set of data. The advantage of doing this is that the estimate of variation is fairly accurate, whether or not the distribution is normal. Thus, you do not need to make elaborate transformations of the original data to complete the capability study.

Conclusion

The capability study is a fundamental source of information for quality, production, and engineering functions. Quality personnel use capability studies to evaluate and certify new and existing processes and products using both process performance and process potential studies. Production personnel use capability studies as the first step toward statistical control of processes. A process performance study can help establish control limits and identify possible assignable causes. Engineering professionals need the information from a capability study to determine if tolerance will work within an assembly. Using scientific methods, the engineers develop tolerances, but a capability study is still conducted to see if the inherent variation in a process can cope with the tolerance. In short, capability studies are one of the most widely used tools of information gathering in manufacturing today.

Probability Plotting Paper

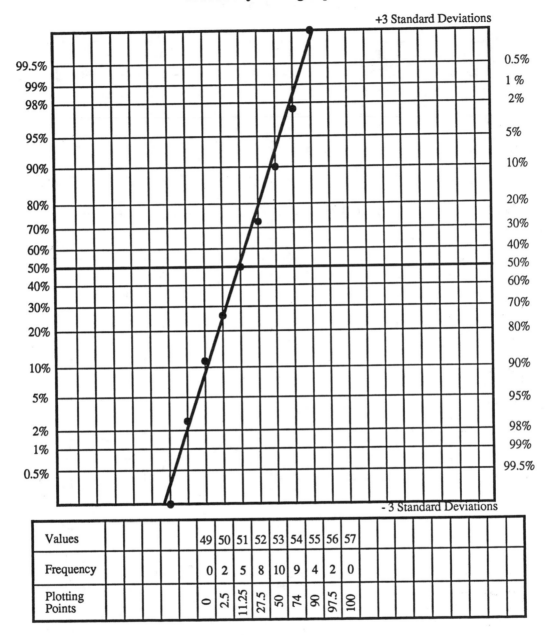

Figure 3-6: A completed capability plot.

69

Probability Plotting Paper

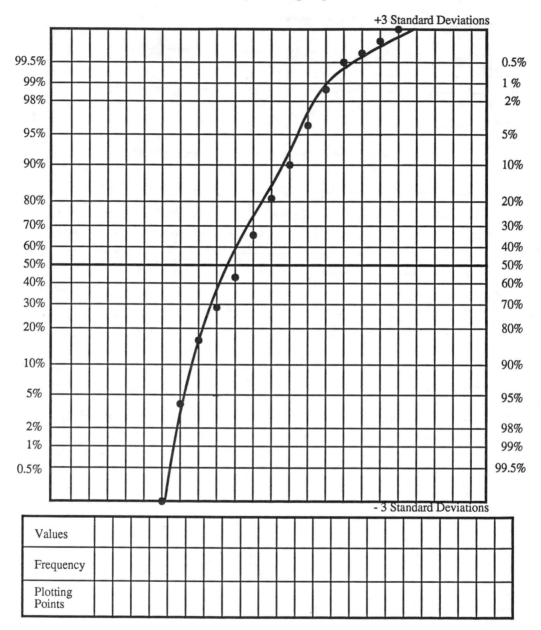

Figure 3-7: Capability plotting of a nonnormal distribution.

CHAPTER 4

Using Statistical Process Control Instead of Product Inspection

Any manager of a manufacturing process should be critically interested in the performance of the production processes. In the environment of world-class manufacturing, management must certify each process in the plant as capable of maintaining engineering tolerances. But before this can be accomplished, the processes must be shown to be under statistical control; that is, they have to be stable and predictable. Statistical process control (SPC) is the most frequently used tool in industry to demonstrate statistical control.

SPC is also a method for involving machine operators in the process of quality assurance. Used as a replacement for on-line inspection, SPC employs control charts to monitor the stability of process variation. Coupled with reaction plans, the control charts give machine operators the ability to detect alterations in the capability of a manufacturing process and to make corrections during production.

Today, a large number of companies and the Department of Defense require the use of SPC as part of a company's quality assurance program. To implement an SPC program successfully, a company must have the commitment of top management. In addition, the manufacturing manager and the quality manager must work closely with each other and other departments.

The Function and Benefits of SPC

In Chapter 3 we discussed the concept of process capability. A capability study looks at the variation within a process by examining a critical characteristic of the product. The inherent variation within a process is assumed to be the result of random causes. Assignable causes create intermittent additions to the variation within a process. Assignable causes can also be found and removed, thus decreasing the overall variation within a process.

SPC strives to detect the occurrence of assignable causes while the process is running. The data for control charts is taken as production proceeds. This allows the machine operator to detect the occurrence of an assignable cause much sooner than the alternative of waiting for an inspection of a finished lot of goods. The sooner an assignable cause can be found and corrected, the more consistent the resulting production.

The concept of SPC monitoring and correcting a production process in real time presents several possible benefits.

1. It replaces in-process inspection that usually waits until a large quantity of product is produced. By looking at the process more frequently, there is less chance of having to scrap or rework large amounts of product.

2. SPC brings quality awareness to a larger number of employees.

3. SPC encourages machine operators to document their production problems and their corrective actions. This helps the company to learn how to operate more efficiently by attacking problem effectively.

4. Assignable causes are usually detected as points landing outside of the control limits or as unusual patterns on the chart.

5. SPC can demonstrate the statistical control of a process. Statistical control is required before a process potential study can be completed.

6. SPC represents a key tool for a company pursuing continuous improvement.

An Example of SPC Encouraging Continuous Improvement Rather Than Traditional Inspection Techniques

A manufacturing situation can best illustrate the differences between inspection, SPC, and continuous improvement. Consider the example of a small company that produces an electric fan. Under a quality system of pure inspection, the components of the fan are inspected after they are assembled. This tells the management of the company how many of the components are not acceptable and must be scrapped. The manufacturing process is corrected after scrap has already been produced.

SPC is an alternative to the inspection system. As each piece is manufactured, the manufacturing processes are continually monitored. Using simple statistical methods, the operator is able to detect when a process is producing usable parts and when a problem begins to develop. If a problem is detected, it can be corrected before unusable pieces are produced.

Continuous improvement uses SPC as a tool of intelligence. The machine operators, using SPC, are able to receive feedback on the stability of the production process. With this knowledge, the operators, engineers, and managers can form work teams that further study the source of production problems and work to eliminate them. For example, the SPC chart in the plastic injection area may find that the molding of fan blades results in some short shots (incomplete molding of a blade). By studying a control chart for defective blades, they can identify when an unusually high number occurs and use this information to trace the assignable cause. Thus, every day the employees of the company are striving to find another improvement of their current situation.

Implementing SPC through Control Charts

A control chart is a statistical tool that graphs the actual variation of a process against the expected variation for that process. Control charts alone do not make an SPC system. As we shall see later in this chapter, reaction plans and other techniques are required to make the SPC system complete. However, the posting of a control chart is the central activity that marks the beginning of implementing an SPC system.

Control charts are created using the following steps:

Step 1: Select a control item.

A control item is a critical quality characteristic of the product produced by a particular process. Sometimes, specific process characteristics are used as control items. The variation in the control item is what the control chart will monitor. The theory is that the stability of the process variation will be represented by the variation in the control item.

Which processes to monitor and which control items to select are dictated by two rules of thumb. A typical process requires that only one, and usually no more than two, control items be monitored. This control item should be something that directly affects the performance of the finished product and is created by the selected process—for example, the outside diameter of a shaft after it is turned on a lathe.

Processes are selected on a scale of economic importance. Characteristics of a product that a customer requires be monitored must be charted as a primary concern. An example of such a characteristic would be a weld that is marked as a safety item on the blueprints. Secondary are characteristics that directly affect the economy of the production process. One possibility would be the location of positioning holes. If they are out of position, it could cost the company considerable amounts of money to fix each assembly. Only when these first two concerns are addressed are charts placed on characteristics of interest to production that do not have an immediate economic benefit. However, when implementing SPC, you should avoid the temptation to plaster the walls with control charts. Start with a few charts and let the demand for information determine the growth of the program.

Step 2: Sample 25 subgroups of data.

To estimate the amount of process variation, 25 small samples have to be taken during the production run. Each of these samples are called subgroups. The size of the subgroup is determined by the type of control chart to be used. For example, a control chart for variable data usually requires 4 to 10 parts per subgroup. A chart for attribute data requires at least 50 parts per subgroup.

Once the size of the subgroup is selected, you must select the timing of the samples. The interval between the drawing of a subgroup is usually determined by the speed of the production process and the difficulty of making the required measurement. For example, an easily measured part being produced at 100 units per hour could be sampled every hour.

Step 3: Keep a process log.

Critical to the use of a control chart is the documentation of any changes in the production process. This written record is kept in a process log. When a change in material, procedure, environment, or operator occurs, it is logged along with the corresponding date and time. In this way, if a significant improvement or decay in the process performance is noted on the control chart, you can read the process log to find possible changes in the process that may be the assignable cause.

Step 4: Compute trial control limits and the process average.

Averaging the 25 subgroups of data will give an estimate of the process average. This is drawn on the control chart as a solid line. On both sides of the line will be control limits. Control limits represent the random variation of the process. Each control chart will have a set of formulas that are used to create the control limits.

Step 5: Chart the subgroup values.

Each subgroup average, and sometimes variation, is plotted on the control chart and compared to the control limits. If the 25 subgroups are plotted within the control limits, the process is said to have statistical control. *Statistical control* means that the variation in subgroup plottings is the result of random causes. If one or more points are found to be over a control limit, it is assumed to be the result of assignable causes. If statistical control is not found, then you must search for and eliminate the assignable causes.

Step 6: Once statistical control is achieved, continuous improvement can begin.

At this point, the control chart continues to be filled in by the machine operator at the process. After 30 days of statistical control, a process capability study is conducted using the data from the chart.

A critical part of the control chart is its reaction plan. A reaction plan is a written set of instructions to the machine operator on what steps to take if statistical control is lost during production. It usually instructs the operator to circle the point out of control and to note the possible cause of the problem on the back of the control chart. Then each corrective action is noted, especially the action that brought the process back into statistical control. This record allows both operators and management to spot more effective ways to solve common problems. In addition, it also will highlight a problem that occurs repeatedly, such as the loss of pressure in a pneumatic line. These abilities allow you to pursue the continuous improvement of the process by exploiting the opportunities the control chart uncovers.

How to Select the Right Control Chart to Use Based on the Type of Data You Are Collecting

SPC charts are used for two different types of data, variable and attribute. These two types of data create two families of SPC charts. Variable data is any information that can be measured on a variable scale, such as time, pressure, temperature, and size. The SPC charts that monitor such characteristics are called the variable data control charts and include the average/range chart and the chart for individual readings.

The average/range chart is also called the x-bar/R chart, named after the statistical shorthand for average and range. This control chart requires subgroups of two or more data points. Most x-bar/R charts use between 4 and 10 pieces in a subgroup for cases of nondestructive testing. Destructive testing tends to use two or three pieces and to spread out the sampling intervals. A chart for individuals is used when one data point can be taken with each sample, such as the temperature of a furnace in a heat treating plant.

Attribute data results from classifying objects. The SPC charts that monitor this type of information are called the attribute data control charts and include the p-bar, np-bar, u-bar, and c-bar charts.

Attribute data comes in two forms. One form is the measurement of nonconforming production called defectives. The number of defective units are charted on an np-bar chart. The percentage of defective units found within a sample is plotted on a p-bar chart.

Another form of attribute data is the measurement of nonconformities, or defects on a product. The raw number of defects is plotted on a c-bar chart. The ratio of defects to the sample size is plotted on a u-bar chart.

How to Control a Metal Stamping Process by Creating and Using the Average/Range (*x*-bar/*R*) Chart

For the purposes of illustration, we will examine the case of a stamping press that shapes flat pieces of steel into a radiator housing. Once shaped, the critical characteristic is the distance between two mounting holes on opposite sides of the housing. The distance must be 300 mm. Since variation is unavoidable in production, a usable tolerance range for the hole positions has been set to plus or minus 2 mm. If the two holes are too far apart or too close together, the housing cannot be assembled with a mating part.

Step 1: Select the control item.

The specifications tell us that we must keep the hole positions to 300 +/- 2 mm. If the hole locations are not correct, then the final assembly will probably not work and you will suffer a financial loss. It is important to know that the tolerances for the position were correctly set using proper engineering techniques.

Step 2: Take 25 subgroups of data.

For this example, assume that an operator has sampled the process every hour for 10 hours. This will make our example calculations easier to follow. Make sure that in practice you take all 25 subgroups.

Each sample contains five housings, in which an average is calculated and recorded. Assume that the following 10 averages were reported along with the corresponding range of measurements.

Average	Range
300.2	2.3
299.7	2.2
300.8	2.5
298.8	1.1
300.8	3.2
298.5	2.4
299.9	3.3
301.1	1.1
299.3	2.2
298.9	2.4

Step 3: Log process changes.

Any changes in the stamping process, its environment, operator, or the materials being used would be noted in a process log.

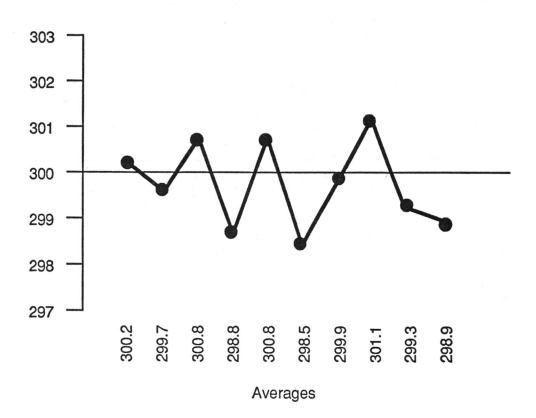

Figure 4-1: Averages plotted over time.

Step 4: Compute trial control limits and the process average.

As you can see, none of the samples achieved the target of 300 mm; instead, they all were close to the target. If we plot these averages over time we can see how they tend to follow our target value (see Figure 4-1).

The variations from the target value are probably due to the chance errors occurring when we take such a small sample as five parts. However, how far could one of the averages vary before we were sure that chance variations were not involved? In other words, at what point would an extreme average be known to result from an assignable cause, and not a random error?

The answer to that question is the control limits of the chart. The control limits mark a zone of variation for the averages and ranges—specifically, the amount of variation that would occur from random, natural causes. The actual limits correspond to where a sample average or range is expected 99.73% of the time.

You begin by calculating the grand average of the subgroups. Each subgroup average is totaled and divided by the number of subgroups. The result is called the *grand average* $(\bar{x})$.

$$\text{grand average} = \frac{\text{total of averages}}{\text{number of subgroups}}$$

The grand average of the 10 averages in our example is 299.8, very close to the 300 mm target.

Next, we need to calculate the average range for all of the samples. The range was found by taking the highest reading and subtracting the lowest reading. For example, in sample one the highest reading was 301.3 and the lowest was 299.0. This gave us the range of 2.3 mm.

Averaging together all of the ranges results in an average range of 2.27 mm. The formula for the control limits for the average is

upper control limit (UCL) = process average + (chart factor A_2 x average range)

lower control limit (LCL) = process average – (chart factor A_2 x average range)

The chart factors are found by examining Table 4-1.

For a sample size of five, the A_2 factor is 0.58. Thus, the control limits for our example data are calculated as follows.

$$\text{UCL} = 299.8 + (0.58 \times 2.27) = 301.1$$

$$\text{LCL} = 299.8 - (0.58 \times 2.27) = 298.5$$

Sample Size	A_2	D_3	D_4	d_2	E_2
2	1.880	0	3.267	1.128	2.66
3	1.023	0	2.574	1.693	1.77
4	0.729	0	2.282	2.059	1.46
5	0.577	0	2.114	2.326	1.29
6	0.483	0	2.004	2.534	1.18
7	0.419	0.076	1.924	2.704	1.11
8	0.373	0.136	1.864	2.847	1.05
9	0.337	0.184	1.816	2.970	1.01
10	0.308	0.223	1.777	3.078	0.98

Table 4-1: Control Chart Factors

This tells us that any sample of five housings should have an average between 298.5 mm and 301.1 mm. If an average beyond these values is found, then an assignable cause is probably present.

However, an *x*-bar/*R* chart is really two control charts. In addition to checking the stability of the averages, you monitor the stability of part-to-part variation. This variation is expressed in the ranges. The average range of 2.27 is plotted as a straight line across a second graph. The control limits for the range are calculated using the following formula.

$$\text{UCL} = \text{average range} \times D_4$$

$$\text{LCL} = \text{average range} \times D_3$$

As before, the *D*4 and *D*3 factors are found in Table 4-1. Using these values, we can calculate the control limits for the range chart.

$$\text{UCL} = 2.27 \times 2.11 = 4.79$$

$$\text{LCL} = 2.27 \times 0 = 0$$

These control limits are drawn across the range chart and the range of each sample is plotted. The resulting chart can be seen in Figure 4-2.

Step 5: Plot the values of the subgroup data.

By plotting the control limits onto our original graph of the data, we create an SPC chart for averages and a second chart for the ranges (see Figure 4-2). Since two of the points on the average chart seem to just meet the control limits, the process is not in statistical control.

At this point, you would have to examine the process and the process log further to determine the assignable causes that created the loss of statistical control. Once these causes are eliminated, another 25 subgroups are examined. This process is repeated until statistical control is achieved.

Step 6: Use the control chart for continuous improvement.

Once all of the plotted values are within the control limits, the control limits are extended on a chart beyond the plotted points. If necessary, the control limits are plotted onto a blank chart. The operator of the process is now able to continue to sample pieces at regular intervals and plot them on the SPC chart. In this example, five housing units would be checked every hour and the average and range of the sample would be plotted on the chart. If a plotted point crosses a control limit, this alerts the operator that the process may be developing a problem. The operator is then able to correct the process. The *R* chart should be checked first to see if the variation within the subgroup is roughly the same as past subgroups.

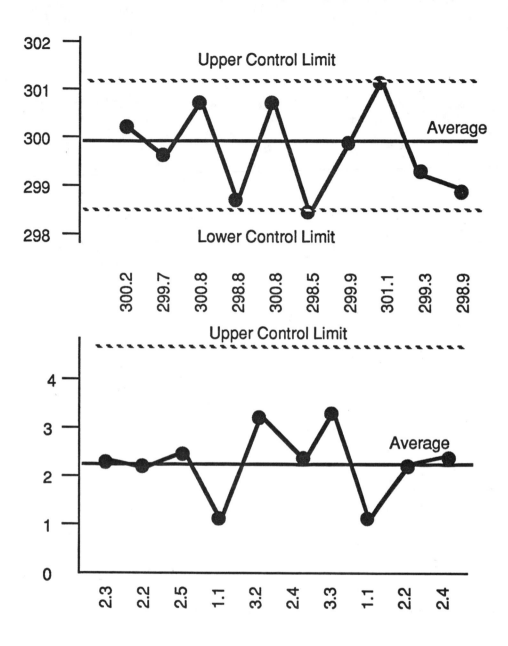

Figure 4-2: The range chart added to the average chart.

The cause of the problem and how it was corrected is noted on the back of the control chart. A reaction plan is attached to the control chart to guide the operator. The documented causes of problems and their solutions are then used in the process of continually improving the process. If a significant improvement is made, the control limits can be recalculated.

If a process can maintain plottings within the control limits for 30 cumulative days of production, the process is said to be within statistical control.

Once statistical control is obtained for a process, a second capability study is performed. This time, data is taken directly from the SPC chart. The last 100 to 150 readings are compiled into the same sort of capability study discussed in chapter 3. If the process exhibits a normal distribution and has an acceptable *Cpk* ratio, then the process is certified as capable.

The theory of SPC is that all processes in manufacturing should be certified as capable of producing parts where critical characteristics are well within tolerance. Once all processes are under statistical control, the company has a consistent database about the performance of manufacturing. With this information it becomes possible to solve problems, redesign processes, and conduct experiments on the factory floor, with greater ease.

In reality, many companies are struggling to reach this objective. The use of SPC charts usually reveals a large selection of problems that went unnoticed in the past. In our example, the process average was slightly different from the target value of 300 mm. The process would have to be adjusted until the process average equalled 300 mm. Naturally, we would also move the control limits to match the target.

In other cases, some processes are not capable, and management must decide whether to replace, redesign, or stop using the particular process. This usually leads to a make-or-buy decision—that is, whether it would be cheaper to contract the job to a company with a capable process, or to sort bad production parts.

How to Sample a Process When Only One Data Reading Is Possible: The Case of a Heat Treatment Oven

In many industrial processes an operator can only sample the process once at regular intervals. Examples include the viscosity of a glue, the temperature of an oven, the percent carbon in iron, or the pH in a chemical batch. With a single data sample it is not possible to calculate the range as with a normal average/range chart. The solution is a chart designed for individual readings, which we will call the individual chart.

The individual chart resembles an average/range chart. However, it calculates a moving range. To see how this is done, consider the following temperature readings taken at regular intervals from a heat treatment oven.

Time	Temp.	Range
8:00	375	—
9:00	350	25
10:00	360	10
11:00	400	40
12:00	375	25

Note that there is one less range than readings. This is due to how the ranges are calculated. The process is called a moving range. A moving range is calculated by taking the difference between the current reading and the last reading. For example, at 8:00 there was no previous reading so no range can be calculated. However, at 9:00 the temperature was 350 degrees, a change of 25 degrees since 8:00; therefore, the moving range is 25.

The steps for creating a control chart for individual measurements are as follows.

Step 1: Select the control item.

In this example, we have selected the oven temperature. Should the temperature of the oven vary too far, the resulting heat-treated material will be out of specification.

Step 2: Gather 25 subgroups of data.

Normally, at least 25 readings have to be taken before the control limits can be calculated. In our example, we will use the five aforementioned samples for illustrative purposes.

Step 3: Log process changes.

This step is critical for a chart for individual measurements. Because our sample size is one, this chart is greatly influenced by assignable causes and other unseen errors. Therefore, every change in the process must be thoroughly documented.

Step 4: Calculate trial limits and the process average.

First we calculate the process average by finding the mean of the temperatures.

$$\bar{x} = \frac{375 + 350 + 360 + 400 + 375}{5} = 372$$

The average range is also calculated.

$$R = \frac{25 + 10 + 40 + 25}{4} = 25$$

Note how the amount of numbers in the range is one less than that of the individual readings. This is always true on an individual chart because the first one or more ranges cannot be calculated. For example, some people choose to average the last three or more readings to calculate a moving range. This gives increased precision but reduces the total number of ranges.

The average and the average range are used in formulas similar to those used for the previous control chart. The control limits for the individual readings are found with the following formulas.

$$\text{UCL} = \text{process average} + (E_2 \times \text{average range})$$

$$\text{LCL} = \text{process average} - (E_2 \times \text{average range})$$

The control limits for the ranges are found using the following formulas.

$$\text{UCL} = \text{average range} \times D_4$$

$$\text{LCL} = \text{average range} \times D_3$$

As before, the E_2 and other correction factors are found in Table 4-1. Also, the control limits and process averages are plotted on graph paper (see Figure 4-3). The control limits are drawn across the end of the chart so that continued monitoring of the process is possible.

Step 5: Chart the individual and moving range values.

If the 25 values and the 24 ranges are within the control limits, then the control chart can be posted. However, if one or more points land outside of the control limits, a careful search for assignable causes must begin. The individual chart contains less information per subgroup than other control charts. Therefore, points over the control limit can occur due to random causes.

Step 6: Begin continuous improvement.

As noted, the individual chart is not as sensitive as the average/range chart. Therefore, the individual chart should be treated with more suspicion. Trends and loss of statistical control may occur from random events. Therefore, real trust in the chart comes only after a few months of use.

In addition, a capability study has to wait until at least 100 individual readings have been taken and statistical control is demonstrated. Even then, the capability ratios will tend to be slightly inaccurate—all of which makes the individual chart seem unreliable, but in practice, it works better than most alternatives for monitoring situations where only a single sample can be drawn.

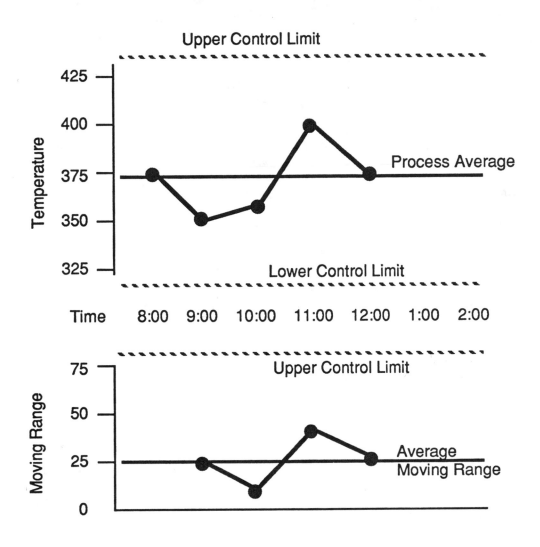

Figure 4-3: The SPC chart for individual readings.

How to Control and Reduce Defects
and Defective Goods Using the *p*-bar Chart

Attribute information requires a precise written definition of when a product has a defect or when a unit of production is defective. This document is usually called the defect checklist, and it helps standardize the appraisal of production pieces. Otherwise, it is easy for defective pieces to be accepted when they are needed badly by the customer, but rejected when there is no pressing need.

Much of the attribute data a company needs to track and control is already recorded in the form of scrap reports, sorting counts, and engineering studies. Even simple go/no-go gauges represent a source of attribute data.

In a situation where the percentage of defective material is reported and varying sample sizes are possible, the *p*-bar chart is used. The following example illustrates the creation and use of a *p*-bar chart.

Step 1: Select the control item.

Assume that a company is tracking the scrap rate within the welding department. For years, the line supervisors have counted the number of production pieces produced within the department and how many of these were rejected because of faulty welds.

Step 2: Collect 25 subgroups of data.

In practice, at least 25 samples of the production process should be taken over time to form the chart. In our example, we will use only five samples to simplify the illustration. The proportion of pieces rejected represents the *p* in the *p*-bar chart. To find a single day's *p*, the number of pieces rejected would be divided by the total production. If 87 pieces were rejected from a daily production of 320 units, the *p*, would be

$$p = \frac{87}{320} = 0.2719$$

This represents just over 27% scrap. This calculation would also represent one subgroup of data.

To create a *p*-bar chart to monitor the daily scrap rate, you would need samples of at least 50 pieces. In our example, the daily production is easily over 100 pieces every day, so the daily scrap report can be used as data. However, caution must be used with this data. The company must have a welding defect checklist so that the definition of a faulty weld is clear in the minds of those checking the parts. This welding defect checklist should describe and have a photograph of major weld problems that make a unit defective, such as spatter, cracks, porosity, and burns.

Step 3: Log process changes

Any change in the welding gas being used, operators, welding wire supply, atmospheric conditions, and other factors related to a successful weld should be noted. An attribute chart can detect an improvement in a process as easily as it can an increase in defectives. Therefore, the process log is critical for finding assignable causes and possible improvements for the process.

Step 4: Calculate trial limits and the process average.

The following are the scrap reports from five consecutive days. (Normally, at least 25 samples are taken.)

Production	Scrap
350	40
400	35
375	27
350	33
350	29

For each of these lines of data, we need to calculate the p. For the first day, the p would be 40 divided by 350, or a p of 0.1143. Repeating this calculation results in the following:

Percent Scrap
0.1143
0.0875
0.0720
0.0943
0.0828

To find the average of these five percentages, we would calculate the p-bar. The p-bar is found by the total of all defectives divided by the total of all samples. We had a total of 1,825 parts produced, of which 164 were scrapped.

$$p\text{-bar} = \frac{164}{1,825} = 0.0899$$

This is roughly an average scrap rate of 9%. To find the control limits around this 9% scrap rate, we first need to calculate the average sample size taken.

$$\text{average sample size } (n\text{-bar}) = \frac{\text{total of all sampless}}{\text{numberrof sampless}}$$

Defects

Spatter	20	35	20	25	20			
Cracks			7	5				
Pores	10				9			
Burns				3				
Other	10							
Total Defects	40	35	27	33	29			
Sample Size	350	400	375	350	350			
% Defective	.114	.088	.072	.094	.083			

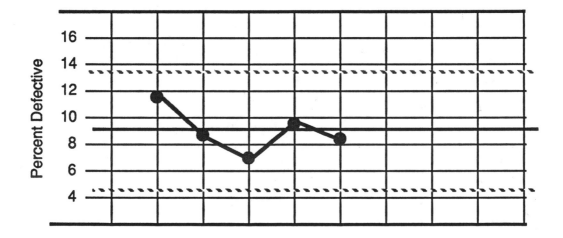

Figure 4-4: A Completed P-bar chart for defectives.

or

$$n\text{-bar} = \frac{1,825}{5} = 365$$

The formula for the control limits is

$$UCL = \bar{p} + 3 \times \sqrt{\frac{\bar{p}(1-\bar{p})}{\bar{n}}}$$

$$LCL = \bar{p} - 3 \times \sqrt{\frac{\bar{p}(1-\bar{p})}{\bar{n}}}$$

With a p-bar of 0.0899 and an n-bar of 365, the resulting control limits are

$$UCL = 0.0899 + 3 \times \sqrt{\frac{0.0899 \times 0.9101}{365}}$$

$$UCL = 0.1348$$

$$LCL = 0.0899 - 3 \times \sqrt{\frac{0.0899 \times 0.9101}{365}}$$

$$LCL = 0.0450$$

Rounding off our figures, we can say that the normal scrap rate for the welding department averages about 9% and can vary from 4.5% to 13.5%. In other words, any scrap rate reported from 4.5% to 13.5% is considered a normal day's worth of scrap.

Step 5: Chart subgroup values.

The use of an attribute chart differs slightly from the variable data family of charts. To begin with, the cause of the scrap would be recorded at the bottom of the chart. This helps the operators to identify quickly the cause of a loss of statistical control. In addition, it provides management with valuable information on the major causes of scrap (see Figure 4-4).

Step 6: Use the chart for continuous improvement.

Another interesting characteristic of the *p*-bar and other attribute charts is that you do not want to maintain statistical control. A 9% scrap rate is not acceptable in today's manufacturing environment. Instead, the goal of any attribute chart is to drive the process average down toward zero.

However, for the first 25 subgroups, the objective is to have all of the plotted points inside of the control limits. Physical control of the process will be difficult until statistical control is demonstrated. Only then will you have a good idea of why scrap rates change each day. You will focus your attention to assignable causes, instead of every high scrap rate on the chart.

When Sample Sizes Change on a P-bar Chart, You Must Use Stepped Control Limits.

Both the p-bar and the *u*-bar charts can work with sample sizes that vary widely. However, whenever these sample size vary by more than 25%, the control limits must be modified. When the sample size increases significantly, the control limits are drawn closer together. When the samples size decreases significantly, the control limits are expanded.

To illustrate this stepping of the control limits, consider the information from the preceding example. Our *p*-bar is roughly 0.09, and the normal control limits are 0.045 and 0.135 with an average sample size of 365. Assume that one day welding is very productive and welds 500 units. This is more than 25% larger than the average sample size.

If 54 of the 500 units had to be scrapped, we would plot a *p* of 0.108. However, the control limits for this single point would be recalculated based on the sample size of 500.

$$\text{UCL} = 0.0899 + 3 \times \sqrt{\frac{0.0899 \times 0.9101}{500}}$$

$$\text{UCL} = 0.128$$

$$\text{LCL} = 0.0899 - 3 \times \sqrt{\frac{0.0899 \times 0.9101}{500}}$$

$$\text{LCL} = 0.052$$

Notice that the control limits are closer to the process average when the sample size increases. These tighter limits would be drawn on the *p*-bar chart using steps (see Figure 4-5).

In contrast, a smaller sample size would have the opposite effect. Suppose that a light production day of 200 pieces resulted in 18 defective units. The *p* for that day would be 0.09. However, the control limits would be calculated as

$$\text{UCL} = 0.0899 + 3 \times \sqrt{\frac{0.0899 \times 0.9101}{200}}$$

$$\text{UCL} = 0.151$$

$$\text{LCL} = 0.0899 - 3 \times \sqrt{\frac{0.0899 \times 0.9101}{200}}$$

$$\text{LCL} = 0.029$$

Defects

Spatter	20	35	20	10	20			
Cracks			7	5				
Pores	10	19			9			
Burns				3				
Other	10							
Total Defects	40	54	27	18	29			
Sample Size	350	500	375	200	350			
% Defective	.114	.108	.072	.090	.083			

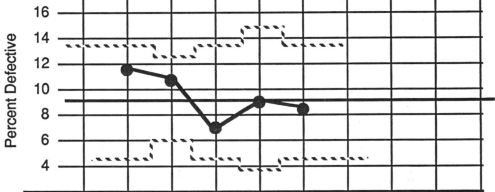

Figure 4-5: A P-bar chart with stepped control limits.

Note that the control limits are stepped out for the smaller sample size (see Figure 4-5). It is a time consuming process to step the control limits by hand, but today most SPC software packages can perform the calculation automatically.

How to Improve the Quality of Purchased Items Using the NP-Bar Chart

The *np*-bar chart is identical to the p-bar chart except that it reports the number of defectives found in a consistent sample size. The term *np* refers to the number defective (as well as *n* x *p*, the total number produced times the percent defective).

An illustration of its application will better define its role. Assume that a shop-by-mail company inspects incoming catalog items by drawing 100 items at random and looking for defective goods. They would be armed with a defect checklist of what makes a particular product defective.

Step 1: Select the control item.

Assume that they are examining make-up display mirrors. If a major problem is found, such as a cracked mirror or nonfunctioning light, the unit is rejected.

Step 2: Collect 25 subgroups of data.

We will again use only five inspection reports for our illustration. In practice, at least 25 samples would be used as the basis for creating the *np*-bar chart. After five inspection reports, we find the following information.

Number Inspected	Number Rejected
100	7
100	3
100	4
100	0
100	11

As you can see, the sample size stays the same. The *np*-chart is easier to work with than the *p*-bar chart because you plot the number rejected instead of performing a proportion calculation.

Step 3: Log changes in the process.

Because this is a purchased item, it is almost impossible to note changes in the vendor's production processes. However, the data gathered on the defects found will be shared later with the vendor to encourage improvements.

Step 4: Compute trial limits and the process average.

If we average the number rejected, we calculate the *np*-bar.

$$np\text{-bar} = \frac{7 + 3 + 4 + 0 + 11}{5} = 5$$

Thus, we have an average of five rejected mirrors in every inspection of 100 mirrors. The control limits around this average of five are found using the following formulas.

$$\text{UCL} = n\overline{p} + 3 \times \sqrt{n\overline{p}\left(1 - \frac{n\overline{p}}{n}\right)}$$

$$\text{LCL} = n\overline{p} - 3 \times \sqrt{n\overline{p}\left(1 - \frac{n\overline{p}}{n}\right)}$$

When the *np*-bar is five and the sample size is 100, the control limits are

$$\text{UCL} = 5 + 3 \times \sqrt{5\left(1 - \frac{5}{100}\right)}$$

$$\text{UCL} = 11.54$$

$$\text{LCL} = 5 - 3 \times \sqrt{5\left(1 - \frac{5}{100}\right)}$$

$$\text{LCL} = 0 \quad \text{(since, -1.5 defectives is impossible)}$$

Step 5: Chart subgroup values.

The first 25 subgroups should be plotted on the chart as the number of defectives found. All of the points should be inside the control limits. If they are not, then the company should take steps to audit the vendor and encourage the implementation of SPC at the vendor plant.

Step 6: Use the chart to pursue continuous improvement.

These control limits tell us that whenever a sample of 100 mirrors are checked, if more than 11 are found defective the process has lost statistical control. Corrective action should be taken in cooperation with the vendor.

An *np*-bar chart is not restricted to vendor products. It can be used anywhere a p-bar chart is possible. When used in-house, the corrective actions are a job for management and the process operators. Otherwise, like the *p*-bar chart, the objective is to drive the process average down to zero.

How to Strive for Zero Defects Using the *C*-Bar Chart: An Example Using the Manufacturing Process for Typewriter Keyboards

Both the *c*-bar chart and the *u*-bar chart monitor the number of defects occurring in a process. Therefore, the first step for both of these charts is to have a defect checklist that groups nonconformances into levels of severity. A typical arrangement is into three groups called critical, major and minor defects. This allows the operators not only to monitor the number of defects occurring, but to also be alerted when a critical defect is present.

Although many schemes exist to define the level of a defect, the military definition tends to be the most widely used. Paraphrasing from several sources, the intensities of defects break down into one of three categories.

1. *Critical:* The defect will cause harm to either the customer or the manufacturer.
2. *Major* : The defect will adversely affect the ability of the company to sell the product.
3. *Minor*: Although not a major problem, the defect is still an annoyance.

The first role of any company that wants to keep defect charts should be the creation of a defect checklist that classifies all possible defects on a scale similar to this.

Step 1: Select the defects to monitor.

The *c*-bar chart begins with the counting of defects in a fixed sample size of parts. For example, assume that the manufacturer of a typewriter keyboard has five keyboards randomly selected each hour for examination. The operators of the keyboard assembly process are responsible for locating defects and they are armed with a defect checklist.

Step 2: Collect 25 subgroups of data.

To create the *c*-bar chart, you must check 25 samples of production. For our example, we will once again use only five samples.

The sample size for a *c*-bar chart can be as low as a single unit of production. The sample size to use depends on the complexity of the production unit and the time needed for a thorough examination. For example, a *c*-bar chart for a finished car would require only a single sample, perhaps every few hours. A car takes a long time to examine, and it has the potential for thousands of defects. In contrast, a solder connector on the end of a wire has little potential for defects and is easy to examine. In such a case, a bundle of 50 wires may be used as the inspection sample.

Assume that the operators have found the following number of defects.

$$
\begin{array}{c}
14 \\
11 \\
9 \\
10 \\
15
\end{array}
$$

This is a total of 59 defects. As the operators find various defects, such as badly molded keys, paint marks, and so on, they would record both the number and type of defects at the bottom of the *c*-bar chart (see Figure 4-6).

Step 3: Log changes in the process.

As with other control charts, a careful history of process changes must be kept.

Step 4: Calculate trial limits and the process average.

Calculate the average number of defects found for every five keyboards. The formula for this calculation is

$$
c\text{-bar} = \frac{\text{total number of defects}}{\text{number of samples drawn}}
$$

In our example, the process was sampled five times. Thus the *c*-bar is

$$
c\text{-bar} = \frac{59}{5} = 11.8
$$

In other words, this process produces about 12 defects for every five keyboards. To find the control limits around the *c*-bar, the following formula is used.

$$
\text{UCL} = \bar{c} + 3 \times \sqrt{\bar{c}}
$$

$$
\text{LCL} = \bar{c} - 3 \times \sqrt{\bar{c}}
$$

Inserting our example's *c*-bar value of 11.8, we calculate the control limits.

$$UCL = 11.8 + 3 \times \sqrt{11.8} = 22.1$$

$$LCL = 11.8 - 3 \times \sqrt{11.8} = 1.5$$

As before, these control limits are drawn across the chart and used for the ongoing monitoring of the process.

Step 5: Chart the subgroup values.

This process has the capability of producing about 12 defects per five pieces. On a normal day the number of defects can vary from about 2 to 22. If more than 22 defects are found, immediate corrective action is required. If one or zero defects are found, the chart has detected a significant improvement in the process. This too must be investigated.

Once statistical control is shown, the chart is posted. The operators responsible for keeping the chart should also be formed into a work team assigned to finding ways of improving the keyboard manufacturing process to reduce defects.

Step 6: Use the chart for continuous improvement.

As with any attribute chart, the final objective is to drive the process average down toward zero. The chart serves as a feedback mechanism for continuous improvement. As the work team tries new manufacturing techniques, the *c*-bar chart, like other attribute charts, reflects improvements and problems. Improvements must be exploited and problems attacked.

How to Reduce Defects Using the *U*-Bar Chart

Sometimes it is difficult to get a consistent sample size when monitoring defects. Restrictions on time, production, or lot size will require a varying sample size. In these cases the *u*-bar chart is used. The *u* in the *u*-bar chart represents the average number of defects per unit of production. The following example illustrates how a *u*-bar chart is created.

Step 1: Select the defects to monitor.

In this instance, we will assume that the manufacturer of circuit boards requires the wave solder operator to examine as many boards as time permits

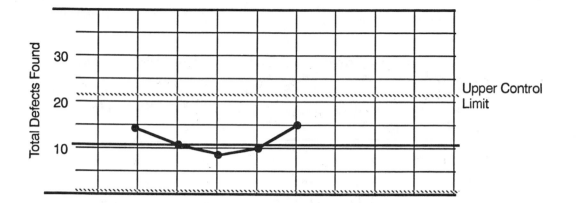

Defects

Sinks	1	1		2				
Cracks	4		1		2			
Missing Ltrs.		10		6	1			
Burrs	9			2	2			
Other			8		10			
Total Defects	14	11	9	10	15			
Sample Size	5	5	5	5	5			

Figure 4-6: A completed C-bar chart for defects.

at the end of each hour. Therefore, the sample size will vary from hour to hour depending on the demands of the production schedule.

Preliminary studies have listed over a dozen defects that can occur during wave soldering. These have been compiled into a defect checklist that includes photographs and written descriptions of each defect.

Step 2: Collect 25 subgroups of data.

During the first hour, the operator has time to look at five boards and he finds 13 defects. The u is calculated using the following formula.

$$u = \frac{\text{number of defects}}{\text{number of units examined}}$$

or

$$u = 13 / 5 = 2.6$$

As with any SPC chart, 25 samples should be drawn before the control limit calculations are made. For simplicity, we will use only five samples as an example.

The operator continues to record both number and type of defects along with the sample sizes. The resulting record is as follows.

	Sample Size	Defects
	5	13
	3	9
	12	22
	10	18
	7	11
Total	37	73

Step 3: Log process changes.

Again, any change in the wave soldering process should be duly noted.

Step 4: Calculate trial limits and the process average.

The u-bar is found by dividing the total number of defects by the total number of units sampled.

$$u\text{-bar} = \frac{\text{Total Defect Count}}{\text{Units Sampled}} = \frac{73}{37} = 1.97$$

In our example, we divide 73 by 37 to get an average number of defects per unit of 1.97. This is our u-bar. To calculate the control limits, we use the following formulas.

$$UCL = \bar{u} + 3 \times \sqrt{\frac{\bar{u}}{n}}$$

$$LCL = \bar{u} - 3 \times \sqrt{\frac{\bar{u}}{n}}$$

With an average sample size of 7.4 units (37/5 = 7.4), the control limits are

$$UCL = 1.97 + 3 \times \sqrt{\frac{1.97}{7.4}}$$

$$UCL = 3.5$$

$$LCL = 1.97 - 3 \times \sqrt{\frac{1.97}{7.4}}$$

$$LCL = 0.4$$

Naturally, these control limits are plotted across the SPC chart for the ongoing monitoring of the process (see Figure 4-7). Like the *p*-chart, if the subgroup size changes more than 25%, stepped control limits have to be calculated and plotted.

Step 5: Chart the subgroup values.

This process is capable of producing about two defects per unit. On a typical day, there should be an average of between 0.4 and 3.5 defects per unit. Defect ratios beyond these levels in the first 25 subgroups indicate a loss of statistical control. Statistical control must be achieved before the chart is posted.

Step 6: Use the chart for continuous improvement.

As with the other attribute charts, a *u*-bar chart can detect both improvements and problems. The chart is a feedback mechanism on whether work team efforts are helping, hurting, or having no effect on a process. Any of these three possibilities are important information for pursuing continuous improvement.

How to Interpret a Control Chart
and Use a Reaction Plan
to Make an SPC System Profitable

As stated earlier, statistics never stand alone. Nowhere is this more evident than with the use of SPC. Until this point, we have created charts that can monitor the quality of a process in real time. However, used by themselves, these charts are nothing more than pretty pictures.

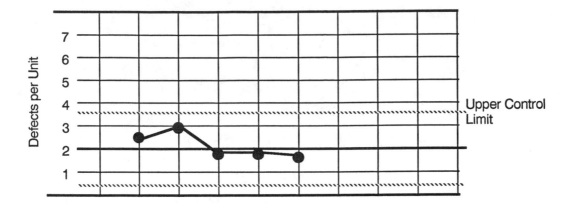

Defects

Missing solder	3	3	11	10	5			
Dirt	5	3	9	4	4			
Pores	5	3		3	2			
Flux residue			2	1				
Other								
Total Defects	13	9	22	18	11			
Sample Size	5	3	12	10	7			
Defect / Unit	2.6	3.0	1.8	1.8	1.6			

Figure 4-7: A U-bar chart for defects.

What makes an SPC chart a real SPC tool is the addition of a reaction plan. A reaction plan is the sequence of steps an operator should take when the SPC chart indicates that the process has lost statistical control. The most obvious case would be a point plotted outside of the control limits. We will look at the more subtle losses of statistical control.

When statistical control is lost, the operator must circle the point in question and flip over the SPC chart to record the date, time, and the problem experienced. Then the operator takes a series of steps to correct the situation. When the SPC is new to the manufacturing area, the steps toward correction are probably unknown. For example, a plastic injection machine operator would probably have little idea which of the dozens of controls would correct a deviation in part size. The operator would try many actions, recording each on the back of the chart. The successful action would be noted. By noting the successful action, and also through experimentation, the operator slowly builds up a record of the correct steps to take for various problems. For example, the plastic injection operator would soon learn that injection speed will radically affect part size.

Management benefits from the reaction plan by being able to collect finished SPC charts and summarize the sources of major manufacturing problems. For example, the management at a plastic injection plant could collect all of the *c*-bar charts and add together the number and types of defects experienced plant- wide. This exercise, also called Pareto analysis, would identify the few defects that create the most problems for manufacturing. Thus, management would have clearly identified specific problems to attack. For example, they may find that part shrinkage is a frequent and costly problem. Therefore, they might assign an engineering study to determine how to reduce shrinkage through the use of new methods and materials.

How to Track When You Are Losing Statistical Control

Sometimes the loss of statistical control is more subtle than the crossing of a control limit. For example, a trend might develop on an average and range chart. Suppose that a grinding operation is monitoring the outside diameter of a shaft. Examination of the average/range chart reveals that the last seven plotted points are forming a slowly rising trend. Whenever seven or more points form a rising or falling trend on an SPC chart, this indicates a loss of statistical control. The pattern is no longer fairly random. Instead, a definitive pattern has emerged. This trend could mean that the grinding wheel is wearing down or that a bracket is coming loose. In either case, there is a change in the process, and action should be taken. In the case of a grinding shop, if the trend is from grinding wheel wear and it remains consistent, they may "tilt" their average chart to match the rate of decay. This would allow them to predict when to change grinding wheels and when a factor other than the wear is present.

Another subtle loss of statistical control is when a run of seven points occurs above or below the process average. This indicates a change in the process average. This is a common phenomenon in the metal stamping industry. A new roll of steel is mounted on a press and the plottings on the chart suddenly move away from the process average. This indicates a change in the thickness of the stock steel. Such a change will naturally change the basic dimensions of a stamping. If the change is too great, the company may have to buy a better grade of certified steel.

As a rule of thumb, an SPC chart that is in statistical control will have no recognizable pattern, and two-thirds of the plotted points will be within the center third of the area between the control limits. This is called the rule of *zone analysis*. If two out of three points are found to be very near the control limits, the process is treated as though it is out of statistical control. If most of the points are near the process average, an out of statistical control situation is assumed. If you look again at Figure 4-2, you will see that less than one-half of the plotted points are near the process average.

How to Ensure Profitability through Continuous Improvement with SPC

An SPC chart with a reaction plan is the basic tool of the larger system of continuous improvement. The next link in the system is the process log. Each manufacturing process keeps a log of its activities. Every time an operator, tool, machine setting, or material changes, it is noted in the log. Then when the SPC chart detects a change, the log can be consulted to see what was different.

The attribute charts are an excellent example of how this system of record keeping contributes to continuous improvement. Suppose that a *p*-bar chart is being kept on scrap rates in a manufacturing area. One day the scrap rate falls below the lower control limit. This represents a significant improvement in the performance of the process. A quick investigation should take place to find the cause of the improvement. Imagine that an inspection of the process log finds that a new type of material is being used. It would be in the best interest of the company to exploit this opportunity to improve the scrap rate.

A specific example of such an occurrence is the manufacturing of wood furniture. Suppose a furniture company has made desks and bookcases for years, but for the past few years the number that had to be scrapped has grown steadily. Imlementation of an SPC chart revealed that warping of the wood caused over 85% of the scrap rate. An examination of past records revealed that engineering had changed from birch to a less expensive pine board for construction. The senior woodworkers indicated that the birch was resistant to warping. The pine boards needed strict climate control to prevent warping. The company decided that expensive birch was still cheaper than new climate controls and a high scrap rate.

How to Use Work Teams to Achieve Maximum Efficiency with SPC

This brings us to the final link between SPC and continuous improvement, the use of problem-solving work teams. SPC is only a tool for gathering the facts of a situation. The real solutions lie with the knowledge of the workers, managers and engineers. Therefore, to obtain a system of continuous improvement, a company must put these knowledgeable people together into work teams that are allowed to address and solve problems.

Consider another example from attribute charts. Suppose that a c-bar chart is being kept on the number of defects found in the final assembly of a weapon guidance system. Assume that the system had proved to be faulty in field use and the *c*-bar chart bears this out by detecting an average of 12 minor defects per unit.

The company might assemble a work team of about nine people made up of operators, engineers, and customer representatives. This group would begin by examining the types of defects experienced in manufacturing against field complaints. Perhaps the work team finds that dust is getting into the gun sight, and during manufacturing the seals on the gun sight are consistently cracked. Such an investigation has focused the group's attention on a particular problem.

The next step would be to talk with the operators about how the seals become cracked. Perhaps this further investigation finds that rough handling of the seals causes the cracking. The work team may then suggest to management that a new handling system be developed. The success of the new handling system can be measured directly on the SPC chart. If the plotting of defects falls below the process average, the new system is a success. The SPC chart control limits are reset to the new, lower process average and the work team moves on to the next problem.

In this example, the SPC chart is being used as a problem-solving tool as well as a way to monitor the ongoing quality of production. The work team can use the attribute charts as a feedback mechanism on the success of their efforts. The process average is a baseline for evaluation. The objective is to drive the plottings down to zero. When zero defects are experienced regularly, the control limits are abandoned and only the recording of the type and number of defects continues. Each occurrence of a defect is then treated the same as the loss of statistical control. In short, SPC becomes continuous improvement.

Conclusion

The SPC chart can be a valuable tool in the pursuit of continuous improvement in manufacturing. However, the statistics alone are not enough to reap a benefit from SPC. Reaction plans, process logs, and work teams are also required to make the system work to produce a higher quality product at a lower cost.

SPC is also used to establish statistical control so that a final capability study can be conducted on the process. Between SPC and capability studies, the manufacturing manager has a firm grip on the hows and whys of variations in the production process. With this information, intelligently planned improvements are possible.

CHAPTER 5

Using Statistical Methods to Ensure the Quality of Manufacturing Processes

Quality is an inverse function of costs. That is, as the quality of the product is improved, generally the cost of its production diminishes. Therefore, quality is a critical concern for the manufacturing manager because a primary goal of the manufacturing department is to find ways to make a product better at a lower cost.

As we have seen in chapters 3 and 4, the manufacturing manager has several motivations for seeking statistical control of a process and then certifying the capability of the process. These actions help assure the quality of the product during start-up and early production.

However, the quality priority actually stretches from the moment a product is conceived until it has finished its useful life in the hands of a consumer. Therefore, every department within a company should have some priority in investigating its own responsibilities for the quality of the product.

In the manufacturing area this priority breaks down into three general areas of concern: planning for quality during production, controlling the quality during manufacturing, and continuous improvement of the manufacturing process. In this chapter we will examine simple statistical techniques that will aid you in fulfilling the quality priority for manufacturing.

How to Plan for Quality Before Manufacturing Begins

The introduction of a new product to the manufacturing area is prefaced with a considerable amount of work and research. Prints have to be drawn up, tolerances set, reliability estimated, marketing research conducted, legal restrictions reviewed, and so forth. The complexity of these steps will be directly proportional to the complexity of the final product.

There will be some specific questions among these tasks that you will want to investigate as the manufacturing manager. For example, you may use a technique such as quality function deployment to translate customer needs into actual production operations, checks, and procedures. As part of this manufacturing planning process, questions will arise as to which customer characteristics are important, what qualities you seek, and which production situations will cause problems during manufacturing.

At the same time, the quality department will be investigating the fitness for use of the product. Engineering may be conducting value analysis to increase the manufacturability of the product. Research and development may be running experiments on prototypes. Therefore, as you answer your own questions using the techniques presented in this chapter, remember to coordinate your results with the flood of data produced by other departments.

How to Find the Critical Qualities of a Product Using Failure Mode and Effects Analysis

Failure Mode and Effects Analysis (FMEA) is a tool to assist you in the development of a new product. The method involves a listing of all possible causes of problems with the product by component. By examining the impact of each potential problem, you can create of list of problems by their economic impact on the company. This provides information on which quality characteristics of the product have to be monitored and strictly controlled. This also gives your development team further information to use in the design of countermeasures.

For each potential problem listed, the probability of occurrence and its economic impact is estimated. Thus, the steps of an FMEA are as follows:

1. List all possible problems with a product by component.
2. Calculate the probability of each occurrence and its economic impact.
3. Use this information to design countermeasures where needed.

An Example of FMEA Benefiting a Company in the Development of a Gasoline Engine

A company is developing a new 3.5 horsepower gasoline engine. This powerplant is intended for powered tools, generators, and miscellaneous small vehicles. Therefore, a wide application of the product must be considered when conducting an FMEA.

Step 1: List all possible problems by component.

The first step would be to list each component of the engine and the potential problems that could be experienced. Even though a small gasoline engine does not need to be a complex product, the list of components can be extensive. Therefore, we shall restrict our example to just two areas, the ignition system and the piston assembly.

Component	Potential Problem	Cause
Ignition System	Failure to start	Broken wire
		Cracked spark plug
		Failed condenser
		Timing poorly set
		Broken flywheel key
		Wrong air gap on fly-wheel
	Fire	Short
		Cracked wire
Piston	Rings crack	Rings too tight
		Low motor oil
		Runs too fast

As you can see, such a list can easily become very large. To avoid this problem on more complex products, you can usually restrict the FMEA to only critical and major problems.

Step 2: Calculate the probability of problem occurrence and economic impact.

The next step in the FMEA is to follow each cause with its probability of occurrence and the economic impact. One way to calculate the economic impact is with the following formula.

impact = cost x probability of occurrence x number of units produced

The probability of occurrence can be found through reliability methods, safety analysis, fault tree analysis, and other such methods.

Assuming that the company plans to build 100,000 engines, you can calculate the economic impact of each problem given the following probabilities of occurrence.

Potential Problem	Cause	Probability
Failure to start	Broken wire	0.001
	Cracked spark plug	0.001
	Failed condenser	0.0005
	Timing poorly set	0.01
	Broken flywheel key	0.0001
	Wrong air gap on fly-wheel	0.001
Fire	Short	0.0001
	Cracked wire	0.0007
Rings crack	Rings too tight	0.0000039
	Low motor oil	0.001
	Runs too fast	0.00005

If we take a moment we can see how one particular probability was calculated using simple statistical methods. Specifically, we shall examine cracking rings. The first potential cause would be rings that were too tight for the cylinder. This can be caused by oversized rings or an undersized cylinder. In most cases, it would be a combination of both.

To find the chance of large rings being placed in a small cylinder, you would begin with the capabilities of the two parts. Assume that the rings average 1.995 inches in size with a standard deviation of 0.002 inches. Also assume that the cylinders average 2.005 inches in diameter with a standard deviation of 0.0015 inches.

Using this information, you can calculate the probability of a large ring being assembled into a small cylinder. The Z-score formula can find this probability.

$$Z = \frac{\text{average} - \text{target}}{\text{standard deviation}}$$

In our example, you would begin by drawing a picture of the two distributions (see Figure 5-1). The probability of occurrence would be where the two tails of the distributions overlap. Begin with the tail for the cylinders. The critical point is where the distribution begins to overlap the plus-three- standard-deviation limit of the rings (in this case 2.001 inches).

The area under the curve for cylinders lower than 2.001 inches represents cylinders that will be too small for the rings produced a little too large. The Z-score for this area is as follows.

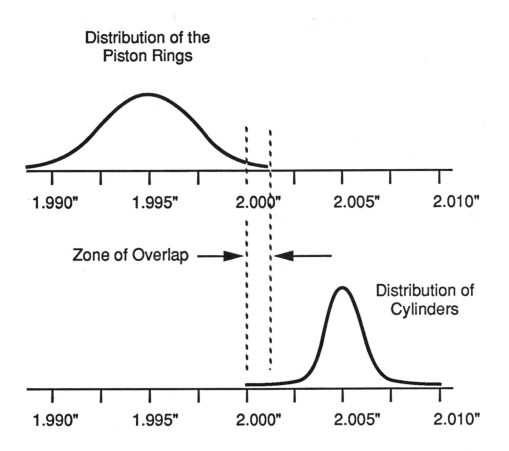

Figure 5-1: Illustration of tolerance overlap.

$$Z = \frac{2.005 - 2.001}{0.0015} = 2.67$$

Using Appendix A, we find that 49.62% of the area is between the average and 2.001 inches. Therefore, the remaining 0.38% of the area lies beyond. This is multiplied into the area for rings above 2.001 inches. This limit represents the top of the three standard deviation range for rings.

In our example, the average size of the rings is 1.995 inches. Our target value of interest is 2.001 inches, and the process has a standard deviation of 0.002 inches. This results in a Z-score of -3.0.

$$Z = \frac{1.995 - 2.001}{0.002} = -3.0$$

Using Appendix A, the area under the normal curve for a Z-score of 3.0 is 49.865%. That means that only 0.135% of the area lies beyond this point. Therefore, the probability of a ring being manufactured larger than 2 inches is 0.00135.

Combined with the 0.38% chance of an undersized cylinder being used, the final probability is

probability of occurrence = 0.0038 x 0.00135 = 0.0000051

In other words, the change of the manufacture of rings and cylinders resulting in an assembly that will crack is about 0.51 in 100,000 engines.

The economic impact of the ring crack due to misassembly can be calculated by taking the cost of cracked rings times the number of expected occurrences. If we assume that the cost of repairing cracked rings is $40.00, then the final economic impact would be about $20.52.

impact = 0.0000051 x $40.00 x 100,000 = $20.52

Step 3: Use the information to design countermeasures where necessary.

The preceding analysis finds that the current capabilities of the manufacturing processes pose very little economic threat to the quality of the engine. Therefore, a countermeasure, such as tighter tolerances, is not needed for this particular problem. You know that it is not needed because the increased cost of maintaining tighter tolerances is far larger than the economic impact of misfitting rings.

In the case where a particular problem will pose too great of a threat (for example, a fire), the engineer has to pursue possible countermeasures. For example, the fires may occur from leaking gasoline. Therefore, tighter connections and gas lines that are resistant to cracking are designed into the product.

If some of the parts for the motor are supplied by an outside source, these same methods may be applied to initial samples to evaluate their qualities. For example, the piston rings were supplied by another company. If an initial sample of 30 rings were required for qualification and the same average and standard deviation were observed, then the same economic impact of large rings would result.

How to Audit Blueprint Tolerances to Assure Quality Before Manufacturing

Although the engineering department frequently evaluates the manufacturability of parts according to tolerances and the quality department serves as the auditor, you can still confirm their work quickly based on knowledge you have on process capabilities.

How to Compare Mating Parts: An Example Using a Bolt and Nut Assembly

For example, let us look at the evaluation of mating parts to see if tolerance for the assembly will be upset by the combined effect of the capability of each process for each part. The steps for such an audit are as follows:

1. Determine if one or many parts are involved.
2. List the mating parts by size and tolerance.
3. Calculate combined tolerance range.
4. Compare calculated range to those specified.

Suppose that part of an assembly requires the threaded end of a bolt to have a washer, a spring, another washer, and a locking nut fastened, in that order. These four parts, stacked together, must be 15 mm in combined width, plus or minus 0.10 mm to ensure that part of the bolt end is past the end of the locking nut.

Step 1: Determine whether these are one or many parts.

If only a single part is involved, go to the next example on evaluating tolerances on an individual part. Otherwise, continue with the following steps.

Step 2: List size and tolerance requirements.

If the size and tolerance of each part are assembled as follows, will they exceed the assembly specifications? You can also substitute the actual six-standard-deviation spread of the process in place of the tolerance. This allows you to compare the stacking effect of multiple process capabilities.

First washer   3.00 +/- 0.02 mm
Spring   4.00 +/- 0.01 mm (when compressed)

Second washer   3.00 +/- 0.02 mm
Locking nut   5.00 +/- 0.05 mm

Step 3: Calculate the combined tolerance range.

The formula for the variation for combined tolerances is,

$$\text{combined tolerance} = \sqrt{T(A)^2 + T(B)^2 + T(C)^2} + ...$$

where $T(A)$ = tolerance of the first part
       $T(B)$ = tolerance of the second part, and so on.

For our example, there are four tolerances to consider.

$$\text{combined tolerance} = \sqrt{0.02^2 + 0.01^2 + 0.02^2 + 0.05^2} = 0.0583 \text{ mm}$$

Step 4: Compare calculated range to specifications.

Compared to the assembly tolerance of plus or minus 0.10 mm, this assembly of parts will work fine. The calculated tolerance range for the assembly is 0.0583 mm. If the amount had been more than specified, engineering would have to reevaluate the tolerances.

How to Evaluate the Tolerance for an Individual Part: An Example Using the Capacitor in an Electronic Circuit

The engineering department usually has set functional specifications for a tolerance, but you may want these compared to the process capabilities.

Suppose that a manufacturer of electronic components wants to set the tolerances for a new type of capacitor. The functional specifications call for 500 microfarads (mfd) plus or minus 50 mfd. Your process performance study samples 10 of the first capacitors produced and finds an average of 500 mfd and a standard deviation of 10 mfd.

The formula for setting the tolerance limits is

$$\text{tolerance} = X \pm (K \times s)$$

where X = sample average
       s = sample standard deviation
       K = limiting factor

To calculate statistically based tolerance limits, a corrected area under the curve factor (K) is used that accounts for the sample size and the confidence you can have that 99% of the parts will be manufactured inside of the calculated tolerances. The typical confidence factor is set to 95%. This combination of confidence and area under a curve results in the following factors.

Sample Size	K Factor
5	6.63
10	4.43
30	3.35
100	2.93

The preceding sample sizes are typical of conventional capability studies.

For our example, 10 parts were sampled. Therefore, the following tolerance can be calculated.

$$\text{tolerance} = 500 \pm (4.43 \times 10)$$

or

$$\text{tolerance} = 500 \pm 44.3$$

In other words, the suggested statistical tolerance is close, but lower than the functional tolerance. The company could either retain the functional specification or lower it to 45 mfd.

How to Find Potential Production Problems Before Manufacturing Begins—Using the Pareto Analysis

In industry, the least expensive way to solve a production problem is to make sure it never happens. This is called prevention. One way to promote the prevention of problems is to examine the history of making a similar product when a new product is being introduced. A simple but effective tool for such an examination is Pareto analysis.

An Example of Pareto Analysis Used to Prevent Production Problems in the Manufacture of Magnesium Oxide.

Magnesium oxide is a chemical compound used in a wide variety of applications from metal working to animal feed. It is produced in a continuous process; that is, instead of individual parts or batches being produced, a continuous chemical compounding process creates the product.

A chemical compounding company receives word that a new substitute for pure magnesium oxide will be introduced in six months. As manufacturing manager, you have received the process instruction sheets from research and development. These sheets are based on models of the process developed using a scaled-down pilot plant. From experience, you know that scaling up to actual volumes your plant can produce will require some adjustments to the process.

What a Pareto analysis does is examine the economic impact of all possible problems. The analysis is based on the Pareto principle that most problems will be trivial, while a few problems will be vital to your successful launch of the new product line.

Step 1: Look into the history of production.

The SPC and process logs kept during past production runs of the magnesium oxide show that dozens of problems were encountered that required many different adjustments to the process. Your goal is to organize these problems in the order of importance so that work teams can address the problem before full-scale production begins.

Step 2: List each problem.

From your historic data you find problems such as the following:

Problem
Kiln temperature fluctuates too much.
Slurry quality is bad.
Line speed is too slow.
Particle size distributions are off.
Some particle sizes are too large.

Naturally, a complete analysis would create a list much longer than this.

Step 3: List the frequency of occurrence for each problem.

The occurrence must be expressed as some sort of ratio of the event happening versus the opportunities for the event to occur. For example, a parts manufacturer may find that 1.3% of all production parts have a particular problem. Another company may find that a machine has 25 hours of downtime for each 1,000-hour production run. In our example, we report the percentage of the total production that has experienced the listed problem.

Problem	Frequency
Kiln temperature fluctuates too much.	2% of production
Slurry quality is bad.	10%
Line speed is too slow.	1%
Particle size distributions are off.	25%
Some particle sizes are too large.	10%

Step 4: List the economic impact of each problem.

Economic impact refers to the cost to correct the situation when it occurs and the cost of scrapping or reworking the affected product. Therefore, each problem must have its economic impact calculated separately.

For example, you find that when slurry qualities are bad, the process will produce a lower yield and will require a chemical adjustment. The cost to the company if all production runs occurred with bad slurry is $100,000 per year.

Problem	Frequency	Impact
Kiln temperature	2%	$200,000
Slurry quality	10%	$100,000
Line speed	1%	$ 10,000
Particle size	25%	$ 10,000
Large particles	10%	$ 2,000

Step 5: Multiply occurrence by impact.

For example, the 2% (0.02) occurrence of the kiln temperature problem is multiplied by the impact of $200,000. The resulting impact is $4,000 per year.

Problem	Frequency	Impact	Results
Kiln temperature	2%	$200,000	$ 4,000
Slurry quality	10%	$100,000	$10,000
Line speed	1%	$ 10,000	$ 100
Particle size	25%	$ 10,000	$ 2,500
Large particles	10%	$ 2,000	$ 200

Step 6: Sort problems by resulting scores.

Problem	Results
Slurry quality	$10,000
Kiln temperature	$ 4,000
Particle size	$ 2,500
Large particles	$ 200
Line speed	$ 100

Note that the priority of the results is different from the frequency of occurrence.

Step 7: Assign corrective actions in order of Pareto priorities.

Using a list such as the preceding one, you can assign work teams to the problems that would create the greatest negative economic impact if left unchecked. By eliminating problems in the order of their impact, you are making the most effective use of your resources to create the greatest efficiency. Specifically, you are spending a low amount of money to reap the highest return on your efforts.

Summary of the Quality Planning Function for Manufacturing

Auditing the tolerances of parts, performing FMEA, and using Pareto analysis to prevent the most damaging potential problems in production are all part of planning quality into manufacturing. When planning is carefully coordinated with the quality concerns of other departments, you create a higher quality product that is produced at a lower cost by avoiding costly corrections to the design and the process. The next step is to control the quality you have planned for the product during production. We have seen in chapters 3 and 4 that SPC and capability studies play an important role in establishing control. Now we will look at a few more techniques you can use to increase the efficiency of your control.

How to Design Sampling Plans for Maximum Information at the Lowest Cost

In the early part of this century, the quality control department would select 10% of any production lot for inspection. However, with the advent of statistically based methods in the 1930s, it quickly became clear that there is a point where taking more samples does not increase the amount of knowledge gained.

How to Find the Best Sample Size Using Variable Data: An Iron Casting Company Selects a Sample Size for Flywheels

Formulas were developed to determine the smallest sample that would provide enough information to make a decision on the quality of a production lot. For example, the following formula is used with dimensional data to find the smallest number of parts to sample to be sure that an inspected lot meets specifications.

$$n = \left(\frac{Z \cdot s}{E}\right)^2$$

where, E = allowable error
Z = Z-score of confidence
s = sample standard deviation

Suppose that an iron casting company is producing flywheels that must have an outside diameter of 5 inches. The tolerance on the diameter is plus or minus 0.01 inches.

Step 1: Make sure that you are using variable data.

Variable data is taken on a measuring device that has a variable scale, such as inches, temperature, or pounds per square inch. Attribute data involves counts, percentages, and other ratio or attribute scales. In this example variable data is being used, therefore you continue on to the next step. If you have attribute data, you should use the attribute procedure described later in this chapter.

Step 2: Find the standard deviation of the population.

The standard deviation of the production population you wish to sample can be estimated using historic data—for example, the capability studies and the SPC charts kept on the process.

In this example, you examine production history for the flywheel and find a typical standard deviation of 0.001995 inches. This is rounded off to a standard deviation of 0.002 inches to ease calculations.

Step 3: Estimate amount of tolerable error and confidence.

After meeting with the engineers, you decide that a sampling plan must give an accurate picture of where the process mean is to within 0.001 inches. This would be your allowable error. It represents how far off your estimate might be from reality.

The next decision is that you want 95% confidence in the results. The higher the level of confidence you select, the larger the resulting sample size. Therefore, you will have to balance the economy of the sample size against the precision of the estimate.

The amount of error you can tolerate and the confidence intervals determine the resulting sample size. Do not be afraid to suggest several different levels of these values and their resulting sampling sizes to decision-makers. By demonstrating that a different combination of factors may create a better sampling plan, you can avoid unnecessarily large samples.

Step 4: Calculate the sample size.

The first step is to look up the Z-score for 95% confidence using Table 2.1 in chapter 2. The value is 1.96. Inserting these values into the formula gives an answer of 15.3664.

$$n = \left(\frac{1.96 \times 0.002}{0.001}\right)^2 = 15.3664$$

The results of a sample size formula are always rounded off to the next higher number, since the answer represents a minimum.

Step 5: Draw up the sampling plan.

In our example, we would need to examine 16 flywheels to get an accurate picture of the quality of the outside diameter. This information is inserted into a complete plan for sampling the flywheels. Such a plan would indicate how often the wheels are sampled, which dimensions to measure, how to record the readings, and what to do if a problem is detected.

How to Design a Sampling Plan for Attribute Data: A Bottling Company Finds an Effective Sample Size for Checking Incoming Bottle Caps

In many cases, the quality department has to inspect attributes of a production lot, such as the number of defects or defectives. Although they are losing popularity, attribute sampling plans are still used widely for lot-by-lot inspection. The most famous of these plans is Military Standard (MIL) 105-D (also known today as ANSI Z1.4-1981). Today, with the need for 100% quality, these types of plans are becoming obsolete.

When an attribute sampling plan *is* used, it usually falls upon the quality department to design and evaluate specific plans. In most cases, the lot size determines the sample size to be drawn and how many defective units are detected before the entire lot is rejected.

As manufacturing manager, you must be able to review quickly the robustness of the sampling plan suggested by the quality department. This is done using an operational characteristic curve, or simply OC curve. The following is an example of creating such a curve. You should refer to how OC curves are created and interpreted to help you evaluate a new or existing sampling plan.

To create the proposed sampling plan, the quality department needs only to determine the acceptable quality level (AQL) for the sampling plan. The AQL is the level of defective material at which the sampling plan will still accept up to 95% of the inspected lots. For example, if the AQL is set to 1.0%, then the sampling plan will accept up to 95% of incoming material that has 1 in 100 defective units.

To evaluate a specific sampling plan, it is necessary to examine its performance across a range of overall lot quality. The resulting data forms the OC curve. The OC curve is created by calculating the probability of accepting a lot at various proportions of defectives.

Step 1: Determine the suggested sample size.

A standard attribute sampling plan (MIL 105-D for single sampling under normal inspection) would suggest that 125 caps be sampled and the entire lot rejected if more than three caps are found to be defective. The AQL for such a plan is assumed to be 1.0%.

Step 2: List a range of percent defectives.

To create the OC curve, you begin by listing a range of percents defective in the production lot and multiplying these by the sample size (in our example the sample size is 125). Usually, the range begins at 0.005 and can go as high as 0.15 and more.

Proportion Defective	Sample Size x Percent Defective
0.005	0.625
0.01	1.25
0.02	2.50
0.03	3.75
0.04	5.00
0.05	6.25
0.06	7.50

Step 3: Calculate the probability of accepting a lot with a given proportion of defectives.

The probability of accepting a lot of with a specific amount of defective caps is given in the following formula.

$$P_a = P \text{ (sample size x percent defective)}$$

where P_a = probability of acceptance
P = Poisson probability

The Poisson distribution is used for cases with a fairly large sample but in which the likelihood of a specific event is slight. In other words, even though we look at 125 caps, the chance of any one cap being defective is quite small. Appendix D lists Poisson probabilities for many different situations.

Step 4: Calculate the Poisson for each value.

For each of the values in the right-hand column, look up the corresponding cumulative Poisson probability. Consider the first number as an example. The np is equal to 0.625, and the c value in our example 3 (the maximum number of defectives allowed under the sampling plan). In Appendix D, the value of $np = 0.6$ and $c = 3$ corresponds to a probability of 0.977.

This same procedure is repeated for each of the np values listed earlier.

np	Probability
0.625	0.997
1.25	0.966
2.50	0.757
3.75	0.494
5.00	0.263
6.25	0.151
7.50	0.060

Step 5: Plot out the OC curve.

These values are now plotted on graph paper to form the OC curve. Figure 5-2 shows the finished OC curve.

Interpretation. An examination of the OC curve reveals several characteristics of the sampling plan for management's evaluation. To begin with, with an AQL of 1.0%, there is a 95% chance of accepting lots with up to 1% of the products defective. Conversely, there is a 5% chance that a good lot will be rejected using this plan.

Another way to look at the OC curve is to check for the chance of accepting lots of materials that exceed the 1% AQL. Even though the AQL is only a guideline for the creation of a sampling plan, the OC curve can show that lots with many defective goods might be accepted. For example, a shipment with 5% of the goods defective has a 15.1% chance of being accepted. Therefore, the AQL does not represent the cut-off point in acceptable quality the sampling plan will tolerate. Instead, it represents a standard that the supplier should meet and then exceed.

Sampling plans can be designed to reject a lot if any defective goods are detected in the sample. These are called $c = 0$ plans because the acceptance level is set to zero. These enforce the idea of zero defects, and they require smaller sample sizes. However, they also produce an OC curve that drops sharply at the beginning. This means that the supplier is under tremendous pressure to produce zero defective units.

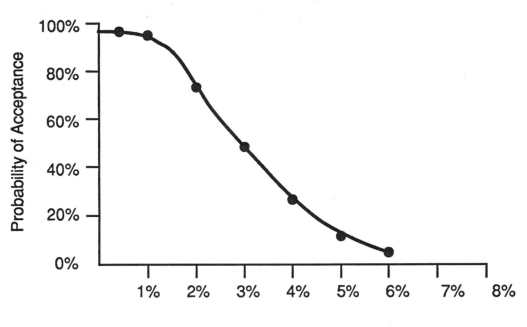

Figure 5-2: An operational characteristic curve.

How to Assure the Measurement Accuracy of Gauges in the Manufacturing Area Using Repeatability and Reproducibility Studies

In the mid-1980s, a new task emerged for many companies—the evaluation of measuring equipment. A number of large customers began to require the study of measurement gauges' repeatability and reproducibility. This test came to be called the R&R study.

Repeatability refers to how well a measurement gauge repeats the measurement of a part. For example, a hand caliper might be used to measure the diameter of a valve. If the measurement is repeated on the same valve, will the reading still be the same? The answer turns out to be no; usually the reading will vary with each repetition.

Reproducibility refers to the variations observed when more than one person measures a single part using the same instrument. For example, if the valve was measured by the first-shift inspector and then by the second shift inspector, would they record the same readings? Again, the typical answer is no.

As noted earlier, these two major sources of measurement error are called the repeatability and reproducibility (R&R) of a gauge. The statistical test of these sources of error is called an R&R study. It requires a target measurement gauge, the most important part the gauge measures, and two or three gauge operators.

An R&R study is conducted after the accuracy of the gauge is determined using conventional calibration. The steps for conducting an R&R study are as follows:

1. Select a gauge, a matching production part, and at least two gauge operators.
2. Measure 10 parts, three times by each operator.
3. Calculate the range between readings on the same part.
4. Calculate the average reading for each operator.
5. Calculate the R&R error.

An Example of Calculating an R&R Error for Metal Stamped Parts

Suppose that a manufacturing firm owns several dozen metric micrometers used for measuring the thickness of the parts produced by the metal stamping department.

Step 1: Select a gauge, part, and the operators.

The most widely produced of these parts is a bracket used in the auto-motive industry. Micrometer 2938-002 is normally used to measure the critical thickness of the bracket at the point where the part mates to a hinge.

To test the R&R of this gauge, the three shift inspectors that normally use this micrometer are called into a testing area.

Step 2: Measure 10 parts, three times by each operator.

One by one the inspectors are handed what they each think are 30 parts to measure. In reality, the tester has given them the same 10 parts, three times over. The tester has coded the parts so that he or she knows which part the inspector is measuring.

Specifications for the part call for 2.45 mm, plus or minus 0.05 mm. Each reading taken by an inspector is coded by how many hundredths of a millimeter it is above or below the target of 2.45 mm. For example, the first inspector measured the first piece as 2.46 mm; thus it was coded as being +1.

For the first inspector, the following readings were recorded.

Part	Trial		
	1	2	3
1	1	2	1
2	1	1	1
3	0	−2	−1
4	2	−1	0
5	−2	−1	−1
6	−1	0	−1
7	1	1	0
8	1	1	0
9	0	−1	1
10	1	0	1

Step 3: Calculate the range between readings on the same part.

As you can see, there are variations in the readings for the same part as it was remeasured. This amount of variation is used to calculate the re-peatability. The average reading for this inspector will be compared to the averages for the other inspectors to evaluate reproducibility. Therefore, the range for each row of data and the average for all 30 measurements must be calculated for each inspector. Inspector 1 has the following results.

Part	Trial			Range
	1	2	3	
1	1	2	1	1
2	1	1	1	0
3	0	−2	−1	2
4	2	−1	0	3
5	−2	−1	−1	1
6	−1	0	−1	1
7	1	1	0	1
8	1	1	0	1
9	0	−1	1	2
10	1	0	1	1
Overall total = 5		Total range = 13		

Step 4: Calculate the average reading for each operator.

Dividing the overall total by 30 results in an average measurement of 0.167. Dividing the total range by 10 results in the average range of 1.3. These two numbers are used to help complete the R&R study.

For the sake of keeping this example brief, we will assume that the other two inspectors were tested as previously stated and had the following results.

Second inspector: average = 0.37; average range = 2.7
Third inspector: average = 0.20; average range = 2.0

Step 5: Calculate the R&R error.

To complete the R&R study, the repeatability is calculated by obtaining an overall average of the average ranges.

$$\text{average of average ranges } (\overline{\overline{R}}) = \frac{1.3 + 2.7 + 2.0}{3} = 2.0$$

The difference between inspectors (reproducibility) is calculated by taking the difference between the highest average and the lowest average.

$$\text{difference between averages } (X \text{ diff.}) = 0.37 - 0.17 = 0.20$$

These figures are placed into the formula for R&R.

$$R\&R = [(\overline{\overline{R}} \times 3.05)^2 + (X \text{ diff.} \times 2.70)^2]^{1/2}$$

Substituting the information from our example,

$$R\&R = [(2.0 \times 3.05)^2 + (0.20 \times 2.70)^2]^{1/2} = 6.124$$

To evaluate the importance of this number, it has to be divided into the tolerance range. The idea is to find the percentage of the tolerance range as the magnitude of gauge error. In our example, the tolerance was plus and minus five hundredths of a millimeter. Therefore, the tolerance range, in coded form, is 10.

$$R\&R\% = \frac{R\&R}{\text{tolerance range}} \times 100$$

Thus,

$$R\&R\% = \frac{6.124}{10} \times 100 = 61.24\%$$

For most precision measuring instruments, the gauge R&R should be less than 10% of the tolerance range of the part in question. Clearly, the preceding gauge fails to meet this criterion. The error in the example micrometer is so bad that readings can vary over two-thirds of the tolerance range from measurement error alone. When the variation of the process is added in, the resulting data makes the process look wildly out of statistical control.

How to Begin the Process of Continuous Improvement by First Reporting the Quality Costs to Management

Planning for quality and controlling manufacturing quality are two necessary functions for the manufacturing manager. However, the added expense of planning and control must be offset by competitive gains and productivity improvements. Therefore, the third critical component of a manufacturing quality plan is continuous improvement. You must be able to demonstrate in hard dollars the gains from your quality efforts.

The system of quality cost reporting was developed and promoted by experts in the field of quality assurance, such a Joseph Juran. It is based on standard cost accounting techniques using classifications of expenses related to the quality function.

In general, these classifications are grouped into four areas:

1. Internal failure: The expenses for many of the items used for COQ, such as scrap, rework, sorting, downtime, and so on.

2. External failure: The costs a company incurs after the product is shipped. This includes such line items as customer complaints, lawsuits, out-of-court settlements, returned items, and warranty costs.

3. Appraisal: The expense of testing, inspecting, evaluating, and auditing the products and processes of manufacturing.

4. Prevention: This includes the activities of any department devoted to preventing quality problems. Line items include quality planning, product review, SPC, data collection, experimentation, and training.

Therefore, the following steps are used:

1. Establish standardized costs.
2. Break down costs by type and subject.
3. Evaluate results for possible improvements.

An Example of Calculating Quality Costs for a Small Manufacturing Firm.

Assume that you are the manufacturing manager of a small firm that has assembled the following summary of quality costs for the previous year. By examining how these costs were obtained and how they are categorized, you can evaluate the total impact, both positive and negative, for any quality improvement.

Step 1: Establish standardized costs.

The accounting department has used the definitions of quality costs to distribute the quality-related expenses as follows.

Quality Cost Source	Cost
Internal Failure	$175,000
External Failure	100,000
Appraisal	200,000
Prevention	25,000
Total	$500,000

Step 2: Break down costs by type and subject.

To clarify the sources of the quality costs, the report would add a summary with a breakdown of each category by line items. Consider the example of internal failure costs. Perhaps the line items look something like this:

Internal Failure	
Scrap	85,000
Rework	15,000
Downtime	10,000
Sorting	25,000
Disposition	15,000
Repair	20,000
Overtime	3,000
Misc.	2,000
Total	175,000

Step 3: Evaluate the report for possible improvements.

Such a report would indicate room for improvements in several areas. Almost all of these costs could be avoided if aggressive problem solving and continuous improvement are pursued. However, that would add to the prevention costs. Thus, quality costs are a balancing act for management.

In addition, you can use crosstabulations and Pareto analysis to further evaluate the quality costs. For example, a crosstabulation table of products by quality costs can identify targets for future improvement efforts.

		Product	
Cost	Gear Box	Motor Drive	Reduction Box
Internal	10,000	20,000	15,000
External	50,000	5,000	10,000
Appraisal	30,000	10,000	10,000
Prevention	4,000	1,000	2,000
Total	94,000	36,000	37,000
Units produced	10,000	50,000	40,000
Cost/unit	9.4	0.72	0.925

Using this method, it becomes clear that the gear box is a major source of quality costs. Specifically, the gear box has high external failure costs. A Pareto analysis of the causes of this high expense will pin down specific targets for improvement. Below is an example of a Pareto analysis.

Cause of External Failure Costs		
Returned Goods	Failure	$20,000
	Pins breaking	5,000
	Gears stripping	3,000
	Unknown	2,000
Lawsuits	Injury	10,000
	Other	5,000
Warranty	Failure	4,000
	Jamming	1,000
	Total	50,000

As you can see, assessing quality costs is a technique that is flexible and able to adapt to the standard cost accounting procedures used at most companies. Therefore, it serves as an excellent tool for examining and responding to the expenses of maintaining a high quality of production.

How to Find Assignable Causes and Other Sources of Improvement Using a Scattergram

As mentioned in chapters 3 and 4, one of the primary purposes of statistical controls on a process is to find and eliminate assignable causes to improve the process. Sometimes the assignable cause is easy to find. For example, an operator loads a new roll of steel into a stamping press and statistical control is immediately lost. However, finding the actual cause is not always an easy task.

An Example of Using a Scattergram to Find the Assignable Cause of a Welding Defect

When the assignable cause is not so easy to locate, the simple tool called a scattergram can help. Consider the case of a welding assembly area.

Suppose that you discover one day that the welding strength of an assembly sporadically fails its pull test. The pull test states that the assembly should survive a pull of 1,000 foot-pounds. Some days the parts are fine, but about every five or six days the parts fail.

Step 1: *Gather data from the SPC system.*

Using the control chart data for pull strength, or the pull test results and the process log, look for changes in the proecess that correspond with days when the parts fail. Unfortunately, many things are changing at the same time in a welding process—the welding wire used, the temperature settings, the gases, and so forth.

Step 2: Break down changes into assignable time units.

The process log should note every change in the process. Each type of change should be listed by identifiable time units. In this case, you decide to list by day. You base this decision on the fact that the pieces are only tested once a day; thus the resolution of the data is in days.

You create a list for each change with the raw data. For example, the list for changing the type of welding wire might look like this:

Day	Type of Wire Used
2/23	Xeron
2/24	Baker
2/25	Baker
2/26	Creaton
2/29	Baker
3/1	Xeron

Step 3: Match results to the list.

Using the pull strength results from the test, the data is matched by day to the list of changes. For example, on February 23, when Xeron wire was used, the pull strength results for that day were an average of 1,100 foot-pounds. The revised list should now look like this:

Day	Type of Wire Used	Pull Test Results
2/23	Xeron	1,100
2/24	Baker	1,000
2/25	Baker	1,200
2/26	Creaton	1,000
2/29	Baker	950
3/1	Xeron	900

Step 4: Use the scattergram to look for associations.

Your task in searching for an assignable cause is to find a change in the process that associates with a change in the quality characteristic you are

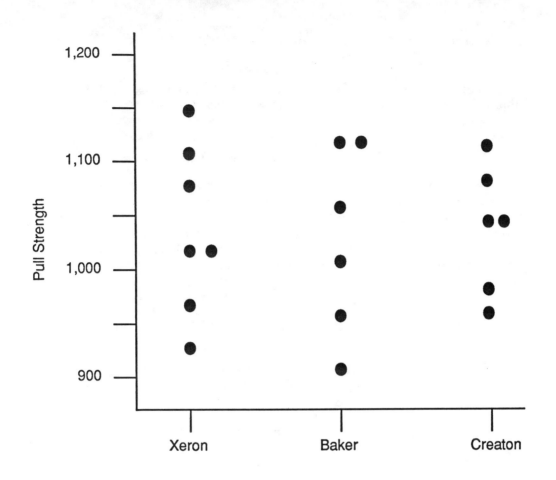

Figure 5-3: Scattergram of wire type.

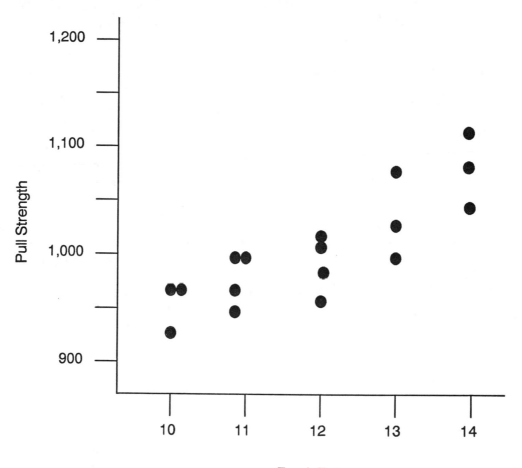

Figure 5-4: Scattergram using feed rate.

investigating. For example, is there a correlation between wire type used and pull strength results?n A scattergram can detect such an association.

The changes are noted on the x-axis of the scattergram. The results are noted on the y-axis (see Figure 5-3). Each pair of change and result is plotted on the scattergram. For example, the first change was to use Xeron wire on February 23. The matching result is 1,100 foot-pounds. Thus, a point is placed where Xeron and 1,100 foot-pounds correspond on the chart. This is repeated until a finished chart is created. The more data you have the better.

Figure 5-3 shows a situation where there is little association between the type of welding wire used and the resulting pull strength of the assembly. The dots on the scattergram do not form a strong pattern.

Figure 5-4 shows a case where the feed rate of the welding wire associates strongly with the pull strength of the assembly. The dots form a strong linear pattern on the page. The more linear the arrangement, the stronger the correlation. Thus, an association has been discovered. By studying the effect of wire feed rates on pull strengths, you can also optimize the process.

The scattergram is repeated for each probable cause until the associations are found. If none are found, a designed experiment may be necessary (see chapter 9).

Conclusion

New quality assurance functions are being developed every day. Accordingly, the role of the quality assurance department is also changing. Some companies are increasing their quality staff, while other have practically eliminated theirs by reassigning tasks to departments closer to the problem. Specifically, the manufacturing department continues to be given greater responsibilities in monitoring and improving the quality of production.

In addition, the manufacturing manager is expected to document and demonstrate continuous improvement and its economic impact. The techniques reviewed in this chapter are intended to be used as the basic set of tools for a manufacturing manager to begin accomplishing the quality function. The information in chapters 3 and 4, and in all the chapters in this book, should add to this basic set of tools and make you an effective manager of manufacturing quality.

CHAPTER 6

How to Use Statistics to Predict the Reliability of Products and Processes

Reliability is the quality of a product over time. Quality assurance, in contrast, is the quality of a product at the time of inspection. Therefore, reliability testing is an extension of the engineering and quality functions of a manufacturer.

Reliability engineering is a science by itself, involving accelerated life testing, stress tests, probability analysis, field surveys, and a host of other activities. This chapter is an introduction to the basic methods used to estimate the reliability of a product and how reliability can be part of the design process. In addition, the most commonly used terms in reliability work will be defined and discussed.

How to Perform Reliability Testing Effectively

The reliability of a production process is usually stated as the mean number of failures over a given period of time. The reliability of a product is the probability that a product will not fail within a given time frame. In both cases, the reliability is given for a particular set of environmental conditions.

How to Define a Failure: An Example Using a Steel Slitting Process

A failure occurs when a product or process does not perform its specified function when called on to do so. For example, a steel bolt might be designed to hold together two sheets of wood. If the bolt snaps, you would say that the bolt has failed.

In manufacturing, the specified role of every product and process must be carefully defined so that you know exactly what constitutes a failure. For example, if the bolt holding the wood together came loose but still held the wood, is that a failure? Questions such as this must be answered to assure that the data gathered for a reliability study is consistent and will give you an accurate picture of the situation.

Consider how you would define failures for a production process, such as a steel slitting machine. The first step would be to define the operating specifications for the process—in simple terms, what you expect from the steel slitting machine.

Your list might include items such as the continuous slitting of each roll at no slower than 6 inches per minute. The time to load a roll of steel should be less than an hour. The slitting tool should last through the slitting of 10,000 feet of steel. Anything that stops the process from performing these tasks is considered a failure.

When writing or reading a reliability report, begin by looking for the definitions of failures. In our example, you may find that the slitting tool breaking is considered a failure with the time it takes to replace the tool considered downtime. At the same time, if the tool wears down after cutting 11,000 feet of steel and the machine is stopped to replace the tool, that may be considered normal operations and may not count as a failure. However, if one of the rollers in the machine should seize up suddenly, that would be considered another failure.

As you will see, this list of failure definitions and performance expectations serves a critical role in measuring the reliability of a product or situation.

How to Write a Reliability Specification Sheet

The central component of a reliability report is the reliability specification sheet. This document spells out the performance requirements for a product or process using reliability terms. In most situations, the sheet uses plain language to describe reliability requirements.

The following are some examples of reliability specifications. Note that they state the maximum number or probability of failures over time under given conditions.

1. For a plastic injection molding machine, the total downtime should be less than one hour for every 100 hours of molding.

2. Connected to a standard 120-volt household outlet, a personal copy machine should produce at least 100,000 copies without the failure of the copy drum.

3. The average time until the failure of a personal computer's hard disk should be an average of 30,000 hours of normal operations.

4. An air-to-air missile used under combat conditions should have a 90% chance of finding and destroying its target.

You may find that a long list of reliability statements are necessary for a particular product or process. Each reliability statement should be referred back to the operational specification where it originated.

An Example Reliability Specification Sheet for a Personal Computer's Hard Disk

One possible way to structure reliability statements is to list each performance specification and then the related reliability requirements. This is similar to the FMEA described in Chapter 5.

Performance Specification	Reliability Statement
20,000 hours of operation	Mean time until first failure of 30,000 hours
99.99% accuracy in reading/writing data	Tracking accuracy of the read/write head on first pass of 99%
	Tracking accuracy on three confirming passes of 99%
	No less than 1.5 megohms of data read during reading pass
	99.99% accuracy of data confirmation algorithm
	No more than one failure from line noise during 1,000 hours of read/write transmission

Naturally, this list would continue for other operational characteristics. Note that these requirements are the result of precision calculation of reliability effects for individual parts and complete systems.

How to Calculate Common Reliability Measures

There is a standard language of expressing reliabilities. By understanding the basic terms of that language you can quickly read and understand most reliability requirements.

The proper reliability term to use depends on several conditions, such as whether the failure can be fixed and whether you are dealing with individual parts or the entire system. Each of the following measures will also define the proper application of the measure.

Calculating the Mean Number of Failures: An Example of an Electric Toaster

Suppose that a reliability engineer for a firm that makes electric toasters selects five toasters at random and gives them to employees to use. Each employee makes toast every morning and brings the toaster back if it needs repair. After 1,000 days, the following information is gathered.

Toaster	No. of Repairs
1	3
2	2
3	5
4	2
5	1
Total	13

To calculate the reliability of the toasters over 1,000 days, you calculate the mean number of failures because the failures are repairable. Therefore, you would want to know the average number of repairs for each 1,000 days of ownership. This would provide you with valuable information on how reliable the toasters are, how they compare to other brands for reliability, and how much money you will have to spend in warranty costs.

$$\text{mean failures} = \frac{13}{5} = 2.6$$

Thus, we can say that the average toaster will need repair 2.6 times every 1,000 days under normal consumer usage conditions.

How to Calculate the Mean Time Between Failures

We can also report the reliability of the electric toasters using a terminology more familiar to reliability studies: mean time between failure (MTBF). It is used as a reliability measure for repairable items and processes. MTBF is perhaps the most widely used designation of reliability. It is also one of the least understood. Our example illustrates this point. To calculate the MTBF, we divide the time period by the mean number of failures.

$$MTBF = \frac{total\ time\ period}{mean\ number\ of\ failures}$$

or

$$MTBF = \frac{1,000\ days}{2.6\ failures} = 384.6\ days$$

This tells us that the toasters will last, on average, 384.6 days until they need repair. This does not mean that every toaster will last this long. In this case the MTBF could mean that approximately 50% of the toasters will need repair within 384.6 days if the probability distribution of failure is fairly normal.

How to Calculate the Mean Time Until First Failure

The distribution of failures can be quite uneven. Thus, the toasters that are expected to last an average of 384.6 days between failures may last considerably more or less time until the first failure. This is called the mean time until first failure, or MTFF.

If the MTFF is longer than the MTBF, you can expect the product or process to need repair more often as it gets older. On the other hand, if the MTFF is much shorter than the MTBF, the product or process needs most of its repairs early in its life.

The calculation for MTFF is similar to the MTBF. You collect information from the toaster test on when the first failure occurred. The average of these data is the MTFF. You will also want to note the causes of each failure for later analysis by product design personnel.

Toaster	Time Until First Failure
1	123 days
2	256
3	495
4	380
5	350
Total	1,604 days

The MTFF is

$$MTFF = \frac{total\ days}{number\ of\ units\ tested}$$

or

$$MTFF = \frac{1,604}{5} = 320.8\ days\ until\ first\ failure$$

This represents a slightly shorter time than the MTBF. Thus, there may be some components in the toaster that are wearing out or breaking down too quickly. Your list of failure causes might point out these components for corrections in the design.

How to Translate the MTBF Into a Failure Rate

If desired, the MTBF can be translated into a failure rate. The failure rate of a product is the inverse of the MTBF.

$$\text{failure rate} = \frac{1}{\text{MTBF}}$$

In our example, this would be

$$\text{failure rate} = \frac{1}{384.6} = 0.0026$$

This failure rate indicates that there is only a 0.0026 (or 0.26%) chance of a toaster failing on a single day. As we shall see later, failure rates are critical to evaluating the reliability of product designs and other systems.

How to Calculate the Mean Time Until Failure

The calculations presented so far make a basic assumptions, that is, they assume that the product in question can be repaired and placed back into service. In reality, there are many products that can only fail once and cannot be repaired. Examples include transistors, diodes, light bulbs, ink ribbons, and fuses. For nonrepairable products, a slightly different set of formulas is used to measure reliability.

The basic description of the reliability of a nonrepairable item is the mean time until failure (also called the mean time till failure, or MTTF). This is the same calculation as MTFF except it is used only for nonrepairable items. To calculate this figure, you would measure the life span of nonrepairable items and report the average life span until failure.

Assume that the aforementioned reliability engineer discovers that the in-line fuse for the toasters is the major cause of failure in the product. Therefore, he decides to test the life span of the fuses. Submitting five fuses to constant electrical current simulating constant usage of a toaster on a typical household electrical line, he obtains the following numbers.

Fuse	Life (in hours)
1	1,200
2	1,850
3	1,050
4	1,300
5	1,450
Total	6,850 hours

The mean of these numbers is the MTTF.

$$\text{MTTF} = \frac{6,850}{5} = 1,370 \text{ hours}$$

In other words, the in-line fuses from the toasters have an average life span of 1,370 hours.

How to Calculate a Hazard Rate

If we inverse the MTTF, we obtain a hazard rate for the product. A hazard rate is different than a failure rate. While the failure rate is the probability of a repair, the hazard rate is the probability of total failure.

$$\text{hazard rate} = \frac{1}{\text{MTTF}} = \frac{1}{1,370 \text{ hours}} = 0.00073$$

If the hazard rate is multiplied by a time span of interest, you can obtain the probability of a failure during the specified period. For example, you may have specified that the fuses should have 99% reliability after 100 hours of operation. With 99% reliability, the engineer is really saying that there should be less than a 1% chance of failure.

A quick check of the fuse reliability shows that this specification is not being met.

$$\text{time x hazard rate} = \text{probability of failure}$$

or

$$100 \text{ hours x } 0.00073 = 0.073 \text{ or } 7.3\% \text{ chance of failure}$$

Thus, the fuse is found to be insufficient for meeting one of the reliability requirements for the toaster.

Reliability for Processes: How to Predict Breakdowns and When to Schedule Preventive Maintenance

The time it takes to repair or adjust a process is called the maintainability of the system. When a production process is making product or waiting to make product, we call this uptime. When the same process is being repaired, changed, or waiting for repairs, we call this downtime. These periods of time can be described in one of several ways to reflect the reliability of the process.

How to Calculate the Mean Time Between Maintenance

Mean time between maintenance (MTBM) is a measure of the average time between a specific type of maintenance activity. For example, if a drill press has to be stopped from time to time to sharpen the drill bit, then the average time between these stoppages would be the MTBM.

Number of Cycles Until Sharpening
250
270
260
230
240
1,250 total

$$MTBM = \frac{cycles\,(\,or\,time\,)}{number\,of\,repairs}$$

or

$$MTBM = \frac{1,250}{5} = 250 \text{ cycles}$$

By having such a measure, you can accurately schedule repair and maintenance times. As in the case of the drill press, you know that the bit has to be sharpened every 250 cycles. Using confidence intervals around this estimate, you can schedule time into the production timetable to allow for the sharpening. This prevents overstressing the tool or creating bad holes from a dull tool.

How to Calculate the Number of Repairs Needed for Each 100 Hours of Operation

If the drill press used in the previous example needs one hour to complete 100 cycles of drilling, then there would be a repair every two-and-a-half hours on the average. The phrase *repairs per 100 hours* is a standard unit for measuring how often a product or process has to be repaired. In the case of the drill press, 40 resharpenings would be required for every 100 hours of production.

This figure is helpful in calculating the total uptime and downtime for a process. If it takes 10 minutes to remove, sharpen, and remount the drill bit, then 400 minutes of additional production time can be expected for this process.

How to Interpret the Mean Life of a Production Machine

Taking the idea of calculating the production time one step further, you would want to know the mean life time of the machine or product involved. In other words, how long will the drill bit and the drill press last under normal production conditions?

In the case of the drill bit, you would count how many times the bit could be resharpened before it had to be thrown away. This information can come from the process logs already being kept for the SPC system. Again, you would take the average of the number of sharpenings a tool could withstand.

As for the drill press, you could choose to measure the length of its life until it is no longer usable or repairable, or you could measure the time between major overhauls of the press. Either way, the mean life rating for a product is usually given in time, and it can be used to calculate the depreciation of the equipment or product involved.

How to Calculate the Availability of a Process: An Example Using a Metal Stamping Press

Availability is a measure of how often a product or process is ready for use when it is needed. For example, when a consumer reaches for a cordless screwdriver, he or she expects it to be ready and able to drive screws. As a manufacturing manager, you expect a production process to be ready to produce. The following example illustrates the value of knowing the availability of a product or process.

An automotive metal stamping plant operates several 100-ton presses. Past studies of production runs have shown that the presses have an MTBF of 240 minutes. When they do need repair, it is almost always because of the failure of one of three components—the die mounts, the stroke control cylinder, or the stock feeding mechanism. A reliability tester estimates the failure rate for each component of the machine.

Component	Failure Rate	Time to Repair
Die mount	0.90	30 minutes
Stroke control	0.80	20
Stock feeder	0.95	15

With this information, it is possible to calculate the availability of the press and thus schedule both production and maintenance time more accurately.

The formula for availability is

$$\text{availability} = \frac{\text{MTBF}}{\text{MTBF} + \text{MTTR}}$$

MTTR stands for mean time to repair, which is the time from the breakdown of the process until the repair is completed. These are the times to repair reported in the foregoing table. To calculate the MTTR, you would use the following formula.

$$\text{MTTR} = \frac{\text{total of repair times}}{\text{total of failure rates}}$$

Adding up the repair times and failure rates already stated, we can complete the calculation.

$$\text{total repair time} = 30 + 20 + 15 = 65 \text{ minutes}$$

$$\text{total failure rate} = 0.90 + 0.80 + 0.95 = 2.65$$

thus

$$\text{MTTR} = \frac{65}{2.65} = 24.5 \text{ minutes}$$

Notice that the MTTR is not the average repair time (65/3 = 21.7). Each repair time is weighted by the probability of the need for repair.

With the MTTR calculated, you can complete the availability estimation.

$$\text{availability} = \frac{240}{240 + 24.5} = 0.907 \text{ (or } 90.7\%)$$

The resulting percentage is a statement of the probability that a press will be available at a specific time. In other words, if the press is needed at a particular time of the day, there is a 90.7% chance that it will be available.

This calculation also tells a production scheduler that for every 240 minutes of production on the press, 24.5 minutes of maintenance should be added. The availability function also says that 9 times out of 10, the machine will be available for immediate use after it completes a job.

How to Calculate the Reliability of a Product as a System

As we have seen, many of the measures of reliability can be reported as a probability, such as the chance of success or failure over a stated period of time. When individual parts in a product are combined, or when we examine the process as a whole, the probabilities of the parts can be combined to estimate the reliability of the system.

The concepts of MTBF and failure rates can be extended to more complex problems of reliability. Consider an example of complex assembly, such as a washing machine. A washing machine has dozens of moving parts that can break down and need repair.

Assume that a reliability technician has measured the reliability of each moving part and found that they can be grouped into one of three families of failure rates.

Parts Used	Failure Rate (after 1,000 hours)
15	0.03
30	0.15
29	0.11

The failure rates reported in this example represent the percentage of parts that have failed after 1,000 hours of use. With this information, we can determine the failure rate and MTBF for the entire washing machine, assuming that moving parts are the sole cause of failure.

Assuming that there are no redundant parts, the failure rate for the machine is the sum of the failure rates. To find this sum, you must first multiply each failure rate by the number of parts involved.

Parts Used	Failure Rate	Total Part Failure Rate
15	0.03	0.45
30	0.15	4.50
29	0.11	3.19
	Total	8.14

Thus, the failure rate for the washing machine is 8.14% for every 1,000 hours because of moving part failures.

$$\text{failure rate} = \frac{8.14}{1,000} = 0.00814 \text{ per hour}$$

The inverse of the failure rate will determine the MTBF.

$$\text{MTBF} = \frac{1}{0.00814} = 122.85 \text{ hours}$$

Therefore, if the engineers were evaluating the reliability of the design of the washing machine, they would know that the MTBF would be 122.85 hours. If it takes about 30 minutes (0.5 hours) to complete a wash load, the average machine would complete about 246 loads before needing repair.

$$\text{wash cycles} = \frac{122.85}{0.5 \text{ hours}} = 245.7$$

If the average family does four loads of laundry per week, the machine would work for a little over one year before it needed repair. Using the more advanced techniques of reliability, the engineers could determine the number of one-year warranty claims that would be experienced with this design and price the product accordingly.

How to Calculate the Reliability of a System with Interdependent Parts: An Electrical Circuit Example

Another example of using failure rates is determining the reliability of a system of interdependent parts. For example, a simple electrical circuit may have four transistors. If any one of the transistors fails, the circuit will fail. Each transistor has the following failure rate for 100 hours of operation.

Transistor	Failure Rate
1	0.003
2	0.007
3	0.011
4	0.001

To find the reliability of each transistor, you could subtract the failure rate from 1.00 to obtain the probability of the transistor functioning properly over 100 hours. The resulting information would be as follows.

Transistor	Reliability Rate
1	0.997
2	0.993
3	0.989
4	0.999

The reliability of a system where the failure of any one part will cause the failure of the system is the product of each probability of reliability.

system reliability = 0.997 x 0.993 x 0.989 x 0.999 = 0.978

In other words, this electrical circuit would be about 97.8% reliable over a 100-hour period of operation. This is the same method used for the probability of success for a circuit in series.

How to Determine the Life of a Product

The median life of a product—the time it will take until half of the population being studied has failed—is represented by the b_{50} rating. Consider the previous example of an electrical circuit that is 97.8% reliable over a 100-hour period. This means that in 100 hours we can expect about 2.2%, or 0.022, probability of a failure. What the b_{50} life will tell us is how long it will take for half of the circuits in use to fail. The answer could be, for example, 2,200 hours.

The b_{50} rating is used in many toxicity studies. If a new drug is slowly exposed to a colony of mice, the toxicity level is defined as when half of the population dies from overdose.

The b_{10} has similar uses. It marks the time until 10% of the population has failed. In general practice, this measure is used as a standard for expressing the reliability of many products and processes. The figure gives you a benchmark of performance. A reliability engineer would use probability curves and the distribution of failures to calculate survival times for a range of total failures.

How to Measure the Effectiveness of a System

There are several models available to measure the effectiveness of a system. A simple model is

$$P_{se} = P_a \times P_r \times P_c$$

where P_{se} = effectiveness of the system
P_a = probability of availability
P_r = reliability
P_c = probability that the design is adequate for the specified function

System effectiveness tells you how well the product or process will satisfy the demands of the user. For example, suppose that you manufacture television sets and you want to know the effectiveness of the set over a 10,000- hour period. Using some of the measures of reliability already presented, you obtain the following information.

MTBF = 16,000 hours

MTTR = 72 hours

Reliability = 0.535

First, you would calculate the availability.

$$P_a = \frac{\text{MTBF}}{\text{MTBF} + \text{MTTR}}$$

or

$$P_a = \frac{16,000}{16,000 + 72} = 0.995$$

The probability of reliability is already known as 0.535. We will assume that if all of the television's parts are working, the set will deliver the performance the customer expects. Thus, a 1.00 probability will be used. The wearing out of a power supply or capacitor could degrade the performance of the set until the customer is no longer satisfied. In such cases, the probability of design capacity would be lower.

The three probabilities are multiplied to estimate the system effectiveness.

$$P_{se} = 0.995 \times 0.535 \times 1.0 = 0.532$$

This measure of system effectiveness can be used to compare competing designs, products, or production methods. The cost of the product or system can be divided into the system effectiveness ratio to obtain a cost-effectiveness scale. The higher the resulting number, the more cost-effective the system.

How to Predict the Life Time Failure Rate for a Typical Product Using the Bathtub Curve

So far, the formulas we have used assumed a constant rate of failure. For some products, this assumption would be true. However, in the real world, many products go through periods of changing rates of failure. The typical model is called the bathtub curve.

The bathtub curve represents the failure rates of a product over its entire life span. During the early part of its life, basic flaws in production create a high rate of failure for a few components. Although the rate of failure is high, it decreases rapidly as the major flaws fail soon after production. This is true of many electronic components. If they are defective, they will fail within a few hours of use. This is why many electronic manufacturers have what they call a burn-in period. Electronic assemblies are turned on and operated for 24 hours or so to sort out the components that will fail right away.

After this initial burn-in period, the immediate failures occur and the surviving products usually have a period of constant failure rates that are very low. Near the end of the useful life of a product, the failure rates begin to increase as the components surrender to time and wear. Thus, the bathtub curve begins with rapidly decreasing failure rates, followed by a constant rate, and ends with a steadily increasing failure rate (see Figure 6-1).

Which reliability calculation and model of failure to use depends on which part of the bathtub curve you are studying. If you are interested in the early burn-in period, use a descending curve of probability. If you are studying the end period of a product's life, use an increasing curve of probability.

Another consideration is the nature of what you are studying. A product made up of many parts may experience repairable failures over its lifetime. Therefore, a continuous curve of probability should be used. On the other hand, an individual part will either fail or succeed when tested. For situations such as this, a discrete probability model should be used.

Each of these models of probability should be calculated by reliability professionals. As a manufacturing manager, you are critically interested in whether the reliability specifications have been developed and that the basic reliability measures are being collected. This information will give you an estimate in advance as to whether a design or process will work as intended.

How to Predict the Future Performance of a Product Using Accelerated Testing

Reliability testing and engineering involves more than the use of statistics. Much of the technique relies on the knowledge of physics and chemistry, as well as the use of mathematical models to predict the performance of a product. In accelerated testing, mathematics and personal experience are used to obtain data for the statistical techniques described in this book.

Consider the example of electrical circuits. Some are designed to last for 100 years or more without repair. The problem is trying to test the reliability of such a circuit when a reliability engineer may have only a few weeks before the final design is approved and put into production.

Personal experience and knowledge are used to solve such a problem. The engineer looks for a factor that can be accelerated to simulate accelerated time. In the case of electronic components, increased voltage creates increased heat that simulates the failures due to decay over time. Thus, stressing the product beyond normal operating conditions accelerates what would normally be the effect of time.

The second step is to find and describe the relationship between the accelerated factor and time. This is usually formed into a mathematical model based on the results of previous tests. For example, the relationship between higher voltage and time is usually given as

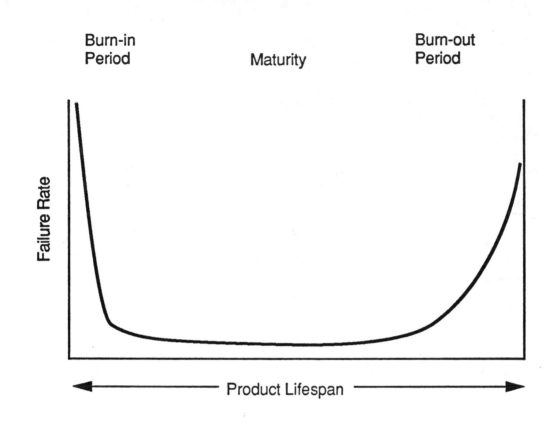

Figure 6-1: The "bathtub" curve of reliability.

$$\frac{T}{T_a} = \left(\frac{V_a}{V}\right)^3$$

where T = time

T_a = accelerated time

V = normal operating voltage

V_a = accelerated voltage

The following example illustrates how this function works. A new electronics product normally uses 25 volts DC as its internal operating current. As an accelerated life test, it is exposed to 100 volts DC until it fails after 100 hours. How long should it last at 25 volts DC?

Substituting the preceding information into the formula, we find the following.

$$\frac{T}{100 \text{ hours}} = \left(\frac{100}{25}\right)^3$$

or

$$\frac{T}{100 \text{ hours}} = 64$$

Multiplying each side of the equation by 100 hours to solve yields

$$T = 6,400 \text{ hours}$$

Thus, the estimated life span of the product under normal operating conditions is 6,400 hours. Naturally, such estimates should be used with caution. However, you can see that usable results are available in 100 hours, instead of having to wait for 6,400 hours (267 days) for a failure.

Derating: Reliability Information Used to Improve a Product

Derating is the practice of assigning components to a design when they are used below their rated performance. For example, a bumper on a car that can withstand a 10-mile-per-hour impact with a fixed object may be used to meet a 5-mile-per-hour bumper requirement. In another case, a bearing rated for 1 million revolutions while loaded with 10 tons of force is used where only a half-ton of force is expected over a lifetime use of 750,000 revolutions.

By using a component that is more reliable than required, a company assures continued performance when the customer misuses the product, such as improper applications, overload, and undermaintenance. Naturally, you will want a company policy on derating because it can easily lead to unnecessary production expenses. Therefore, the increase in reliability should be calculated as precisely as possible.

Conclusion

Reliability information is critical to successful design and promotion of products. It is also useful for the layout and scheduling of machinery. However, reliability is similar to quality assurance in that it reflects the quality of a product after production.

A manufacturer also must to be able to predict and control the quality and economy of products and processes before they are manufactured. The next few chapters address this problem. Combined with good quality and reliability information, the techniques of forecasting, experimentation, and just-in-time inventory control create a complete manufacturing feedback system for management.

CHAPTER 7

Using Statistical Methods for a Just-in-Time System of Production and Delivery

There are many myths that surround just-in-time (JIT) systems. Popular literature taunts JIT as a revolution in production and delivery scheduling. Many professionals believe that JIT requires the complete redesign of their current methods of management.

There is no single model of JIT. Terms such as just-in-time and Kanban are used in industry to describe any system that strives for maximum effectiveness with inventories. Actually, a typical JIT system is characterized by its abhorrence of waste. The goal is to create a product system where no product or effort is made that is not immediately necessary.

JIT is a philosophy of perfection in planning and scheduling. Therefore, it is commonly used by manufacturers seeking world-class quality of production. JIT strives to reduce inventories, improve quality, streamline production, and involve workers. The following example demonstrates the intent of JIT.

A typical manufacturing plant wants to make a product in large numbers. By making a large batch of parts, the production process runs without interruptions and with fewer set-ups. This reduces the costs per part. However, the large inventory of parts creates an inventory carrying cost. Thus, management wants shorter runs for less carrying costs. The conflict is usually resolved using the economically optimal quantity (EOQ). This is the size of a production run that balances set-up and order costs against inventory costs to obtain the minimal production expense.

With JIT the costs for set-up and ordering are not accepted as fixed. Instead, management encourages employees to seek out new ways to cut the cost of set-up and ordering dramatically. For example, some large stamping dies are redesigned so that they can be mounted into a press in a few minutes instead of the more typical several hours. This is not accomplished quickly. Management and workers must strive continually to improve the set-up process until it happens so quickly that it involves little cost.

When the cost for set-up is reduced to near zero, the economically optimal quantity of production drops to one part. This is one of the goals of JIT. With the ability to produce products in lot sizes of one, a company is able to build to match orders with little lead time. In addition, custom orders can be accommodated with little trouble. This allows the manufacturer to satisfy customer needs at a lower cost than competitors.

JIT can only be successful when you have 100% quality. If machinery is making just enough production to cover demand, then no defective products can be tolerated. Therefore, you should have implemented the statistical controls for production outlined in chapters 3, 4, 5, and 6 before attempting to implement JIT. Without a system of total quality based on the principle of continuous improvement, your efforts at JIT are likely to be fruitless.

How Statistics Help Implement JIT

JIT is not implemented all at once. Achieving JIT is a process of transition that takes years to accomplish. The manufacturing resources planning (MRP II) system is not thrown out. Instead, it remains in place to assist in the day-to-day production planning. Management plans the strategic changes in the current production and inventory systems, but statistical tools help guide the company through the period of transition.

Every step in the implementation of JIT requires that the people involved are monitoring critical characteristics of the process in real time. This is exactly the type of work intended for SPC. In addition, by using a more complete range of statistical tools, a company intent on JIT can guide itself toward its final goal.

How to Record and Reduce Machine Set-up Times Using the Time/Cost Chart

The time/cost chart is actually a form of control chart. The difference is that the critical characteristic is the time or costs involved in a process. To illustrate how the chart is created and used, we will examine the process of reducing the set-up time for the mold for a plastic injection machine.

Suppose that you are the manufacturing manager for a medium-sized plastic injection molding shop. One of your customers has just informed you that the parts you make for them are going onto a JIT schedule of production. This means that you will receive quantity orders five days before they are due for delivery at the customer's plant. The customer will also be asking for daily deliveries of parts with each day's order specifying which parts are needed. This means you will have little time for coordination of orders and set-up of the process.

While examining the plastic molding log for the machine making this particular set of parts, you discover that the quality of production is high but set-up of the mold is taking two to three hours. A typical day's order will be around 10,000 parts, and that requires about 18 hours constant production with two to five set-ups of molds. When the current set-up time per mold is added into the equation, it quickly becomes clear that you will not be able to keep up with the orders.

The answer to this problem is to reduce the set-up time to make it possible for you to cope with this schedule of smaller, more frequent orders. Since time is the critical factor, a time chart will be created.

Step 1: Determine the critical characteristic.

In this example, it is the time for set-up.

Step 2: Establish the current capability of the process.

Consulting the time record for the set-up engineer, you sample at least 30 time records for the set-up of the mold. Suppose that you find the following 30 times recorded for set-up.

321	340	337	320	335
338	316	333	312	321
321	318	328	336	318
316	335	318	339	320
328	326	331	311	322
326	325	321	341	314

Using the formulas for mean and standard deviation introduced in chapter 1, you obtain an average of 325.6 minutes with a standard deviation of 8.98 minutes.

Step 3: Keep a log of process changes.

As you gather time data, record any special events that may occur—for example, if one of the set-ups took over 400 minutes because a tool was lost and another had to be secured. The exceptional time would not be recorded in the calculation of capability. Instead, a note would be made that the special cause, the loss of a tool, should be prevented in the improved system. That is, you might design a special mold change tool cart to assure that all of the necessary tools stay in one place.

Step 4: Compute and plot the average.

You have already determined the process average to be 325.6 minutes per set-up. This is plotted onto your time chart (see Figure 7-1). Plus and minus three standard deviations will give you a good estimate of how far normal times for set-up might deviate. These can be noted on the chart for reference. However, the idea is not to establish statistical control but to reduce the set-up time consistently.

Step 5: Plot time readings.

Starting with the original 30 time readings, plot each time report on the chart (see Figure 7-1). (Only 21 readings are plotted in Figure 7-1.)

Step 6: Pursue continuous improvement.

Now you can assign a work team to look into ways of reducing the set-up time. The objective of the chart is to get seven points in a row below the process average. When this occurs, you calculate a new process average based on the seven points and draw the new average on the chart (see Figure 7-1).

Suppose that the manufacturing engineer, production supervisor, and the machine operator start their improvement effort by designing a better coupling system for the mold. After considerable discussion, they agree to mount quick-release couplings on the mold. This eliminates the need to mount hydraulic lines with wrenches. Instead, the lines just snap into place.

With the new mold design, the team tries a few set-ups and discovers that the average time has plunged to less than 100 minutes. This is noted on the chart, and a new average is plotted just below 100 minutes.

Some Japanese companies have been known to push their set-up times down by designing rapid change molds and then holding mold change practices on weekends. The effort resembles a pit stop at a road race. The team practices the set-up again and again. Each time they try to find and eliminate every unnecessary movement. For example, plastic molds might be staged on one side of the machine so that as one mold is pulled from the machine, the next mold is pulled into place. Using time charts, they have slashed set-up times from hours to less than 10 minutes in many cases.

How to Reduce the Cost of Ordering Parts Using a Cost Chart

Besides set-up time, the time and effort involved in processing orders from a customer represent another large cost of smaller, more frequent or-

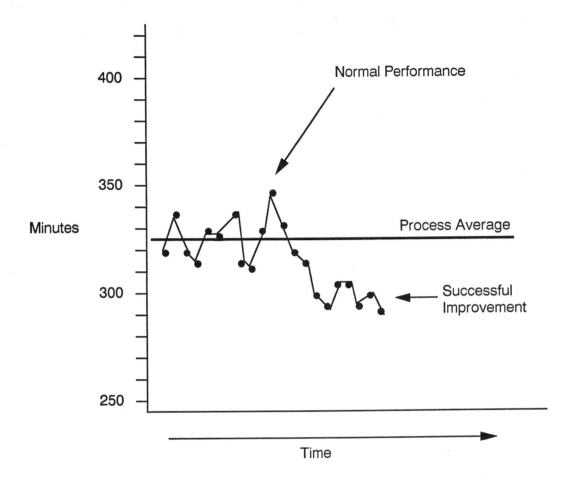

Figure 7-1: Time chart for set-up delays.

dering. Office workers can also be organized to attack these sources of costs to make JIT possible.

Consider the example of the order processing department of a manufacturing firm. Under normal circumstances, an order from a customer is received and logged by a clerk. A purchase order is updated, the customer is billed, work is scheduled, packing lists are created, quality reports gathered, and so on. This flow of paperwork requires costly personnel.

Now assume that you have been assigned the task of reducing this cost to process a customer's order. The aforementioned time chart can also be used to track costs.

Step 1: Identify the critical characteristic.

In this case, you decide that the cost to produce the paperwork can be described as the number of work hours spent preparing the paperwork times the average hourly salary of the clerks. For example, you may track a single order and find that it required 6.5 labor hours to complete and file the paperwork. With an average clerk's salary being about $15 an hour, the order then cost $97.50 to process.

Step 2: Sample 30 costs.

Tracking at least 30 orders through processing, you obtain the data needed to start the cost chart. For illustration, assume that the following 30 costs were obtained.

$73	53	70	92	58
134	71	105	115	151
65	89	117	82	88
87	88	82	150	115
50	105	111	140	126
80	108	103	140	111

Step 3: Keep a log.

While tracking and charting costs, be sure to keep a log of any unusual occurrences. An exceptionally large or small order or an order with special requirements should be documented. This information is used later to determine if new systems of order processing would also help in exceptional cases.

Step 4: Compute the average cost.

In this example, the average cost is $98.63. This is drawn on the cost chart the same way the time average was drawn on the time chart.

Step 5: Chart the costs.

The original 30 costs are charted to establish the normal pattern of variation in the costs. Then new cost figures are obtained for randomly selected orders. That is, at regular time intervals (for example, once each day) an order is selected and tracked for its costs. The resulting cost figure is plotted on the chart.

Step 6: Pursue continuous improvement.

Now the objective is to drive downward the average cost to process an order. For example, you may decide to start a list of customers that have shown a consistent record of paying their bills. A blanket purchase order may be issued. Then when an order is received, the order is placed in manufacturing and only a single confirmation invoice is sent with the parts. The reduction in costs can be demonstrated on the cost chart by seven points in a row below the current average costs.

Later, a purchasing agent may program the computer to fill out the necessary paperwork as soon as the basic information from the order is entered. This also drives down the personnel time required per order. Thus, the cost chart again will record a reduction in average cost.

In summary, the cost chart, like the time chart, is a feedback tool to measure your progress in reducing cost and time variables associated with production. The ideal is to eliminate all costs and time delays. This is impossible, of course, but the recent record of many world-class companies has shown that these variables can be reduced so far that it is equivalent to zero.

How to Reduce Work-in-Progress Inventories Using the Control Chart for Individual Measurements

Inventories involve the extensive use of counting. Specific counts that apply to JIT are the number of inventory turns, inventory volumes, work-in-progress volume, number of order changes, and purchasing lead times. Except for the first item, the goal is to drive these counts down to zero.

The method for doing so involves setting up a standard system of measurement that can detect significant changes. Then problem-solving teams and engineering project teams work to find and test improvements to the system. If these changes are successful, they should be detected by the system of measurement. The following example illustrates this detection system.

In the case of counting, only one count can be made at any given time. For example, the number of inventory turns is calculated only once. It is impossible to sample it five times every hour as you can for a production process. Therefore, a different type of SPC chart is used—the chart for individual measurements.

Consider the example of a company that is interested in reducing the work-in-progress inventory to zero. Assume that this company produces office desks. During the production of the desk, sanding and varnishing is required. The current method of production places groups of desks into a waiting area first for sanding and later for drying after the application of varnish. This creates a large, and thus expensive, work-in-progress inventory.

To reduce and eventually eliminate this expense, the company must begin by describing the average size of this inventory and its normal behavior. For illustrative purposes, we will use 10 weeks of data (normally 25 or more would be used).

Work-In-Progress Inventory (per week)
325 desks
330
295
330
300
290
270
350
320
340
3,150 Total

The average number of desks in the work-in-progress inventory is 315. The chart for individual readings is created and used the same as any SPC chart. First the average is plotted across the graph paper and labeled. Next, upper and lower control limits are calculated and drawn. The procedure described in chapter 4 is used. However, the objective of this chart is to drive it out of statistical control toward the goal of zero.

Using the preceding data, we would take a moving range for every two readings.

Work-in-Progress Inventory (per week)	Range
325 desks	
330	5
295	35
330	35
300	30
290	10
270	20
350	80
320	30
340	20
	Total 265

Thus, the average range would be 29.4. This is enough information to complete the chart. Only the chart for the individual readings is necessary. The range chart portion is unnecessary since the objective is to lose statistical control toward zero.

$$UCL = \overline{X} + (E_2 \times \overline{R})$$

where $\overline{R}$ = average range
$\overline{X}$ = process average

$$= 315 + (2.66 \times 29.4) = 393.20$$

and

$$LCL = \overline{X} - (E_2 \times \overline{R})$$

$$= 315 - (2.66 \times 29.4) = 236.80$$

These two boundaries establish the limits of significant change for the problem-solving teams. If the work-in-progress inventory can be cut to 235 desks or less, then the new method of production is seen as a significant improvement. If a new technique increases the inventory above 395 desks, then it can be seen as a significant decrease in the efficiency of the process.

Once the 235 or less barrier is broken, the inventory numbers are allowed to stabilize at their new level and a new set of control limits is calculated. Then the cycle of "improving until significant results are obtained" is repeated.

How to Reduce a Process to Zero Defectives: Using a *p*-bar Chart to Monitor Scrap and Rework Rates

The *p*-bar chart for defectives is an effective tool for monitoring the overall scrap and rework rate within a company. Using the scrap and rework reports from all areas of production, a company can quickly construct a *p*-bar chart using the methods described in chapter 4. At the same time, notes can be kept on the chart describing the cost to inspect the production, fill out related paperwork, and disposition the defective parts.

By tracking this information along with the scrap or rework rate, you can demonstrate that reducing the amount of scrap and rework in a production process will also decrease the need for and expense of inspection. A process that predictably produces no scrap or need for rework can have its inspection requirements reduced or eliminated. Such reduced inspection only helps the implementation of JIT.

For example, suppose that a company is interested in eliminating the creation of scrap pieces. Your first step would be to collect the percentage of scrap created daily.

Scrap as % of Production
10.5
9.2
11.0
8.6
10.1
9.9
12.5
13.0
6.6
8.2

The average scrap rate would be 9.96% or very close to a 10% scrap rate. Normally, you would collect at least 25 days of data before making this calculation, but 10 days of data are used here.

The objective of this company-wide scrap chart is to find the control limits and then drive the scrap rate down, out of statistical control. For example, with a 10% scrap rate, the lower control limit, assuming an average daily production of 1,500 units, is about 7.7%.

With the chart in place, continuous improvement is required. For example, a Pareto chart of the type of defectives found will lead you toward the causes of the most frequent and expensive problems. Work teams assigned to these problems are given the task of finding the assignable causes of the scrap or rework. These causes are, in turn, eliminated.

Using Statistics to Balance Production as Part of Moving Toward Lot Sizes of One

The JIT philosophy considers all production and delivery processes operating in balance with the tasks before and after them in the sequence of manufacturing. The actual system of balance operates backwards from conventional thinking.

This process begins with a unit of measurement called the *cycle time*. The cycle time is the number of units of production to meet that day's demand.

$$\text{cycle time} = \frac{\text{daily operating time}}{\text{required quantity}}$$

For example, suppose that your manufacturing firm sells about 50,000 light switches to the housing industry each month. Assuming 20 work days in a month, that is 2,500 switches per day. If the company operates two shifts producing for 7 1/2 hours each, there is a total of 15 hours of operating time available each day.

Thus,

$$\text{cycle time} = \frac{15 \text{ hours}}{2,500 \text{ units}} = 0.006 \text{ hours}$$

or

0.006 hours x 60 minutes = 1 unit every 0.36 minutes (about 3 units per minute)

This represents a final manufacturing schedule of about three units per minute. This final demand is used to pull along the preceding steps of the manufacturing process. For example, six different people wire the switches before they are boxed and shipped. To meet the three-units-per-minute goal, they each have to wire a unit in two minutes. The process before wiring must maintain a flow of one unit every two minutes to each wiring person, and so on back to the purchase of supplied materials.

However, this entire process assumes that the machinery and people involved will have an almost perfect rate of availability. At the three switches per minute cycle, the plant should produce 54,000 switches. This is 4,000 more than needed. Therefore, the plant could tolerate an overall availability of 0.926. If the entire manufacturing process was available 92.6% of the time, then a final production volume would be 50,000 units.

Therefore, until perfect production without breakdown can be achieved, a company must constantly improve the availability of the manufacturing processes or schedule around availabilities. To calculate the chance of a series of processes functioning correctly involves more probability calculations. Chapter 6 detailed how availability and reliability for a production process can be calculated. We now discuss how these measures of the probability of reliability can be used to calculate the probable success of tighter production schedules.

How to Predict Production Performance Using Probability in Series: The Series Production of a Drive Shaft

Consider the example of a straight series of machines. Suppose that a drive shaft is being produced through a series of machining processes. First the shaft is turned for overall diameter, then it is lathed for cam positions, and then another turning machine completes the landings and polishes the finished shaft. Overall, the shaft is handled by three machines, one right after the other.

If each machine has an availability of 99% (0.99), then the availability of the entire shaft production process is 97% (0.97). This is found using the probability formula for processes in series.

$$P = R^n$$

where, P = probability of successful operation
R = reliability of each stage of the operation
n = number of stages in the operation

If unequal reliability figures exist for each stage of production, the formula is

$$P = R_1 \text{ x } R_2 \text{ x } R_3 \text{ ...}$$

where, R_1 = reliability of the first operation
R_2 = reliability of the second operation
R_3 = reliability of the third operation

In our example, the probability of all three stages of the operation working successfully is

$$P = 0.99^3 = 0.970299, \text{ or about } 97\%$$

How to Calculate Probability of Success for Redundant Systems: Increasing the Reliability on a Screw Machine Operation with Backup Equipment

Real-world manufacturing systems usually involve groups of machines where one machine can take over the workload from another machine that has broken down. Therefore, manufacturing usually involves redundancy. Fig-

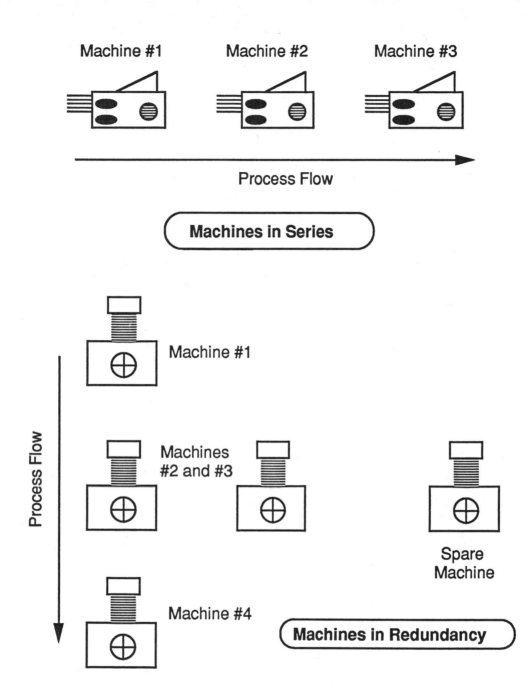

Figure 7-2: Machines in series versus redundancy.

ure 7-2 shows the difference between machines in series and machines in redundancy.

The probability of successful operation when two machines are in redundancy is

$$P = 1 - (1 - R)^n$$

where R = reliability of each machine
n = number of redundancies

For example, assume that two automatic screw machines are assigned to the aforementioned shaft turning job, but only one needs to be operating for production to proceed. If each machine is 99% reliable, the reliability of the screw machine phase of the turning operation is

$$P = 1 - (1 - 0.99)^2 = 0.9999$$

or about 99.99% reliable.

How to Evaluate Production Bottlenecks: Applying Probabilities to a Combined Stamping and Welding Process

For a successful JIT operation, the reliability of the manufacturing processes must either be near 100%, or the occurrence of breakdowns must be so predictable that maintenance is accurately scheduled. The use of probabilities in series and redundancy helps to evaluate the location of bottlenecks and the effect of continuous improvement.

Consider the example of a series of processes in a stamping and welding operation. A series of six machines are used to create a fuel cell for a truck.

Machine	Probability of Success
Stamping	0.99
Folding	0.98
Bending	0.92
Spot weld	0.88
Weld (MIG)	0.78
Painting	0.99

The overall probability of success for this series of manufacturing processes is

$$P = 0.99 \times 0.98 \times 0.92 \times 0.88 \times 0.78 \times 0.99 = 0.6065$$

This represents only about a 60% chance that a single sheet of metal will make it through this process as a finished fuel cell free of major defects. Obviously, the lower rates of success in the welding areas would need improvements. If continuous improvement actions were implemented and the success of spot and MIG welding increased to 0.95 and 0.97 respectively, the following increased reliability of the operation would result.

$$P = 0.99 \times 0.98 \times 0.92 \times 0.95 \times 0.97 \times 0.99 = 0.8143$$

This would be just over 81% reliable, or about a 21 percentage point increase over the former system. Still, the 81% reliability figure would indicate that this system is probably still not good enough to meet the demands of a JIT company.

Using Gangs of Machines.

Another example of the use of the probability series and redundancy formulas is a gang of machines. Suppose that a plastic injection molding company has five molding machines capable of running the mold for fishing lures. Four of the presses are needed at any time to keep up with production demands. The fifth machine is used only if one of the other machines fails. Each machine has proven to be 95% reliable. What is the probability of success for these machines as a gang?

To calculate the reliability of the gang of molding machines, you first must calculate the chance that a single machine might fail.

$$P = 0.95 \times 0.95 \times 0.95 \times 0.95 = 0.8145$$

Using the formula for a series of machines, the chance of a single machine failing is one minus the probability of success.

$$\text{Failure} = 1 - 0.8145 = 0.1855$$

Thus, we have already found that there is just over an 18% chance that one machine may fail during a production run. However, there is still one more machine available to take over in such a case. Therefore, we can use the redundancy formula to calculate the reliability because of an existing back-up machine.

$$R = 1 - (1 - 0.95)^2 = 0.9975$$

The system with a back-up machine is now over 96% reliable. The number of redundancies is set to two because there is the original machine that may break down and the back-up machine. Had we added another back-up machine, the redundancy figure would have risen to three and the reliability of the system would have increased.

$$R = 1 - (1 - 0.95)^3 = 0.9998$$

In other words, a second back-up machine would have increased the reliability of the entire molding process to over 99%.

These examples show how the addition of back-up devices and machines and the improvement of existing processes will increase the reliability and availability of industrial processes. Examining the processes as a series of production stages helps the JIT planner to evaluate where improvements are needed and where they will be expensive to implement. Consider the preceding example. The addition of another back-up molding machine would be a very expensive method of assuring continuous production. A closer study of breakdown occurrences, when they occur, how they occur, and methods to fix them faster would be a less expensive alternative.

Conclusion

Implementation of JIT is a simple process of planning the exact system desired and installing statistical and Material Resource Planning monitoring aids for management feedback. However, JIT implementation takes a long time because of the exacting discipline required and the difficulties of converting from current operational methods. An established company must replace each old method that blocks JIT with a more appropriate substitute. The process is similar to replacing a carburetor on an engine with a fuel injection system while the motor is still running.

Statistics, however, are an invaluable aid in the process of implementing JIT. As we have seen with the use of probability theory, you can form estimates of your probable success using current equipment, or you can estimate your likely success with new equipment and methods. We have also seen that set-up time and ordering expenses have to be drastically reduced to make JIT successful. Time and cost charts can be an important feedback tool for guiding management and work teams toward their goals.

Finally, the instructions for implementing JIT are not to be used by themselves. A JIT system makes a key assumption about your manufacturing process: that it has a total quality system that produces so few defects that they are measured as parts defective per 1 million production pieces. This is why this chapter on JIT follows several chapters on monitoring and improving quality.

CHAPTER 8

How to Improve Production Forecasting Using Statistical Analyses

The ability to forecast is important to a manufacturer for several reasons. For example, the sales forecast is the base of the entire materials planning resource system. This forecast determines the master production schedule for a manufacturer. Thus, the ability to forecast consumer trends allows a company to market its product competitively. Accurately forecasting needs over several years allows for effective facilities planning. In addition, knowing how changes in selected factors will affect production outcomes, such as manufacturability, makes the manufacturing process more predictable.

There are two ways to forecast. The first involves the study of historic information to find a trend that can be extended into the future. We will discuss how this is done later in this chapter. The second method is frequently overlooked by forecasters. It involves the study of one factor's effect on another factor. This method is called correlation and is vitally important to the manufacturing process.

Predictability is the key word in forecasting. A forecaster is not just looking toward the future. A forecaster attempts to find reliable patterns that can be successfully described. This leads to an accurate prediction of an event. For example, if it is found that the sale of your product is directly proportional to current interest rates, the interest rates can serve as a leading indicator of sales—they will foretell your future sales trends.

Method 1: Correlation Analysis: How to Predict Daily Production by Calculating the Number of Job Cycles

A correlation is a statistical test that measures the amount of association between two factors. A classic example of a correlation is between a person's level of education and annual salary. Usually, a person with more education also makes more money. There are exceptions of course, and a correlation does not prove a direct relationship, but the existence of a correlation indicates a predictable trend. As manufacturing manager you can appreciate the importance of having some predictability in your daily life.

Step 1: Begin with a scattergram.

In chapter 5 we talked about the use of a scattergram to see if an identifiable cause associated with quality outcomes. In forecasting, you always begin with a plot of your data. This gives you a visual reference for eyeballing possible trends, patterns, or erratic data. For example, the easiest way to test for a correlation is to plot the relationship of two variables on graph paper. You may wish to study the relationship between the number of job cycles each day in the forming department and the total production for the day. Each job cycle represents the process of set-up, production, and take-down to manufacture a batch of specific parts.

Suppose that monitoring the production process for 10 days results in the following information.

Cycles	Units Produced (in thousands)
12	5.5
15	6.3
22	3.4
14	4.9
3	12.5
9	8.0
11	4.4
15	5.6
25	5.1
21	3.9

You can create a scattergram using a piece of graph paper. On the horizontal axis you draw the scale of daily job cycles. The vertical axis is the scale of production. Each pair of data points is plotted on this graph. For example, the first day of production had 12 job cycles and produced 5,500 parts. The point is plotted where these two coordinates meet. After all of the data pairs are plotted, the scattergram is complete (see Figure 8-1). A slight

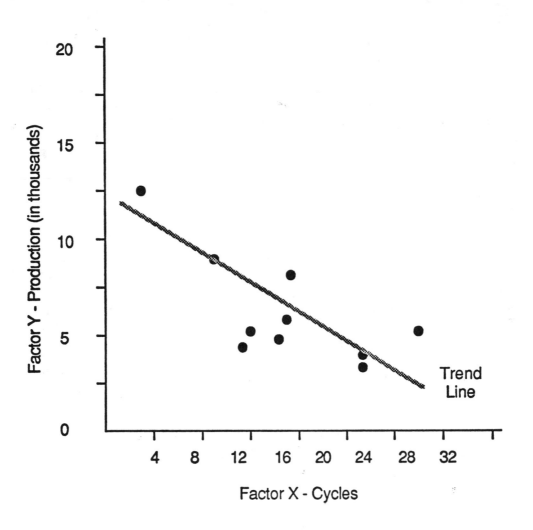

Figure 8-1: Scattergram of job cycles and production.

downward trend is visible in Figure 8.1. Such a trend indicates that as the number of job cycles increases, the total production tends to decrease.

Any elongated pattern of dots indicates a correlation between the two variables. A random pattern, like the pattern of a shotgun on paper, would indicate no correlation. In our example, the pattern is not overwhelmingly obvious. Therefore, a statistical test must be performed to test for correlation.

Step 2: Conduct correlation analysis to find the degree of association between factors affecting productivity.

In our example, the objective is to discover how much the variation in job cycles explains the variation in productivity. This is called finding the amount of determination. In other words, how much does the variation in factor X determine the variation in factor Y? The statistic used is called the *coefficient of determination* (designated as R^2).

For example, if the R^2 is 0.50 (50%), then half of the variation in factor Y is determined by variations in factor X. The remaining variation is a product of other noise factors. As a rule of thumb, any determination above 50% is worth further consideration as a model of prediction.

$$R^2 = \left(\frac{n(\Sigma xy) - (\Sigma x \cdot \Sigma y)}{\sqrt{[n(\Sigma x^2) - (\Sigma x)^2] \cdot [n(\Sigma y^2) - (\Sigma y)^2]}} \right)^2$$

where, Σx = sum of the first factor
Σy = sum of the second factor
Σx^2 = sum of the squares of the first factor
Σy^2 = sum of the squares of the second factor
Σxy = sum of the first factor times the second factor
R^2 = the coefficient of determination

The formula used to calculate this coefficient is as follows. To calculate this formula, you must perform some additional calculations with the raw data. The best way to do this is to extend the original data table to include columns of each factor squared and the product of the two factors. The first factor will be labeled X and the second factor will be labeled Y. Our end goal is to see how much X will predict the behavior of Y.

Cycles	Units			
X	Y	X^2	Y^2	XY
12	5.5	144	30.25	66
15	6.3	225	39.69	94.5
22	3.4	484	11.56	74.8
14	4.9	196	24.01	68.6
3	12.5	9	156.25	37.5
9	8	81	64	72
11	4.4	121	19.36	48.4
15	5.6	225	31.36	84
25	5.1	625	26.01	127.5
21	3.9	441	15.21	81.9
Totals				
147	59.6	2,551	417.7	755.2

These figures can be substituted into the coefficient of determination formula to complete the calculation.

thus
$$R^2 = \left(\frac{10(755.2) - (147 \cdot 59.6)}{\sqrt{[10(2,551) - (147)^2] \cdot [10(417.7) - (59.6)^2]}} \right)^2 = -0.774^2$$

$$R^2 = 0.60$$

This coefficient of determination tells us that about 60% of the variation in factor Y, the production, can be explained by the variation in factor X, the number of job cycles in a day. In other words, by knowing the number of job cycles to be assigned tomorrow, you can make a fairly good prediction of the final productivity of the department. This is a form of forecasting. To make the forecast you need to apply regression analysis and then estimate the error of your forecast. These steps will finally determine the strength of your forecast model.

Step 3: Apply regression analysis to create the forecast model

Regression analysis involves finding the line of best fit to the plotted data points on a scattergram. In a previous example, the number of job cycles per day were plotted against the number of units produced that day. On the scattergram, it appeared that the data formed a downward trend. To see if that is true, you must mathematically fit a straight line to the data. The best method for doing this is called the least-squares method.

A straight line is described with the formula $Y = a + bX$. The factor a is the origin of the line, and the factor b is the slope of the line. Factors X

and Y are the same two factors described earlier: number of cycles and pro-duction. By solving for a and b you form a mathematical model of prediction. Merely enter a value for X, and a Y prediction is created.

To solve for the straight line formula, you begin by calculating b, or the slope of the line.

$$b = \frac{n\left(\Sigma xy\right) - \left(\Sigma x \cdot \Sigma y\right)}{n\left(\Sigma x^2\right) - \left(\Sigma x\right)^2}$$

where Σx = sum of the first factor (X)
  Σy = sum of the second factor (Y)
  Σx^2 = sum of the squares of the first factor
  Σxy = sum of the product of the first factor and the second factor
  n = number of data pairs

Using the data presented on page 171 we can solve for b.

$$b = \frac{10(755.2) - (147 \cdot 59.6)}{10(2,551) - (147)^2}$$

thus

$$b = -0.31$$

A negative result indicates that the data does indeed have a downward trend. Using the results from the b formula, you can now calculate the a factor.

$$a = \frac{\Sigma y}{n} - b\frac{\Sigma x}{n}$$

Substituting the data from our example,

$$a = \frac{59.6}{10} - (-0.31)\frac{147}{10}$$

$$a = 10.52$$

Putting this information together into the line formula creates the **mathematical model of prediction.**

$$Y = 10.52 - 0.31X$$

By placing various values of X into the equation, you can estimate the amount of production that will result. For example, if there are 18 job cycles scheduled for the day, you can predict a production of about 4,940 units.

$$Y = 10.52 - (0.31 \times 18) = 4.94$$

$$4.94 \times 1,000 \text{ units} = 4,940 \text{ units}$$

As we calculated earlier, this correlation has a coefficient of determination of 0.60. There is still 40% of the variation in production that is accounted for by other factors. To evaluate the impact of this unexplained 40%, you calculate an estimate of the forecasting error.

Step 4: Calculate the error of estimation for the forecast.

The linear model we have calculated creates a straight line of specific, forecasted production amounts based on job cycles. For example, we forecasted that 18 job cycles would produce 4,940 units of production. However, we know that in practice the actual amount of production will not be exactly this number but one that is fairly close.

Determining a range for the actual production figure is done the same way as forming interval estimates (see chapter 2). We assume that the forecasted value is the average. Then we calculate a standard deviation for the forecast and form interval estimates around the mean. The standard deviation for regression is called the standard error of the estimate. The formula used is

$$Sxy = \sqrt{\frac{\Sigma(Y - Y')^2}{n-2}}$$

where Y = actual value obtained in our original data
          Y' = forecasted value
          n = number of data pairs in our original data
          Sxy = standard error of the estimate

This standard error is treated just like a standard deviation. If we want to form an estimate around a mean, we use confidence intervals based on the Z-values of the area under a normal curve when the sample size is large. For example, plus and minus one standard deviation around the mean would represent a 68% chance that the actual production figure would fall inside the defined range.

However, use caution with this method of estimating. A key assumption is that the raw data scatters equally along the line of regression. If your scattergram shows a different pattern, such as wide scattering near the ends of the line and tight patterns near the middle, then do not rely on this method of estimating the error.

The procedure for calculating a standard error of the estimate is fairly simple. First list the original data.

Cycles	Units Produced (In thousands)
X	Y
12	5.5
15	6.3
22	3.4
14	4.9
3	12.5
9	8.0
11	4.4
15	5.6
25	5.1
21	3.9

Against this data you list the forecasted values for each factor X value. For example, the first X value listed is 12 job cycles. Using the regression formula from the previous step ($Y = 10.52 - 0.31X$) you calculate the forecasted value, also called the Y-prime (Y').

$$Y' = 10.52 - (0.31 \times 12) = 6.80 \text{ units of production } (1,000)$$

This is repeated for each of the X values listed. Then the predicted values are subtracted from the actual Y value. This is the amount of deviation between prediction and the actual data. By summing the square of these deviations, you can obtain the information needed to complete the formula for the standard error of the estimate.

Cycles	Units			
X	Y	Y'	$(Y - Y')$	$(Y - Y')^2$
12	5.5	6.80	−1.30	1.6900
15	6.3	5.87	0.43	0.1849
22	3.4	3.70	−0.30	0.0900
14	4.9	6.18	−1.28	1.6384
3	12.5	9.59	2.91	8.4681
9	8.0	7.73	0.27	0.0729
11	4.4	7.11	−2.71	7.3441
15	5.6	5.87	−0.27	0.0729
25	5.1	2.77	2.33	5.4289
21	3.9	4.01	−0.11	0.0121
Totals			−0.03	25.0023

Before you calculate the standard error of the estimate, you should check the average of the $(Y - Y')$ column. This represents the average deviation from the line of regression. If the regression model has made a good fit, this value should be very close to zero. In other words, the deviation from overestimates equals those for underestimates.

$$(Y - Y') \text{ total} = -0.03$$

and

$$\frac{-0.03}{10 \text{ data pairs}} = -0.003$$

Indeed, this is very close to zero. This tells you that the average predictions are on target. The calculation of the standard error of the estimate will tell you how much variation there is in the model.

$$Sxy = \sqrt{\frac{25.0023}{10-2}} = 1.76$$

To calculate the range of forecasting error, you first select a confidence interval such as:

$$\pm 1.96 \; Sxy = 95\% \text{ confidence}$$

$$\pm 2.58 \; Sxy = 99\% \text{ confidence}$$

In this example we will form an interval estimate with 95% confidence. Specifically, we will look at the estimate for 12 job cycles. The regression formula predicted an average production of 6.80 units (1,000). The interval estimate would be

$$12 \text{ cycles} = Y' \pm 1.96 \; S_{xy}$$

or

$$12 \text{ cycles} = 6.80 \pm (1.96 \times 1.76) = 6.80 \pm 3.45 \text{ units}$$

Thus, you could expect actual production after a day of 12 job cycles to be around 6.80 units, plus or minus 3.45 units. You have 95% confidence in this estimate.

In this particular illustration, we have used a small data set to clarify how this method works. If you find you have fewer than thirty data pairs, then you are working with a small sample. In such a situation, you use a more extensive formula to form the confidence intervals.

$$\bar{Y} = t \cdot Sxy \sqrt{\frac{1}{n} + \frac{(x - \bar{x})^2}{\Sigma(x - \bar{x})^2}}$$

where, t = the t-value from Appendix B
$\Sigma(x - \bar{x})^2$ = is taken from the data columns previously calculated
Sxy = the previously calculated standard error
$\bar{Y}$ = the mean value of the Y factor

Essentially, this formula corrects each pair for the small sample size involved.

At this point you can evaluate whether this amount of variation in the estimate is too high to suit your purpose. In our example, the actual production range is plus or minus almost half of the expected output. This large amount of error is the result of the weak determination between job cycles and production output.

If this range is too high for your situation, then seek stronger models of prediction. However, stronger methods also mean more complicated and demanding analysis, such as multiple regression models. Therefore, the advanced techniques should be left to the professional production planners and statisticians.

Our example also presents another opportunity. Only ten data point pairs were used in the calculations. The collection of a larger sample would likely reduce the error of prediction.

Method 2: Time Series Analysis: How to Predict Production Output Based on the Passage of Time

The first method of forecasting uses the raw data to make predictions within the range of the original data. In our previous example, the number of cycles in the raw data varied from 3 to 25. Thus, the estimations were restrained to these limits. However, the more popularly known method of forecasting involves making predictions about the future.

This second form of forecasting has two distinct differences from the first method. First, the *X* factor is always time and it is always plotted on the horizontal axis of the scattergram. Second, after the regression line is drawn, it is extended beyond the range of the original data to make a prediction about the future. For example, government economists examine the history of the demand for wheat to predict its demand in the future.

Extending the prediction beyond the original data range is not without dangers. For example, some people take the rate of population growth within a community for the past 20 years and extend it ahead 20 years. This usually creates the impression that cities the size of Grand Rapids will be as large as Detroit in the twenty-first century. Therefore, a forecast should never be made more than 10% farther than the range of the original data. In other words, the population for Grand Rapids can only be predicted with validity for two years in the future based on a 20-year growth record.

Usually, the raw data can best be fitted to a straight line or a simple curve to describe its internal trend. The following example of data on a straight line trend of growth illustrates how time series analysis is conducted.

Straight Line Trends: How to Calculate the Number of Employees Needed in the Near Future

The president of a small manufacturing plant has been enjoying a period of expansion. It seems like every month she has to hire new people to fulfill the growing number of orders. It occurs to this president that being able to predict the number of people needed in the coming few months would allow her to search longer for better people and to train them for their jobs before they are needed. Therefore, she collects the following hiring information for the past 14 months.

Months	Employees
2	50
4	72
6	90
8	105
10	112
12	149
14	150

Plotting these points on a scattergram, she finds a straight line trend in the points. What is the mathematical formula of prediction for these numbers?

To solve this problem you would use the same formulas used earlier to find a and b for a straight line. The coefficient of determination would tell you how much factor X (months since opening) relates to the variation in factor Y (number of employees needed).

To complete these calculations, you must complete the raw data table to include the necessary sums.

Months	Employees			
X	Y	X^2	Y^2	XY
2	50	4	2500	100
4	72	16	5184	288
6	90	36	8100	540
8	105	64	11,025	840
10	112	100	12,544	1,120
12	149	144	22,201	1,788
14	150	196	22,500	2,100
Totals				
56	728	560	84,054	6,776

Solving for *a* and *b*,

$$b = \frac{6{,}776 - \dfrac{56 \cdot 728}{7}}{560 - \dfrac{56^2}{7}}$$

$$b = 8.5$$

and

$$a = \frac{728}{7} - 8.5 \frac{56}{7}$$

$$a = 36$$

These two results are then used to form the regression line.

$$Y = 36 + 8.5X$$

By substituting 16 and then 18 for the X factor, you can form the predicted level of employment for the coming months.

$$Y = 36 + (8.5 \times 16) = 172$$

and

$$Y = 36 + (8.5 \times 18) = 189$$

In other words, 172 employees should be employed within two months and 189 within four months, assuming that the straight line trend continues. The plotting of points on the scattergram could have given you a rough estimate of the trend, but only through analysis will an accurate estimate be formed. To find if the predictive power of time is strong, the coefficient of determination can be calculated.

$$R^2 = \left[\frac{7(6,776) - (56 \cdot 728)}{\sqrt{[7 \cdot 560 - (56)^2] \cdot [7 \cdot 84,054 - (728)^2]}} \right]^2$$

$$R^2 = 0.97$$

Thus, the number of months explains 97% of the variation in employment levels. This makes the predictive power of the regression line strong, but only for the short term. Using the 10% rule of prediction, the 14 months of data would be valid for only the next month or two. Still, it does provide a basis for planning future hiring.

An Increasing, Curved Trend: How to Predict Order Placements by Examining the Sales Trend

A common situation in forecasting is to discover that the data does not fit a straight line as well as it would fit a curve. There is an almost endless variety of curves that could fit different data sets, but most cases will fit one of two curved trends; either an increasing curve or a decreasing curve. We will examine the case of the increasing curve first.

Your manufacturing schedule is driven by the orders placed by your customers. Therefore, the sales forecast is an important document for manufacturing planning. Consider the example of a company that uses sales history as a prediction of future demand for a particular product.

When plotted on a scattergram, these sales figures will create an increasing curve. This occurs frequently in companies that demand a steady rate of growth each quarter (such as 10% sales increases annually). Steady sales rates will create an increasing curve of sales volume. For example, a company has been tracking the sales of a new product since its introduction. For each $10,000 in sales, the company will need to schedule two shifts of production per day.

Month	Sales ($10,000)
1	2.0
2	2.3
3	3.1
4	4.2
5	5.4
6	7.0
7	9.2
8	13.4
9	16.9
10	21.0

If you plotted these figures on a scattergram, an increasing curve of sales volumes would form (see Figure 8-2). This increasing curve of volume is best represented by the exponential curve formula.

$$Y = a \ x \ e^{bx}$$

where e = a logarithm equal to 2.71828
        a = origin of the line
        b = slope of the line
        x = time unit (months in this example)

To obtain the data necessary to complete this formula, the natural logarithm (ln) of factor Y and its square must be calculated. In addition, the ln Y must be multiplied into X. The resulting table of data would look like this.

Month X	Sales Y	ln Y	x^2	ln Y^2	X x ln Y
1	2.0	0.693	1	0.480	0.693
2	2.3	0.833	4	0.694	1.666
3	3.1	1.131	9	1.280	3.394
4	4.2	1.435	16	2.059	5.740
5	5.4	1.686	25	2.844	8.432
6	7.0	1.946	36	3.787	11.675
7	9.2	2.219	49	4.925	15.534
8	13.4	2.595	64	6.735	20.762
9	16.9	2.827	81	7.994	25.446
10	21.0	3.044	100	9.269	30.445
Totals					
55	84.5	18.409	385	40.067	123.787

To calculate the natural logarithms of the data, a scientific calculator, electronic spreadsheet, statistical software, or the ability to use a computer programming language is recommended. The sums of each column are used to complete the calculations for the curve and the coefficient of determination.

$$b = \frac{\Sigma(x \ \ln y) - \frac{1}{n} (\Sigma x) (\Sigma \ln y)}{\Sigma x^2 - \frac{1}{n} (\Sigma x)^2}$$

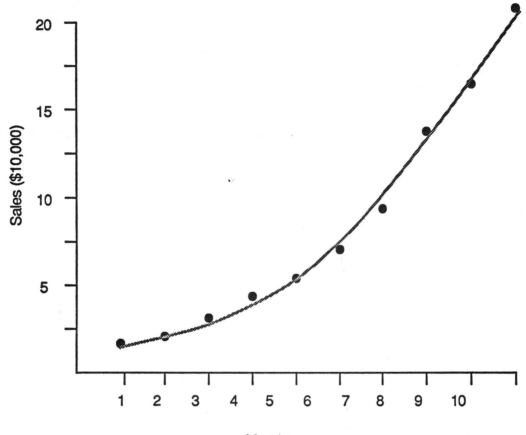

Figure 8-2: Increasing sales curve.

where $\Sigma(x \ln y)$ = sum of X's times ln Y's
Σx = sum of the X's
$\Sigma \ln y$ = sum of the ln Y's
n = number of data pairs

Substituting the data from the preceding table,

$$b = \frac{123.787 - \frac{1}{10}(55) \cdot (18.409)}{385 - \frac{1}{10} \cdot (55)^2}$$

$$b = 0.273$$

And

$$a = e^{\left[\frac{\Sigma \ln y}{n} - b\frac{\Sigma x}{n}\right]}$$

where e = logarithm equal to 2.71828

so

$$a = 2.71828^{\left[\frac{18.409}{10} - 0.273\frac{55}{10}\right]}$$

$$a = 1.404$$

Putting these figures together creates the curve formula.

$$Y = 1.404 \times e^{[0.273x]}$$

By using 11 and 12 to represent the coming two months, the curve formula can be used to make a forecast of sales.

$$Y = 1.404 \times 2.71828^{[0.273x]}$$

$$Y = 28.28$$

and

$$Y = 1.404 \times 2.71828^{[0.273 \cdot 12]}$$

$$Y = 37.16$$

In other words, the next month will have approximately 28,280 units sold, and the following month 37,160 units sold. Naturally, these are estimates and should be treated as such. However, they do fit the increasing curve nicely.

To find the coefficient of determination, the following formula is used. Although it looks complicated, it is fairly easy to calculate once the sums from the data table are substituted into their appropriate positions.

$$R^2 = \frac{\left[\left(\Sigma x \cdot \ln y\right) - \frac{1}{n} \cdot \Sigma x \cdot \Sigma \ln y\right]^2}{\left(\Sigma x^2 - \frac{(\Sigma x)^2}{n}\right) \cdot \left(\Sigma(\ln y)^2 - \frac{(\Sigma \ln y)^2}{n}\right)}$$

where $\Sigma x \ln y$ = sum of X's times $\ln Y$'s
Σx = sum of the X's
$\Sigma \ln y$ = sum of the $\ln Y$'s
Σx^2 = sum of the squared X's
$\Sigma (\ln y)^2$ = sum of the squared $\ln Y$'s
n = number of data pairs

Substituting the data from the preceding table,

$$R^2 = \frac{\left[(123.788) - \frac{1}{10} \cdot 55 \cdot 18.411\right]^2}{\left(385 - \frac{55^2}{10}\right) \cdot \left(40.067 - \frac{18.411^2}{10}\right)}$$

$$R^2 = 0.997$$

Thus, the X factor explains 99.7% of the variation in sales. This is a strong model of prediction.

This method of forecasting can be continued by calculating the standard error of the estimate as before. Then it will be possible for you to calculate interval estimates based on the forecast. However, you are probably noting by now that forecasts such as this one demand a considerable amount of calculation time. Therefore, a good computer software program can go a long way in making forecasting much faster. In addition, by understanding the assumptions involved and statistics generated, you can quickly read and interpret forecasts generated by others.

Forecasting for a Curve with a Decreasing Rate of Growth: How to Forecast the Need for Raw Materials

Although it always seems that forecasters are trying to make the future look bright, there are situations where things are degrading and their demise must be forecasted. For example, consider the case of a product that has been on the market for many months and has a saturated customer base. The growth of sales will soon reach zero and perhaps will even fall. Such a situation represents a decreasing curve. The main trend line in Figure 8-3 represents one possible decreasing curve. Although unit sales are increasing each month, the rate of that increase is slowly falling.

The following logarithmic curve formula fits many of these situations well.

$$Y = a + b \cdot \ln X$$

The following example of decreasing sales illustrates how the logarithmic curve formula is calculated. Assume that the manufacturer of food processors finds that its most popular model is not enjoying strong sales growth as it once did. Instead, the market for this model seems to be saturated. The production schedule for the model bases its schedule on the demand for the product. Part of this schedule will be the order quantities and frequencies for raw materials, such as the plastic resin for molding the case of the food processor. This forecast must try to prevent the overordering of raw materials because slowing sales will leave extra lots of material in the warehouse taking up valuable inventory space. The previous eight months of sales figures are gathered.

Month	Coded Month	Sales
Jan.	1	44.0
Feb.	2	49.0
March	3	51.5
April	4	53.0
June	5	54.0
July	6	55.5
Aug.	7	55.0
Sept.	8	56.0

The formulas for the *a* and *b* factors are as follows.

$$b = \frac{\left(\Sigma y \cdot \ln x\right) - \frac{1}{n} \cdot \Sigma \ln x \cdot \Sigma y}{\Sigma (\ln x)^2 - \frac{1}{n} \cdot \left(\Sigma \ln x\right)^2}$$

where $\Sigma y \ln x$ = sum of the product of *y* times the natural logarithm of *x*
$\Sigma \ln x$ = sum of the natural logarithm of *x*
$\Sigma (\ln x)^2$ = sum of the squares of the natural logarithm x n
n = number of data pairs

$$a = \frac{1}{n} \left(\Sigma y - b \cdot \Sigma \ln x\right)$$

where Σy = sum of the *y*'s

To complete these calculations you need to find the logarithm of X, square each result, square each Y, and multiply Y times the logarithm of X. The following table is created to find the appropriate sums.

Coded Month	Sales				
X	Y	Y^2	ln X	(ln $X)^2$	Y ln X
1	44.0	1,936.00	0.0	0.0	0.0
2	49.0	2,401.00	0.693	0.480	33.964
3	51.5	2,652.25	1.099	1.207	56.579
4	53.0	2,809.00	1.386	1.922	73.474
5	54.0	2,916.00	1.609	2.590	86.910
6	55.5	3,080.25	1.792	3.210	99.443
7	55.0	3,025.00	1.946	3.787	107.025
8	56.0	3,136.00	2.079	4.324	116.449
Totals					
36	418	21,955.5	10.605	17.520	573.844

Once again, access to a scientific calculator, electronic spreadsheet, statistical software, or a computer programming language is required for these calculations. This data is then used to complete the calculations for the curve function.

$$b = \frac{573.844 - \frac{1}{8} \cdot 10.605 \cdot 418}{17.52 - \frac{1}{8} \cdot (10.605)^2}$$

$$b = 5.70$$

and

$$a = \frac{1}{8}(418 - 5.70 \cdot 10.605)$$

$$a = 44.69$$

Thus, the curve function for this data is

$$Y = 44.69 + 5.70 \cdot \ln X$$

By substituting various X's, you can make predictions into the near future. For example, the ninth month would represent a prediction of the sales for the coming month.

$$Y = 44.69 + 5.70 \cdot \ln 9$$

or

$$Y = 44.69 + (5.70 \times 2.197) = 57.21$$

In other words, the sales for the next month will be slightly over the 57,000 units sold this month. The production schedule would be duly reduced and production would be cut back.

The coefficient of determination for a logarithmic curve is found using the following formula.

$$R^2 = \frac{\left[\left(\Sigma y \cdot \ln X\right) - \frac{1}{n} \cdot \Sigma \ln X \cdot \Sigma y\right]^2}{\left(\Sigma (\ln X)^2 - \frac{1}{n}\left(\Sigma \ln X\right)^2\right) \cdot \left(\Sigma y^2 - \frac{1}{n}\left(\Sigma y\right)^2\right)}$$

where Σy^2 = sum of the squares of Y

$\Sigma \ln X$ = sum of the natural logarithm of X

$\Sigma (\ln X)^2$ = sum of the squares of the natural logarithms of X

$\left(\Sigma y \cdot \ln X\right)$ = sum of the product of Y times the natural logarithm of X

n = number of data pairs

Therefore,

$$R^2 = \frac{[573.844 - \frac{1}{8} \cdot 10.605 \cdot 418]^2}{[17.520 - \frac{1}{8}(10.605)^2] \cdot [21,955.5 - \frac{1}{8}(418)^2]}$$

and

$$R^2 = 0.978$$

This is a high coefficient of determination and shows that the raw data fits a decreasing curve very well.

How to Forecast Production Levels When Work Orders Are Fluctuating: Smoothing Raw Data with a Moving Average

Once a strong relationship is found between two factors, a mathematical model can be constructed that will best describe the relationship. Usually this model is in the form of a line that best fits the data. Regression analysis involves fitting a line to the data.

There can be a problem in working with raw data. Specifically, data can vary from outside factors that cannot be controlled. For example, sales volumes and rates of absenteeism can vary according to the season. Information collected daily may vary widely from day to day, but still retain a definite trend. Figure 8-3 shows how a trend is encased in the wild fluctuations of daily quality levels for a large manufacturer.

Although the raw data in such a situation could be used to construct forecast models, it is easier to calculate and work with data when it is translated into a basic trend. For example, suppose that the production scheduler for a small manufacturing facility was interested in whether the number of work orders issued was steady, increasing, or decreasing. The raw data may resemble the following.

Day	Work Orders
1	11
2	37
3	29
4	14
5	33
6	52
7	7
8	19
9	25
10	25
11	29
12	16
13	31
14	40

As you can see, the raw data does not present a clear picture of the trend in work orders. Day-to-day fluctuations are clouding the picture. To develop the underlying trend, the data has to be "smoothed out." This is accomplished using the moving average.

The moving average takes the first few numbers, averages them, moves forward one time period, and averages again. This is easily illustrated using the foregoing raw data. The practitioner begins by arbitrarily selecting the number of periods to average. In this case, we will take a three-day moving average of the data.

The first three days of data are averaged together and recorded.

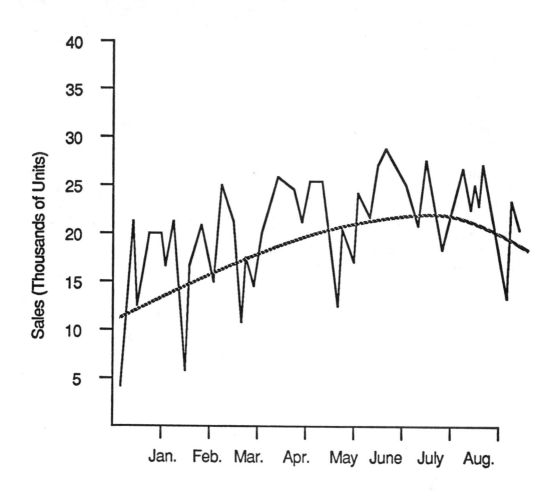

Figure 8-3: A trend hidden in the "noise" of raw data.

Day	Work Orders	Three-day Average
1	11	
2	37	25.7
3	29	

Then the three day bracket is moved down one day and a new three day average is calculated.

Day	Work Orders	Three-day Average
2	37	
3	29	26.7
4	14	

This procedure of moving down a day and calculating a new moving average is repeated for all of the raw data.

Day	Work Orders	Three-day Average
1	11	
2	37	25.7
3	29	26.7
4	14	25.3
5	33	33.0
6	52	30.7
7	7	26.0
8	19	17.0
9	25	23.0
10	25	26.3
11	29	23.3
12	16	25.3
13	31	29.0
14	40	

Note that the moving averages form a much more steady trend than the raw data. In fact, if the moving averages were plotted, a steady or slightly falling trend would appear. If a recurring cycle had been present within the data, the moving average would have brought it to the surface.

How to Deseasonalize Data: Predicting Seasonal Sales Using Monthly Sales Data

Although a lot of data used in forecasting have a definitive trend or cycle, they also can vary according to the season. Sales, employment, and production resources are often involved in a seasonal fluctuation. For example, the quality of natural rubber changes between the dry and rainy seasons of the countries it is produced in. As another example, absenteeism is highest during the flu season.

Therefore, it is necessary to separate seasonal effects from data so that underlying cycles and trends can be studied. In addition, the seasonal pattern must be defined so that forecasts can be calculated more accurately. This process of removing the seasonal effect is called deseasonalizing the data.

Detecting a seasonal pattern within raw data is easy by plotting a few years of data. For example, a manufacturer may believe that the rusting of metal parts is related to the season in which they are shipped. To find out, the number of rusted parts discovered by customers for the past three years could be collected. Using a graph with the 12 months of the year along the x-axis, the company can plot three overlapping years of data. If each year's data rises and falls at the same time, a seasonal trend is present (see Figure 8-4).

To deseasonalize data, you must first create a seasonal index. This index is then used to remove the seasonality from your raw data. To create this seasonal index, you will need two complete cycles of data. For example, to create a seasonal index of monthly sales data, you will need 24 months of data.

The following example illustrates how the seasonal index is created. Suppose that you are interested in the seasonal pattern of the metal parts manufacturer's monthly sales. You have selected the following 24 months of data as a basis for creating the seasonal index.

	Two Years Ago	One Year Ago
Jan.	110	232
Feb.	121	139
March	143	137
April	169	157
May	133	141
June	131	132
July	125	132
Aug.	120	127
Sept.	152	165
Oct.	175	184
Nov.	196	186
Dec.	204	225

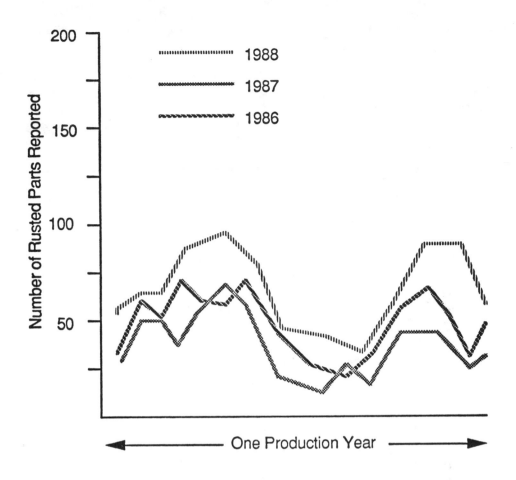

Figure 8-4: Detecting a seasonal trend in overlapping data.

A 12-month moving average must be calculated for the data. This will create 13 averages. Each of these averages must be combined to create 12 final averages. Dividing these into the original data creates the seasonal index. Figure 8-5 demonstrates the process. If you examine Figure 8-5 closely, you will see that the following seasonal index corresponds to the middle spread of months in the figure. Thus, the January seasonal index correction is halfway down the list. Resorting the list into the 12 twelve months of the year creates the following.

Jan.	80.55%
Feb.	92.18%
March	90.36%
April	102.92%
May	92.43%
June	86.27%
July	84.06%
Aug.	80.04%
Sept.	101.05%
Oct.	116.92%
Nov.	131.10%
Dec.	136.11%

This seasonal index indicates the peaks and valleys of sales over the year. The months leading up to the end of the year have the heaviest sales, while the summer months indicate light sales. The seasonal index can also be used to test whether current monthly sales are higher or lower than expected.

Let us continue with our example of the company collecting monthly sales figures. Assume that the first five months of this year produce the following sales figures (in thousands of dollars).

Month	Sales
Jan.	$123
Feb.	129
March	126
April	134
May	137

To detect the underlying sales trends, this data must be seasonally adjusted. That is, the seasonal trend must be removed. This is accomplished with the following formula.

$$\text{adjusted data} = \frac{\text{sales}}{\text{seasonal index}} \times 100$$

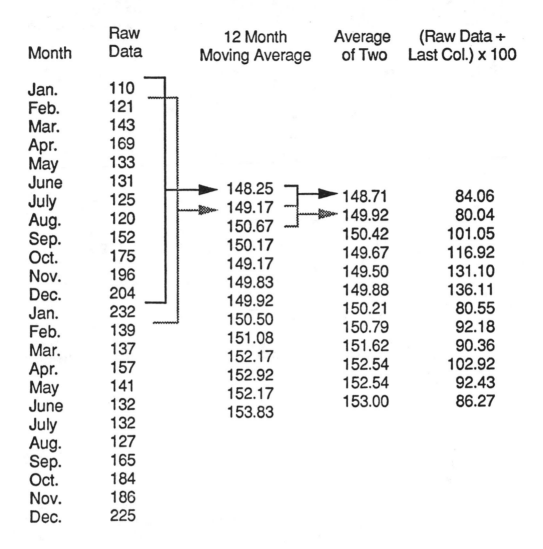

Month	Raw Data	12 Month Moving Average	Average of Two	(Raw Data + Last Col.) x 100
Jan.	110			
Feb.	121			
Mar.	143			
Apr.	169			
May	133			
June	131	148.25	148.71	84.06
July	125	149.17	149.92	80.04
Aug.	120	150.67	150.42	101.05
Sep.	152	150.17	149.67	116.92
Oct.	175	149.17	149.50	131.10
Nov.	196	149.83	149.88	136.11
Dec.	204	149.92	150.21	80.55
Jan.	232	150.50	150.79	92.18
Feb.	139	151.08	151.62	90.36
Mar.	137	152.17	152.54	102.92
Apr.	157	152.92	152.54	92.43
May	141	152.17	153.00	86.27
June	132	153.83		
July	132			
Aug.	127			
Sep.	165			
Oct.	184			
Nov.	186			
Dec.	225			

Figure 8-5: Calculating a seasonal index.

For the month of January,

$$\text{adjusted data} = \frac{123}{0.8055} = 152.7$$

Continuing this calculation for the other four months yields the following results.

Month	Sales	Index	Adjusted Data
Jan.	$123	0.8055	152.7
Feb.	129	0.9218	139.9
March	126	0.9036	139.4
April	134	1.0292	130.2
May	137	0.9243	148.2

Notice that the raw sales figures show an increasing amount of sales, but the adjusted data show a flat trend. The company should pay attention to the seasonally adjusted data, which indicate that sales are basically following the same seasonal trend as past years. Otherwise, without this data, the company might have increased the production schedule in response to a false demand.

Conclusion

Forecasting using statistical methods is a valuable tool for any manufacturing activity. However, the techniques presented in this chapter serve only as an introduction to the subject. Once these techniques are used and the results compared to actual performance, you are ready to employ even more complex models of forecasting. At that point, computer software that can manipulate the data quickly becomes mandatory.

As we have seen, forecasting drives the production planning of a company. Even with the simple methods described in this chapter, you should be able to add more predictability to your manufacturing process.

CHAPTER 9

How to Conduct Statistical Experiments to Improve Manufacturing Designs and Processes

So far we have been discussing the use of statistics in a tactical role. That is, we have shown how statistical methods can be used to track, monitor, and correct problems that already exist. As manufacturing manager, you know that strategic techniques are needed for revolutionary improvements in both processes and designs. Experimentation represents the strategic technique of choice.

Experimentation allows a company to improve the quality of existing products, develop new products, and optimize production processes. Experimentation will pinpoint trouble spots as easily as it will identify opportunities for improvement.

To master experimental research requires years of education and practical experience. However, as a manager it is only necessary to know how to conduct a proper experiment and interpret its results. This chapter contains enough information so that you can conduct simple experiments that will point the way toward more complete research projects. You should be able to solve many process and design problems with the information that follows. As many statisticians and engineers have pointed out, even the simplest experiment will open vast opportunities for improvement.

If your company already has an extensive research and development program, this chapter will help you to understand better how the experimental process works and how the results can best be interpreted. The information in this chapter does not represent a complete discussion of experimental methods. In fact, there is no single book that can cover all possible uses of experimentation. Instead, this chapter serves as an introduction and overview of the use of the scientific method for industrial problems.

How to Conduct a Proper Experiment

You begin an industrial experiment with a goal. Perhaps the quality of a product has to be improved or the performance of a process optimized. You have a good idea of the results you want, but you also know that there is a long list of variables in the product or process that could affect your desired outcomes. An experiment searches for those factors that can control the outcome you desire.

The technique of experimenting is fairly simple if you use your common sense at each stage of the process. We will review the steps of an experiment and then we will discuss some specific examples of experimenting in an industrial setting.

Step 1: Identify a situation that requires an experiment.

Although powerful, an experiment is not always an efficient method for solving problems. As a rule of thumb, exhaust the use of simpler techniques of problem solving before using an experiment.

For example, a problem in the appearance of a finished part might be addressed by the SPC system and problem solving work teams as described earlier. A capability study can be used to detect the presence of an assignable cause. Thus, an experiment is used to probe just beyond the obvious.

Step 2: Investigate the situation and select factors for study.

Do not conduct an experiment until you have talked to 10 people involved with the process. A thorough investigation of the situation by examining SPC and other process records, talking to the people involved, and doing a literature search is highly recommended. A literature search alone may find that the answer to your problem is already known.

When talking to people involved in the process, include the project engineer, a quality department representative, a machine operator, the line supervisor, a top manager, and perhaps the customer. You may also want to talk to purchasing personnel, other engineers, and an outside expert on the process involved.

You will find that many things vary in a given process. For example, different materials are used, operators change, and machine settings drift. Each of these potential changes are called *variables*. In an experiment, you change a select number of specific variables, called *experimental factors*, and hold constant all other variables.

Step 3: Form a central question about the situation you are investigating.

The production manager may want a machine that underproduces brought up to standard, but that is not a specific enough request for an experiment.

You must narrow the goal of the investigation to fundamental questions, such as "How does varying the machine settings affect productivity in this machine?"; "Which machine settings affect quality and productivity?"; and "Does raw material variation adversely affect the process?" These are questions that can be verified using measurable data. As manufacturing manager, you should place half of your manpower and time effort into answering these questions. As a result, many manufacturing problems can be solved without the need of an experiment.

Your objective in forming the fundamental questions is also to list out the variables that will be used as experimental factors and the variables you will measure as your results (response variables). For each factor, the number of levels, or settings, is determined. This list leads you toward the proper design to use for your experiment.

Step 4: Design the experiment.

Your list of factors to experiment with and the levels at which to test these factors must be put into a logical arrangement for efficient testings. The arrangement of these factors and their levels is called the *experimental design*. Each example we will look at in this chapter shows you how these efficient arrangements are created.

Step 5: Conduct the experiment and gather data.

After an experimental design is created, the combinations of factor levels are randomly run and the data is grouped with the corresponding experimental run. Each combination of factors tested is called a *run*.

Step 6: Analyze the data.

Statistical tests are applied to the data to test for significance, association, or pattern fitting. In the simple experiments that we will talk about in this chapter, the analysis of variance will be the primary test. We will also use simple effect diagrams to interpret the data visually.

Step 7: Make adjustments to the design or process based on the analysis.

The statistical tests will tell you whether there are significant effects from the factors under study. However, to make an experiment complete, a mathematical model of the effect of each factor should be created. This helps the experimenter to predict the future results of various settings. It also gives the manufacturer a benchmark to compare against actual production results under the new recommended settings.

Step 8: Verify results.

This step is critical to the experimental process. Unless an experiment is verified, the time, money, and effort expended are probably wasted. If an optimal set of tolerances is found using experimental techniques, these should be tested to see if they produce the response predicted by the mathematical model. The verification confirms and refines the mathematical model so that it can be adopted as regular manufacturing information.

Step 9: Take action.

This step is universally ignored in texts on experimental design. You must present your results to top management so that problems can be corrected and opportunities exploited. If, as manufacturing manager, you make decisions about process changes, then anyone experimenting with the production processes should report their results to you.

For example, an experiment may find that top-grade stock steel is needed to keep a stamping press producing high-quality components. Thus, you must alter the purchasing agreements and supplier monitoring to assure that only high-grade material is obtained.

Be aware that this step introduces a threat to an experiment's validity: internal politics. An experiment is likely to find an answer you did not want to hear, such as the fact that the machinery tested is in need of expensive repair. Some managers will then "bury" the experimental results to avoid having to commit funds to repairs. Avoid this type of thinking at all costs, since it neither solves the problem nor profits the company. When you have chosen to experiment you have also chosen to face the realities the experimentation will uncover.

How to Experiment on Industrial Problems

The end goal of any experiment is to understand how selected factors affect a given response. For example, we may wish to find out how much change in the dimension of stamped parts will result when the thickness of the stock steel changes 0.002 inches. Statistical process control will tell us that a change took place or that the change was significant. A capability study can tell us the final quality of the resulting parts. An experiment will produce a mathematical model of the effect of the changing thicknesses. An experiment can determine whether other factors had a significant effect. Some experiments can determine if two or more factors interact to produce the effect you are seeking.

To accomplish these goals, an experiment must be repeatable. In the scientific community, studies are published so that other groups can try to duplicate the results. In manufacturing, the results of an experiment are tested in a pilot run or during full production.

In addition, an experiment must be designed to avoid problems from bias, testing affects, time, instrumentation problems, and other threats to validity. The most common countermeasure used to prevent a threat to validity is randomization. Experimental conditions, subjects, objects, and other factors are applied or sorted randomly. In addition, measurement equipment should be calibrated, and the conditions the experiment was run under should be documented. Remember, the results of an experiment apply only to the conditions under which it was tested. If shot speed was tested between one second and three seconds, then only the settings inside that range apply with validity.

Using the Classic Approach of Testing One Factor at a Time: Testing a New Method to Increase the Strength of a Welded Part

The classic approach is sometimes called the one-factor-at-a-time experiment because the effect of only a single factor is studied. For example, a company may wish to test a new method of welding. This new method involves cleaning the surface to be welded before the metal pieces are joined. The experimental factor is the method of welding. The first level is the old method; the second level is the new method. The response variable is the increase in the strength of the welded parts.

To ensure that the test is fair, a group of volunteers is randomly divided into two groups. Both groups are assigned to identical work areas with similar production schedules. One group is called the treatment group because they will eventually apply the new method. The other group is called the control group because they will use the old method of welding throughout the experiment.

As a first step, each group welds together 50 units for testing using the old method of welding. The pull strength of the welds is compared. This initial observation of the two groups ensures that they produce equal weld strengths before the new method is tried. For the sake of illustration, we will assume that both groups produced parts with an average pull strength of 1,100 foot-pounds and a standard deviation of 90 foot-pounds.

Then the treatment group changes to using the new method of welding while the control group continues to use the old method. The control group continues the old method to ensure that an unobserved change in the process did not happen while the treatment group was trying the new method. If any changes in the environment or material did occur, both groups would experience the change and the results would retain their validity.

Again, 50 pieces are welded and tested. The results are as follows:

	Old Method	New Method
Average	1,100	1,200 ft. lbs.
Standard Deviation	90	85

As you can see, the new method might have made the parts stronger. However, it is possible that the increase measured occurred by chance. You must test for a significant difference between these means.

A statistical test will lend evidence about whether the change was real. These tests center on what is called a *null hypothesis*, because in experimenting we test to see if our ideas are wrong. That is, we first state that there is no difference between the two averages produced by the two methods of welding. Then we test the data to see if there is enough evidence to reject this null hypothesis.

Since we are dealing with large samples and testing the difference between two means, the Z-test can be used. The formula is

$$Z = \frac{\bar{x}_1 - \bar{x}_2}{\sqrt{\dfrac{S_1^2}{n_1} + \dfrac{S_2^2}{n_2}}}$$

where $\bar{x}_1$ = first group's average

s_1 = first group's standard deviation

n_1 = first group's sample size

$\bar{x}_2$ = second group's average

The population mean of the treatment group is assumed to be equal to the population mean of the control group. To draw a different conclusion (that the treatment does have an effect), your evidence must fail to support the null hypothesis.

We can set the level of significance by selecting the percent confidence in the results. These are the same critical values used in estimations. For example, the 95% confidence level for an average is 1.96 standard deviations from a mean. The test of two means from large samples calculates the ratio of deviations from the separate means. If the result is outside the range from +1.96 to -1.96, you assume a significant difference and are forced to reject a null hypothesis.

Placing our data into the formula,

$$Z = \frac{1,100 - 1,200}{\sqrt{\frac{90^2}{50} + \frac{85^2}{50}}} = -5.712$$

Since the -5.712 value falls outside of the range of acceptance, you would reject the null hypothesis. Your assumption would be that the two methods do not produce about the same average pull strength. Specifically, you have found evidence in this test that the null hypothesis is false.

How to Analyze an Experiment Using Analysis of Variance: What to Do When More Than Two Averages Are Involved

In the previous example, only two averages were compared. In many industrial cases, you will have to compare three or more averages, such as the differences between three possible methods of production.

The analysis of variance (ANOVA) is one of the most commonly used methods of analyzing experiments. It is a flexible and powerful tool of analysis. The mathematics involved require diligence in calculation, yet the way ANOVA works is relatively simple.

In any experiment where several factors are allowed to vary, a situation called *experimental error* exists. Experimental error is the random errors created in the experiment from the chance variations in uncontrollable factors such as the quality of material, environmental conditions, and operators involved. Taken together, this experimental error creates a background "noise" in the data.

ANOVA measures this background noise. Then ANOVA measures the amount of signal each factor under study creates. The signal is the strength of the factor to create a real change in the response variable. If a factor is creating a signal that has more magnitude than the background noise, we say that this factor has a significant effect. Factors that cannot overcome the noise are said to be insignificant. As we shall see, even insignificant factors can be important in improving a process or product.

How to Set Up and Calculate an ANOVA: Comparing Three Types of Cutting Oils

Imagine that you are the manufacturing engineer for a small job shop. One of your big expenses is the purchasing of cutting oil for the lathes. You have been approached by two new oil vendors that claim that their cutting oil can be used in lower quantities than your current brand. You decide to run an experiment to test these claims.

You have one factor, cutting oil, at three levels representing each of the manufacturers. Your current supplier will be called Oil 1. The new potential suppliers' products will be called Oil 2 and Oil 3. A lathe operator is instructed to cut nine drive shafts. For each shaft the operator will be given a supply of one of the oils. The operator will cut three parts for each type of oil used. The number of quarts required will be recorded for each part.

The following results are obtained.

Oil	1	2	3	
Run 1	17	15	13 quarts	
2	16	19	14	
3	11	18	15	
Total	44	52	42	Grand total = 138
Average	14.7	17.3	14.0	

At first, it appears that your current product, Oil 1, requires about the same or less oil than the other two products. However, to be sure that this is correct and that other outside factors are not the real cause of the differences, you conduct an ANOVA.

To calculate the ANOVA, each column must be totaled. This particular experiment requires that the three averages be compared to see if any are significantly different from the others. This is called a one-way ANOVA because it compares data in one direction — across the columns.

The ANOVA method creates a table of variations, called the ANOVA table. It shows the effect of each factor versus the experimental error. Since we only have one factor in this example, the table we will fill in will look like this:

Source of Variation	Sum of Squares	Degrees of Freedom	Variation, or Mean Square
Factor A (oil)			
Error			
Total			

The following calculations complete this table. Once the table is filled in, you can draw conclusions about the data obtained in your experiment. We will discuss those interpretations in detail later.

The first calculation is to derive the correction factor that is used in the other formulas.

$$\text{correction factor} = \frac{\left(\sum_x\right)^2}{n}$$

where $\sum_x$ = grand total of raw data
n = number of numbers

Therefore, the correction factor (*CF*) is

$$CF = \frac{(138)^2}{9} = 2{,}116$$

The next calculation is for the magnitude of the experiment. This is also called the sum squares of the total, or SS_{total}.

$$SS_{total} = \text{grand total of squared data} - CF$$

$$SS_{total} = (17^2 + 16^2 + 11^2 + 5^2 + 19^2 + 18^2 + 13^2 + 14^2 + 15^2) - 2{,}116$$

In our example, the SS_{total} would be

$$SS_{total} = 2{,}166 - 2{,}116 = 50$$

The next calculation is the effect of the factor under study, the cutting oils. This calculation is called the sum square of treatment, or *SST* for short.

$$SST = \frac{\left(\sum_A\right)^2}{n} + \frac{\left(\sum_B\right)^2}{n} + \frac{\left(\sum_C\right)^2}{n} - CF$$

where $\frac{\left(\sum_A\right)^2}{n}$ = sum of each raw data column square, divided by n

n = number of numbers in the column
CF = correction factor

Therefore, the *SST* is,

$$SST = \frac{44^2}{3} + \frac{52^2}{3} + \frac{42^2}{3} - 2{,}116 = 18.7$$

Finally, we must calculate the amount of background noise in the experiment. This is called the sum square of error, or *SSE*. Since we already know the total magnitude of the experiment and the effect of the factor under study, the difference must be caused by experimental error. Thus, the formula for *SSE* is

$$SSE = SS_{total} - SST$$

That is,

$$SSE = 50 - 18.7 = 31.3$$

With these calculations, we are now ready to create the ANOVA table. The ANOVA table lists the sums of squares by their source and then proceeds to calculate their variance and, finally, the F-ratios between factor signals and the background noise of experimental error.

ANOVA Table

Source	Sum of Squares (SS)	Degrees of Freedom (df)
Factor A	18.7	2
Error	31.3	6
Total	50.0	8

The degrees of freedom are almost always one degree of freedom less than the number of numbers or number of levels involved. For example, the degrees of freedom for a factor are

$$df = k - 1$$

where k = number of levels for the factor
In our one-way ANOVA example, the degrees of freedom for the factor are two, since there are three brands of oil being compared.

$$df = 3 - 1 = 2$$

For error, the degrees of freedom are

$$df = N - k$$

where k = number of levels for the factors
N = the number of numbers in the entire experiment

Since there are three brands of oil and nine data points collected, the degrees of freedom for the error are

$$df = 9 - 3 = 6$$

The degrees of freedom for the entire experiment are one less than the total number of numbers in the experiment.

$$df = N - 1$$

Therefore,

$$df = 9 - 1 = 8$$

This is how the degrees of freedom are calculated for a one-way ANOVA. When the degrees of freedom are divided into the sum of squares, we create a mean square, also called a variance, hence the name analysis of variance. Our ANOVA table is expanded by adding a column for the variances (designated as V). The other columns are abbreviated to save space.

$$V_{factor} = \frac{SS_{factor}}{df_{factor}}$$

or

$$V_A = \frac{18.7}{2} = 9.35$$

ANOVA Table

Source	SS	df	V
Factor	18.7	2	9.35
Error	31.3	6	5.22
Total	50.0	8	

Our main concern in this method of analysis is to see if the signal created by the factor (oil type) is stronger than the background noise of the experiment (error). The F-test is used to compare two variances.

$$F = \frac{S_1^2}{S_2^2} = \frac{V_1}{V_2}$$

In this example,

$$F = \frac{V_{factor}}{V_{error}}$$

Since we have only one factor under study, only one F-ratio has to be calculated.

$$F = \frac{9.35}{5.22} = 1.79$$

This F-ratio is added to the ANOVA table to make it complete. As we shall see in later examples, the number of F-ratios increases as we study more factors.

ANOVA Table

Source	SS	df	V	F
Factor	18.7	2	9.35	1.79
Error	31.3	6	5.22	
Total	50.0	8		

The preceding is a completed ANOVA table. Our final step in the analysis is to see if the *F*-ratio is inside the acceptance range of a null hypothesis. To find out, we must look up the critical *F*-value from a table of *F*-values. Appendix E contains such a table for values at the 95% confidence level. However, to find the appropriate value, we have to know how many degrees of freedom there were in the numerator and denominator of the *F*-ratio equation calculated earlier.

An experimental factor is always on top in an *F*-ratio equation, so our numerator had two degrees of freedom. The denominator is always the error variance, and it has six degrees of freedom. Therefore, we look up the value for two by six degrees of freedom in Appendix E and find 5.14. Since our calculated *F*-ratio is 1.79, and it is much less than the critical value of 5.14, we conclude that the differences in the brands of oil are purely by chance. Outside factors seem to affect the total variation in the experiment more than changing oil types.

You can choose to continue the use of your current cutting oil. However, if one of the other oils is less expensive, then that would be a better choice. These results indicate that the difference in oil performance seen in the raw data was the result of chance variation in the sample or outside factors. This is easy to accept considering that only three shafts were cut using each oil.

Using the Modern Experimental Technique to Test More Than One Factor at a Time: Testing the Effect of Speed and Feed on Tool Life

Although the classic experimental design and its derivatives are used widely in the scientific community, they are usually impractical in the manufacturing environment. A scientist can build a laboratory to control all external factors (i.e., heat, humidity, variation in materials, and so on) and vary only the experimental factor. The manufacturer can only create such conditions at great expense and can rarely maintain them during real production runs. Therefore, the manufacturer is forced to study several varying factors at the same time. The experimental design for such situations is called the *factorial experiment*. The factorial experiment is the keystone of modern experimentation. A factorial experiment is usually used when two or more factors are involved. The design tests these factors simultaneously in experimental combinations.

Set-up and Design of the Experiment

The following example illustrates how a factorial experiment is designed. Assume that only two factors will be studied. The situation under study is a milling machine that cuts molding dies for a plastic injection department.

The speed of the cutting tool and the feed rate of the material are two factors that you know are critical to cutting accuracy and tool life.

As part of your investigation of the situation, you find that the manual supplied with the machine recommends a tool speed of 1,500 rpm and a feed rate of 32 inches per minute. You want to determine if these are the optimal feed and speed rates. Therefore, you will vary both factors and measure the resulting tool life, measured as the number of molds cut before tool replacement was necessary.

As a rule of thumb, factors are tested at two levels to find the general effect of each factor. Experiments at three or more levels are used to engineer your final settings. Therefore, each of the factors will be set to two different levels. The first level will be the speed or feed recommended by the manual. The second level will be the fastest speed and feed that would reasonably be used in manufacturing.

When two factors are tested at two levels, the two-squared (2^2) factorial design is used. The designation means that there are two to the second power number of experimental combinations possible; that is, four combinations. The designation is created by stating the number of levels raised to the power of the number of factors. This is also called the 2^n set of designs.

The design can be drawn as follows.

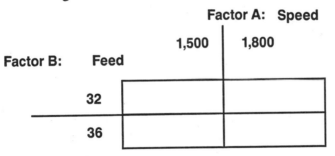

The resulting 2 x 2 array represents the four experimental combinations that will be tried in the experiment. Naturally, the order of experimental combinations will be selected randomly.

How to Read and Use the Design

To aid in the use and interpretation of a factorial experiment, a nomenclature has been developed to standardize the designs. Each run is written out as a row of symbols. The plus sign signifies the upper setting for a factor. The minus sign is used to represent a lower setting. Each column represents a factor. Using our 2^2 example, this creates the following design:

Run	Factor A	Factor B
1	−	−
2	+	−
3	−	+
4	+	+

Thus, run one sets both factors at low levels. In our example, factor A would be tool speed with the low setting being 1,500 rpm. Factor B would be feed rate at a low setting of 32 inches per minute. Therefore, to create your experimental design, you need to translate that basic design of pluses and negatives into the actual settings used by your experiment.

The experimental design then becomes

Run	Speed	Feed	Results
1	1,500 rpm	32 in./min.	
2	1,800	32	
3	1,500	36	
4	1,800	36	

Each run combination is given to the machine operator in random order until every combination is tried. The results are written to the left of the corresponding combinations.

How to Analyze an Experiment

Assume that you count the number of molds cut by a tool before it breaks or needs resharpening for each combination. For example, using the low speed and feed combination in run 1 you cut 25 molds before the tool broke. This is recorded in the results column.

Run	Speed	Feed	Results
1	1,500 rpm	32 in./min.	25
2	1,800	32	24
3	1,500	36	17
4	1,800	36	15

Take a moment to look at the results. Many times, identifiable patterns can be seen merely by examining the data. In this case, more molds were made when the slower feed rate was used.

You can demonstrate to yourself the effect of each factor by adding the results for various low and high settings. For example, when the speed was at 1,500 rpm, 25 and 17 molds were cut. This is a total result for the low setting of 42. When the 1,800 rpm setting was used, 24 and 15 molds were cut for a total of 39. This represents only a three-mold difference when the speed was changed. However, 49 molds were cut at the low feed rate versus 32 at the higher rate of feed. This is a difference of 17 molds. Clearly, the lower feed rate is more productive.

This simple act of adding the results for each factor by level is an easy way to detect large effects from changing levels. We will explore this method of initial analysis in later examples. For now, you can see that the best setting to make for this process is the low feed rate for greater tool life. You can also select the tool speed that is most economical for your operation because, in the range from 1,500 to 1,800 rpm, the tool speed has no real effect.

How Two Factors Working Together May Create More Improvement Than Either Factor Alone

So far, we have been discussing the effect of factors by themselves. In the previous example, we saw that feed rates had an important impact on the number of molds a tool could cut. However, we did not explore the effect that combined tool speed and feed has on the results.

When the variation in one factor is dependent on the level of a second factor, we call this an interaction. A quick and easy way to test for an interaction is to compare the change in levels of one factor against a change in a second factor.

Let us return to the aforementioned mold cutting example. To check visually for an interaction, we would create an effect diagram for the two factors. The effect diagram charts the change in the number of molds cut at each level of two factors.

First, you must summarize the results by the four possible settings of two factors at two levels.

$$
\begin{array}{lll}
A_1B_1 & & \text{speed} = 1{,}500, \text{feed} = 32 \\
A_1B_2 & \text{or} & \text{speed} = 1{,}500, \text{feed} = 36 \\
A_2B_1 & & \text{speed} = 1{,}800, \text{feed} = 32 \\
A_2B_2 & & \text{speed} = 1{,}800, \text{feed} = 36
\end{array}
$$

Using the data from the experiment,

Run	Speed	Feed	Results
1	1,500 rpm	32 in./min.	25
2	1,800	32	24
3	1,500	36	17
4	1,800	36	15

you can divide the data into the four components of interaction.

Factor A (speed)

Level Factor B (feed)		1	2
	1	25	24
	2	17	15

To draw the effect diagram, the number of molds cut is represented by the vertical axis of the graph. Factor *A* is plotted along the *X* axis. Factor *A* is represented as being at either level 1 or level 2. The effect of factor *B* is also plotted on the graph; thus two lines are created. One line represents the change in factor *B* at the low level when factor *A* was moved from its low setting to its high setting. In our example, the change was from 25 to 24 molds cut. The second line is the effect on factor *B* at its high settings when factor *A* was changed from low to high. In our example, this was a change from 17 to 15 molds cut (see Figure 9-1).

To interpret the resulting chart, a set of crossing lines represents an interaction. The shorthand designation of an interaction of these two factors is *A* x *B*. The x sign in the middle of the designation serves as a memory jog for the fact that an interaction on an effect diagram has crossing lines. Parallel lines represent no interaction. Lines that seem to converge somewhere off the chart represent a weak interaction. As you can see from Figure 9-1, there is no interaction occurring between speed and feed.

If interactions are not present, you have a simple job of merely picking the levels for each factor that gave you the best results. When an interaction is found, the table of components must be studied carefully. When you find an interaction, set up a separate experiment to study its effect.

An interaction means that two factors are tied together, and to adjust one factor implies that the other factor is automatically considered. This does mean more work in interpreting an experiment, but at the same time, it also represents the opportunity for revolutionary changes in your process or design. Interactions represent a hidden potential for improvement. If you tested only one factor at a time, you would probably miss any interaction of factors. Therefore, interactions can mean additional opportunities to make a process or product more robust and profitable. In the next example, we will look at the statistical way to test for interactions.

Optimizing a Machine's Settings by Testing Three Factors at Two Levels Each: Evaluating the Quality of a Wave Soldering Process

Suppose that you are the manufacturing manager for an electronics company in California and you are concerned about the wave solder process used to solder electronic components to circuit boards. Over the past few months the quality of the finished boards has been decreasing. Quality assurance reports that most of the problems found are related to the quality of the soldering.

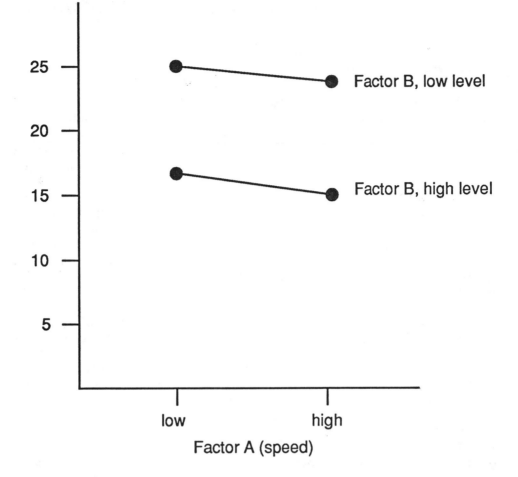

Figure 9-1: An effect diagram for A x B interaction.

How to Investigate the Situation, Select Factors, and Create an Experimental Design

You assemble a team of engineers, quality technicians, and operators from the line to study the wave solder process. Their task is to optimize the machine settings to produce a better quality of soldering. Their initial research reveals that three factors seem to affect solder quality the most: the speed of the wave solder line, the temperature of the solder, and the amount of flux treatment the boards receive before soldering.

Since three factors are involved, a factorial experiment is proposed. Since this is an initial experiment to screen these three factors for their general effect, each of the factors will be set to one of two levels. This will create a 23 factorial design, or eight experimental combinations. The following procedure can be applied to any number of factors where each is set to one of two levels.

The levels are set to the highest and lowest practical settings suggested by the process engineer. For example, the line speed (factor *A*) will be either a low setting of 64 inches per minute or a high setting of 88 inches per minute. The temperature of the solder (factor *B*) will be at either 400 or 500 degrees. The flux treatment (factor *C*) is designated as being either high or low. The high treatment refers to the fact that the board is in the flux for 15 seconds before soldering. The low setting represents 4 seconds of treatment. These settings are used because they are believed to be wide enough apart to create real changes in the results, and they should not produce scrap parts.

To make the design of the experiment and its analysis easier, the high and low settings for each factor are denoted as before: A plus sign indicates a high setting; a minus sign indicates a low setting. The resulting design for three factors at two levels each is as follows. This order was created by professional statisticians and should be adhered to strictly.

Run	Factors		
	A	B	C
1	−	−	−
2	+	−	−
3	−	+	−
4	+	+	−
5	−	−	+
6	+	−	+
7	−	+	+
8	+	+	+

Each row represents an experimental run. The order in which the experiment is run is determined by random selection. For example, run 5 might be selected as the first experimental run. The settings for factors *A* and *B* are set to low and factor *C* is set to high. The data collected for this run is recorded at the far right of row five. This allows for the simple association of data with the experimental run from which it was produced.

How to Collect and Analyze the Data

In our example, the team ran a single board through for each of the experimental setting combinations. The quality of the soldering was then judged by a panel of operators and quality audit personnel. Each board was rated on a scale from zero to 125. The scale was created by awarding a single point to every perfect solder at a critical connection on the board. Since there are 125 connections on a board, only a perfect board could score 125 points.

The results of the experiment were recorded to create the following table.

Run	Factors			Results
	A	**B**	**C**	
1	–	–	–	87
2	+	–	–	62
3	–	+	–	124
4	+	+	–	58
5	–	–	+	89
6	+	–	+	34
7	–	+	+	63
8	+	+	+	37
			Total	554

Even a quick review of the foregoing numbers shows that the settings for row three produced the best results. The temptation would be to set the machine to these settings and stop the experimentation process at that point. However, this would miss the critical nature of experimentation—the ability to learn about how a process works. For example, if we accept these settings blindly, we would still not know which factor accounts for the improvement. Without such knowledge, we would soon find ourselves facing the same problems once again.

Therefore, we analyze the results by creating an ANOVA table. This table will break down the effect of each factor and the experimental error. In addition, as we shall soon see, it will also break down all of the possible interactions of the factors. Thus, the sources of variation on our ANOVA table will increase to the following.

ANOVA Table

Source	Sum of Squares, etc.
A	
B	
C	
A x B	
A x C	
B x C	
A x B x C	
error	
Total	

The procedure to complete the table is the same as before: We begin by using the total of the data to create the correction factor.

$$CF = \frac{\left(\Sigma_x\right)^2}{n}$$

where Σ_x = total of data
n = number of data points

In our example,

$$CF = \frac{(554)^2}{8} = 38{,}364.5$$

The sum square for the total experiment is found by totalling the square of each data point and dividing the results by the number of numbers.

$$SS_{total} = \Sigma_x^{\,2} - CF$$

where $\Sigma_x^{\,2}$ = the sum of each data point squared

For the data in our example, the sum square of the total experiment would be as follows.

$$SS_{total} = \left(87^2 + 62^2 + 124^2 + 58^2 + 89^2 + 34^2 + 63^2 + 37^2\right) - 38{,}364.5 = 6{,}203.5$$

From this point on, the calculations of sums of squares decompose from the experimental results the effect of each factor. The sum of squares for factor A (SS_A) would be calculated using the formula

$$SS_A = \frac{\left(\Sigma_{A_{low}}\right)^2}{n} + \frac{\left(\Sigma_{A_{high}}\right)^2}{n} - CF$$

where A_{low} = low settings of the factor
A_{high} = high settings of the factor
n = number of numbers at this setting
CF = the correction factor

To see where the data comes from to complete this formula, we must re-examine the data table created earlier (see page 213). Looking down the factor *A* column, we see a series of pluses and minuses. Each minus represents a low setting. The data in the results column corresponds to these settings. Therefore, the data that corresponds to the low settings are added together in the formula. Likewise, those data points corresponding to the high settings are also added together.

Run	Factors A	Results
1	−	87
2	+	62
3	−	124
4	+	58
5	−	89
6	+	34
7	−	63
8	+	37

As an illustration, notice how the low settings in the first, third, fifth, and seventh rows correspond to the numbers 87, 124, 89, and 63. These numbers represent the effect of a low setting for factor *A*. Performing a similar addition for the high settings gives us the data we need to complete the sum of square calculation for factor *A*.

low settings = 87 + 124 + 89 + 63 = 363

high settings = 62 + 58 + 34 + 37 = 191

Thus

$$SS_A = \frac{363^2}{4} + \frac{191^2}{4} - 38,364.5$$

or

$$SS_A = 32{,}942.25 + 9{,}120.25 - 38{,}364.5 = 3{,}698$$

This same formula can be used to calculate the effects of factors B and C. For example, to calculate the sum of square for factor B, we would take the plus and minus signs in the factor B column and match them to the corresponding results.

Run	Factors		
	A	B	Results
1		−	87
2		−	62
3		+	124
4		+	58
5		−	89
6		−	34
7		+	63
8		+	37

Therefore, we find the following.

$$\text{low settings} = 87 + 62 + 89 + 34 = 272$$

$$\text{high settings} = 124 + 58 + 63 + 37 = 282$$

Thus, the sum square for factor B is

$$SS_B = \frac{272^2}{4} + \frac{282^2}{4} - 38{,}364.5 = 12.5$$

The effect of factor C is also calculated using these methods.

$$SS_C = \frac{331^2}{4} + \frac{223^2}{4} - 38{,}364.5 = 1{,}458$$

With these sums of squares we can calculate the sum square of error and complete our ANOVA table.

$$SS_e = SS_{total} - SS_A - SS_B - SS_C$$

Thus

$$SS_e = 6{,}203.5 - 3{,}698 - 12.5 - 1{,}458 = 1{,}035$$

ANOVA Table

Source	SS	df
A	3,698	1
B	12.5	1
C	1458	1
Error	1035	4
Total	6,203.5	7

The degrees of freedom for the error effect are found by taking the remaining degrees of freedom from the total after giving one degree to each factor. Each factor receives one degree of freedom because this is one less than the number of levels ($k - 1 = df$).

At this point you can further decompose the results to check for interactions between the factors.

How to Check for Interactions Using an ANOVA Table

The sum of squares for error just calculated had four degrees of freedom. That means that there could be up to four additional pieces of information contained within the error. Those four pieces of information are the interactions of the factors.

An interaction is the effect of two factors working in tandem. For example, the factor A and B interaction (written as $A \times B$) is the effect of the two factors working together. With three factors being tested at two levels each, there are four possible interactions: $A \times B$; $A \times C$; $B \times C$; and $A \times B \times C$. The last interaction is the effect of all three factors working together. Although extremely unlikely to be significant, it is still checked.

The existence of significant interactions will create severe problems in manufacturing. For one thing, interactions are difficult to control by normal process methods. Consider the example of a molding process that has a strong interaction between holding time and injection speed. To create a high-quality part, these two factors would have to be monitored constantly and adjusted together.

To test for interactions in the example of the wave soldering process, we must extend the design of the experiment. Specifically, interaction columns must be created. To do this, we merely multiply together the two or more columns involved in the interactions. Let us begin with the original design and create the $A \times B$ column, the interaction between factor A (the speed of the line) and factor B (the temperature of the solder).

Run	Factors	
	A	B
1	−	−
2	+	−
3	−	+
4	+	+
5	−	−
6	+	−
7	−	+
8	+	+

The first row of columns *A* and *B* have negative signs. If we multiply together two negatives, we get a positive.

$$A\ B \qquad AxB$$
$$-\ - \qquad\ +$$

or

$$-1 \times -1 = +1$$

The second row has a positive and a negative. If we multiply a negative and a positive, we get a negative (+ 1 x −1 = −1). If we continue to use this simple rule for the rest of the *A* and *B* columns, we create the following column for *A x B*.

Run	Factors			Results
	A	B	AxB	
1	−	−	+	87
2	+	−	−	62
3	−	+	−	124
4	+	+	+	58
5	−	−	+	89
6	+	−	−	34
7	−	+	−	63
8	+	+	+	37
			Total	554

The interaction is calculated as the sum of squares that match the plus and minus signs in the *A x B* column. The same formula used for sums of squares for factors applies.

$$SS_{axb} = \frac{\left(\sum_{AxB_{low}}\right)^2}{n} + \frac{\left(\sum_{AxB_{high}}\right)^2}{n} - CF$$

Using the data in the previous table,

$$SS_{axb} = 18{,}360.25 + 20{,}022.25 - 38{,}364.5 = 18$$

This procedure of creating the interaction columns and calculating the sum of squares is repeated for the remaining interactions. The resulting table of factor and interaction columns is as follows.

Run	Factors			Interaction			
	A	B	C	AxB	AxC	BxC	AxBxC
1	−	−	−	+	+	+	−
2	+	−	−	−	−	+	+
3	−	+	−	−	+	−	+
4	+	+	−	+	−	−	−
5	−	−	+	+	−	−	+
6	+	−	+	−	+	−	−
7	−	+	+	−	−	+	−
8	+	+	+	+	+	+	+

Factor A = line speed
Factor B = temperature of solder
Factor C = amount of flux treatment

Run	Results
1	87
2	62
3	124
4	58
5	89
6	34
7	63
8	37
Total	554

Each column for the interactions is treated as if it were another factor column. The sums of squares are calculated and tabulated into an ANOVA table. The following ANOVA table would be created with the foregoing information.

ANOVA Table

Source	SS	df	V
A	3,698.0	1	3,698.0
B	12.5	1	12.5
C	1,458.0	1	1,458.0
A x B	18.0	1	18.0
A x C	12.5	1	12.5
B x C	392.0	1	392.0
A x B x C	612.5	1	612.5
Total	6,203.5	7	

Notice that the error factor is now missing from the ANOVA table. The error factor has been completely decomposed into the four possible interactions. Since all three factors and four interactions use up the seven degrees of freedom in this experiment, there is nothing left over with which to measure the error. This poses quite a problem, because without a variance for error, we cannot calculate F-ratios.

The solution to this predicament is normally solved by taking more than one sample for each combination. This would increase the total degrees of freedom in the experiment and prevent this problem. However, if you find that only a single reading is practical for each combination, then the answer is to pool the effect of nonsignificant factors and interactions. By nonsignificant we mean those factors or interactions that have variances that are so small it is obvious that they have little effect. In our example, factor B and interactions A x B and A x C have very small variances. Therefore, we can pool together their degrees of freedom and their sums of squares.

pool of SS = 12.5 + 18 + 12.5 = 43

pool of df = 1 + 1 + 1 = 3

These pooled figures are removed from their place on the ANOVA table and create a new error factor that is recorded at the bottom of the ANOVA table.

ANOVA Table

Source	SS	df	V
A	3,698.0	1	3,698.0
B			
C	1,458.0	1	1,458.0
AxB			
BxC	392.0	1	392.0
AxBxC	612.5	1	612.5
Total	6,203.5	7	
Pooled error	43.0	3	14.3

Using this pooled error variance, we can complete our calculations of the F-ratios. For example, the F-ratio for factor A would be

$$F = \frac{3,698}{14.3} = 258.6$$

The final ANOVA table would look like this.

ANOVA Table

Source	SS	df	V	F
A	3698.0	1	3698.0	258.6
B				
C	1458.0	1	1458.0	101.9
A x B				
B x C	392.0	1	392.0	27.4
A x B x C	612.5	1	612.5	42.8
Total	6203.5	7		
Pooled error	43.0	3	14.3	

The critical value of an F-ratio at the 95% confidence level is 10.1. This is found by noting that the numerator (factor) of our F-ratio has one degree of freedom and the denominator (error) has three. Thus, in Appendix E, the value of 10.1 lies at the intersection of one by three degrees of freedom. Therefore, all of the remaining *F*-ratios are significant. As we suspected before, factors *A* and *C* are the most important to the process. However, the interaction of factors *B* and *C* seems to be a contributing influence as well. What this could mean is that solder temperature by itself is not important, but when combined with another factor is has great influence. However, with only one reading per combination, interpretations should be made with caution. This example only used one reading per combination to simplify the illustration of calculations.

How to Put the Results to Work

The first step in using the information provided by this experiment would be to investigate the *B* x *C* and *A* x *B* x *C* interactions more fully. Usually a second experiment would be set up to test these interactions more completely by testing at more levels. This is particularly necessary because the large effect from factors A and C might be falsely creating the perceived interactions.

As a second step, you would adjust the factor settings to produce the best production quality and the highest economy.

To determine the best setting for factor *A* (speed of the line), the team goes back to the data associated with the high (88 inches per minute) and low (64 inches per minute) settings. This information is used to calculate the average quality for each setting.

$$\text{average low settings} = \frac{87 + 124 + 89 + 63}{4} = 90.75$$

$$\text{average high settings} = \frac{62 + 58 + 34 + 37}{4} = 47.75$$

Clearly, when the low line speed is used there is a higher quality to the finished product. Therefore, the low line speed is set.

Since factor *B* is insignificant, either setting can be used. Because a higher solder heat requires more expensive energy, the team elects to use a low heat setting. For factor *C* the average quality for the high and low settings is 82.75 and 55.75 respectively. Therefore, the team sets the flux treatment to a short exposure (four seconds). This saves both money and time, as well as producing a slightly better quality.

This leads us back to the original data, which suggested that the third experimental run produced the best quality with factors *A* and *C* set low and factor *B* set high. The final results disagree with the factor *B* setting. The experiment has shown that the original combination in the third row of the design produced good results because of factors *A* and *C*. We now know that factor *B* is irrelevant to the final quality. This knowledge allows us to set the line to its optimal performance and maximum economy.

How to Make a Professional Presentation of Experimental Data

The results of any experiment must be transmitted to other people in the company. Usually, top management should be informed of the discoveries so that designs, standards, and procedures can be changed to take advantage of the new knowledge.

Any presentation of experimental data should be done professionally. Written reports should be produced on desktop publishing equipment using standardized formats. Visual aids should be done on similar equipment following the guidelines of presentation graphics. Oral presentations should be short and to the point. By adopting a professional attitude toward presentation, the validity of your results will be reinforced.

All experimental results should be documented as a written report to management. As manufacturing manager you will want to see a copy of every experiment's final report. This report should contain a description of why an experiment was necessary, what factors were tested, what the results discovered, and the suggested actions for management to implement.

Such a written report for internal use on nonregulated products or processes can be just a few pages in length. However, a regulated product or process should be documented using the publication guidelines issued by the regulating body. These experiments will be critical in any legal situations that may arise, so they must be very detailed and exhaustive.

In most cases, however, you will need short, clearly written summaries of the experiments. As manager you should create a procedural guideline for the format and reporting of these documents. The experimenter should be encouraged to use visual aids to explain effects.

Presentation graphics must be clean and simple. Computer drawing programs and computer-aided design packages can be used to create such illustrations. There are even software packages specifically designed for making presentation graphics. These illustrations must include a title, source, and date. A minimum number of illustrations should be used in any presentation.

The best visual tool for transmitting this information is the effect diagram. Suppose that you have just completed a detailed experiment on the diameter of a drive shaft. You found that the size of the outside diameter of the shaft would significantly affect the life of the connecting rod it drives in a finished engine. That is, the larger the shaft, the longer the connection rod life. Therefore, you need to show the relationship between shaft diameter and product life. These can be graphed on a two-axis chart. The horizontal axis represents the shaft diameter, and the vertical axis represents the life cycles of the product (see Figure 9-2). The average number of expected cycles for each level of factor *A* is plotted on this chart. The resulting diagram creates a clearly understood picture of the relationship between the factor and the re-

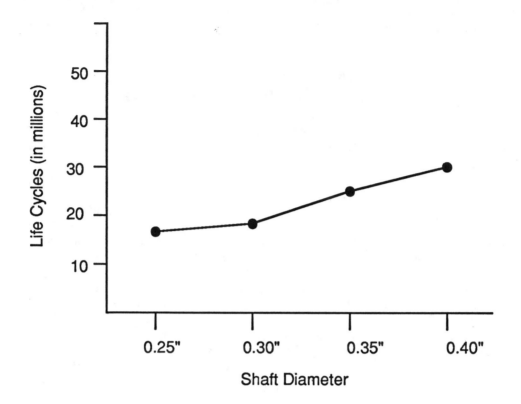

Figure 9-2: Effect diagram of the shaft diameter experiment.

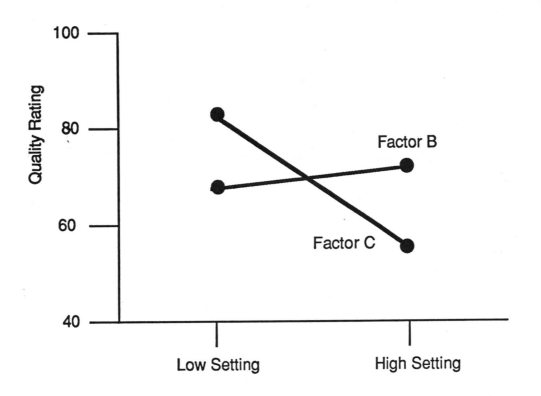

Figure 9-3: An effect diagram showing interaction.

sponse. An almost linear relationship exists between the size of the shaft and its expected life.

The preceding example of the wave soldering process can illustrate the effect diagram. In this case, we found an interaction between factors B and C. This interaction can be seen graphically on an effect diagram. The response of each factor is plotted on the same chart (see Figure 9-3). Whenever two factors have crossed lines on an effect diagram, this is an indication of an interaction. Even to untrained individuals, it is obvious that an interaction is taking place.

Finally, it is a good idea to require an oral presentation of the experimental results to a group of managers. For example, if the foregoing drive shaft data is to be of any use, then the manufacturing manager, the engineering manager, and the production manager should hear about the suggested design changes as a group. In this way, issues such as the manufacturability of the new design can be discussed immediately.

Conclusion

Experimentation is a skill that can only be mastered with practice and knowledge. The information presented in this chapter is adequate to introduce you to the methods of experimentation. These methods are simple and only recommended for uncomplicated situations. However, this does not stop you from conducting exploratory experiments into the workings of the manufacturing process. These results can be used to guide a skilled experimenter toward the important factors and interactions in a process or product.

As we will see in the next chapter, there are also simple ways to study many factors at the same time using designs that are hardly larger than the ones already introduced.

CHAPTER 10

How to Make Manufactured Products Robust Using Taguchi's Philosophy of Engineering

Dr. Genichi Taguchi is the proponent of a method of engineering and manufacturing that is gaining wide acceptance. He suggests that the quality of a product is measured as the loss society suffers after the product is shipped. In simple terms, the quality of a product is directly related to how well it performs for the customer. For example, an automobile purchased by a customer may have no defects, but if it requires frequent repairs, the customer sees the quality of the car as being poor.

What Taguchi recommends for manufacturing managers is to produce products that are robust against the variations of customer use. For example, a lawn mower must be designed to withstand various grades of gasoline, exposure to moisture, infrequent oil changes, and so on. This range of abuse to the product is the normal operating environment for a lawn mower.

We have already mentioned the importance of ensuring that a production process maintain engineering tolerances (see chapter 3). Taguchi says that maintaining a product to specification is not as important as making the product robust against customer use. He hypothesizes that if you concentrate on reducing the number of failures of your product in the field, you will also reduce the number of defectives you experience during manufacturing.

This chapter will show you how this is possible and will look at three examples of how the Taguchi method™ is practiced.

Taguchi's Background

Taguchi was in charge of research for the Nippon Telephone and Telegraph Company after World War II. Americans had ordered the company to increase the quality of telephone communications in Japan to the level of that in the United States. Taguchi estimated that it would take over 20 years to do so using conventional methods of research and development (see chapter 9). Therefore, he created a unique set of experimental designs along with a complete method of deploying them to decrease the research time needed down to a few years. Although these designs and their related methods are officially known as off-line quality control techniques, the phrase *Taguchi method*[TM] has been popularized in the United States. A more correct way to think of his method is "factory as a laboratory." Each engineer and technician in the plant uses this method to study all aspects of products, processes, and plant layout. The objective is to understand the manufacturing process so well that all industrial conditions are corrected to their most economical and robust settings.

Putting the Taguchi Method[TM] to Work: Making a Power Adaptor Robust

The philosophy of Taguchi's experimentation is very different from the modern method of experimentation used extensively in the West. For example, the Taguchi method[TM] is more of a black box approach to experimentation. Designs are standardized so that an experimenter only needs to identify test variables and then follow procedure to conduct an experiment. The techniques are designed for nonexperimenters to use with ease. With the Taguchi method[TM], the experimenter is not looking for the cause of a problem, but for a countermeasure that will make the product or process robust against the cause of the problem.

The following example explains how the Taguchi method[TM] works. Suppose that you are currently manufacturing a small power adaptor that converts the 120 volts of alternating current (AC) from a wall outlet to 9 volts of direct current (DC). The adaptor is sold to a wide variety of companies that produce consumer electronics.

Step 1: Investigate the situation.

Your customers have been complaining that the adaptor fails to produce a steady 9-volt output. You do not find this surprising, since the average wall outlet in a home can vary in voltage from 110 to 130 volts AC. You need to redesign the adaptor to make it robust against these changes in incoming voltages.

Step 2: Select experimental factors.

In the case of the voltage adaptor, you would begin by looking at the electronic parts that make up the design. In this example, you discover six parts in the adaptor beside the stepdown transformer. These six parts are four resistors and two capacitors, as follows.

Resistor 1: 250 ohms

Resistor 2: 500 ohms

Resistor 3: 1,000 ohms

Resistor 4: 100 ohms

Capacitor 1: 50 microfarads

Capacitor 2: 300 microfarads

Further investigation reveals that the tolerance for each of these parts is set to plus or minus 1% of their target value. You find that these tight settings were suggested by engineering to maintain the quality of the unit. These tighter settings also mean that it costs more to buy the higher quality components. Your study will start by determining whether these tight tolerances are called for with every part. Specifically, is there one or more parts that affects the final output of the unit?

Foremost in the selection of experimental factors is the elimination of any factor that has a known interaction with another factor. This can be discovered by simple investigation of the physics and chemistry of the situation under study. For example, the use of Ohm's law could indicate which parts of the adaptor might interact with each other.

After such an investigation, you find no interactions. Therefore, the six parts under investigation become the six experimental factors.

Factor A = resistor 1: 250 ohms

Factor B = resistor 2: 500 ohms

Factor C = resistor 3: 1,000 ohms

Factor D = resistor 4: 100 ohms

Factor E = capacitor 1: 50 microfarads

Factor F = capacitor 2: 300 microfarads

The response variables have to be hard, measurable data, such as volts, pressure, temperature, and so on. In limited cases subjective characteristics, such as visual appeal, can be used, but they should be translated into a variable scale. The use of judges and a scoring scale based on a written list of quality characteristics is suggested.

In this example, you choose to measure a single variable as the response factor—the output of voltage in direct current. The target value you are trying to achieve is 9 volts. Because this is an initial experiment on the design, you want to test each factor at two levels.

Currently, your company is purchasing high-priced components that hold their rated value to plus or minus 1%. There are cheaper components available, but they only hold values to within plus or minus 5% of their rating. For example, a resistor rated at 100 ohms could actually be producing a resistance of from 95 to 105 ohms. In contrast, the current tolerance would purchase the same resistor only if it held a value of between 99 and 101 ohms.

However, a tighter tolerance is no guarantee of quality. In this experiment, you will try components that vary by up to 5%. If the tests discover that these cheaper components have no effect on output voltage, then you have discovered a way to make the adaptor for less money, yet with at least equal quality.

The resulting level settings are found by adding 5% of the rated value of the part for the upper setting and subtracting 5% for the lower setting. For example, the first resistor is rated for 250 ohms. Five percent of this is 12.5 ohms. This would result in an upper setting of 262.5 ohms and a lower setting of 237.5 ohms.

Factor *A* = resistor 1: 237.5 and 262.5 ohms

Factor *B* = resistor 2: 475 and 525 ohms

Factor *C* = resistor 3: 950 and 1,050 ohms

Factor *D* = resistor 4: 95 and 105 ohms

Factor *E* = capacitor 1: 47.5 and 52.5 microfarads

Factor *F* = capacitor 2: 285 and 315 microfarads

Step 3: Design the experiment.

Your proposed experiment has six factors to test. If each factor was varied between two levels, a 2^6 factorial design would normally be required. This would require you to build 64 adaptors where the resistance and capacitance of the parts are varied. This may prove costly and time consuming. In addition, your factorial array will contain 57 additional columns to analyze all possible interactions. Most of these interactions would be unlikely to occur. Thus, when more than four or five factors are being studied, the full factorial design is not efficient.

Taguchi and others recommend that when more than four or five factors are being studied, a fractional factorial design is usually more practical. A fractional factorial design is a small sample of the combinations normally found in a full factorial design. For example, one of the designs popularized by Taguchi is called an L_8 orthogonal array. With this array, we will be able to study the effect of the six electronic parts using only eight combinations of design variations.

We can understand fractional designs and orthogonal arrays more clearly by taking a moment to examine the L_8 design.

L_8 Orthogonal Array

Run				Columns				Results
	1	2	3	4	5	6	7	
1	1	1	1	1	1	1	1	
2	1	1	1	2	2	2	2	
3	1	2	2	1	1	2	2	
4	1	2	2	2	2	1	1	
5	2	1	2	1	2	1	2	
6	2	1	2	2	1	2	1	
7	2	2	1	1	2	2	1	
8	2	2	1	2	1	1	2	

Within the array itself, the low and high settings are represented by the numerals 1 and 2, respectively. Each row of the array represents an experimental run and its combination of factor levels. The order that the experimental runs are made in is selected randomly. The response for each combination is recorded after the corresponding row.

Let us look more closely at just one column to see why this design is called orthogonal. Orthogonality implies a type of mathematical balance. If you look at the first column in an L_8 design, you will see that each level is exposed to an equal number of levels in any of the other columns. For example, look at column 1 compared to column 7.

Columns	
1	7
1	1
1	2
1	2
1	1
2	2
2	1
2	1
2	2

You can quickly see that when a factor in the first column is at a low level, it is tested with a factor in the seventh column twice being low and twice being high. Thus, a representative and balanced sample of possible combinations is tested. This allows you to obtain quickly the main effects of the factors being tested.

To create your experimental design, each of the six factors in your study is assigned to the first six columns of the design. Thus

Run	Columns							Results
	1	2	3	4	5	6	7	
				Factors				
	A	B	C	D	E	F	e	
1	1	1	1	1	1	1	1	
2	1	1	1	2	2	2	2	
3	1	2	2	1	1	2	2	
4	1	2	2	2	2	1	1	
5	2	1	2	1	2	1	2	
6	2	1	2	2	1	2	1	
7	2	2	1	1	2	2	1	
8	2	2	1	2	1	1	2	

The empty column 7 is designated with a small *e*. This represents what is called an error column. The column is analyzed just like a factor column. It is used to test for experimental error caused by leaving a significant factor out of your experiment.

Step 4: Analyze your results quickly.

As reviewed in chapter 9, the experiment is conducted using the combinations represented under columns with factor assignments. For example, run 3 has a combination of 1,2,2,1,1,2. Matching these levels to the corresponding factors, we would design a power adaptor using the following parts.

(Factor *A*, level 1) resistor 1 = 237.5 ohms

(Factor *B*, level 2) resistor 2 = 525 ohms

(Factor *C*, level 2) resistor 3 = 1,050 ohms

(Factor *D*, level 1) resistor 4 = 95 ohms

(Factor *E*, level 1) capacitor 1 = 47.5 microfarads

(Factor *F*, level 2) capacitor 2 = 315 microfarads

This design would be tested for the voltage output it created. For illustrative purposes, assume that it created 8.6 volts DC. This would be placed in the results column of the design on the third row (thus representing the third run). The following are the results of building all eight designs recommended by the orthogonal array.

Run	Columns							Results
	1	2	3	4	5	6	7	
				Factors				
	A	B	C	D	E	F	e	
1	1	1	1	1	1	1	1	9.1 V DC
2	1	1	1	2	2	2	2	9.5
3	1	2	2	1	1	2	2	8.6
4	1	2	2	2	2	1	1	8.2
5	2	1	2	1	2	1	2	9.0
6	2	1	2	2	1	2	1	9.1
7	2	2	1	1	2	2	1	8.1
8	2	2	1	2	1	1	2	8.2

To analyze the data quickly, you break down these results into what is called a level sum table. Simply put, this is a summary of the total effect for each level of each factor. To illustrate, begin by adding up the effect of factor *A* (resistor 1) at its two levels. As before, you match the numerals 1 and 2 in the factor *A* column to the results.

Run	Factor A	Results
1	1	9.1
2	1	9.5
3	1	8.6
4	1	8.2
5	2	9.0
6	2	9.1
7	2	8.1
8	2	8.2

The total response for factor *A* at the two levels is

$$A_{low} = 9.1 + 9.5 + 8.6 + 8.2 = 35.4$$

$$A_{high} = 9.0 + 9.1 + 8.1 + 8.2 = 34.4$$

This same procedure is repeated for each of the other columns. The result is a summary table of effects by factor.

Level Sum Table

Factors	A	B	C	D	E	F	e
Level 1:	35.4	36.7	34.9	34.8	35.0	34.5	34.5
Level 2:	34.3	33.1	34.9	35.0	34.8	35.3	35.3
Range:	1.1	3.6	0.0	0.2	0.2	0.8	0.8

By examining the range between the results at a low setting and a high setting, you can quickly scan this table and see that factor *B* (resistor 2) had the greatest effect on the output voltage. Therefore, this is one of the resistors that you will check more closely in later experiments. The other resistors produce fairly steady output within the plus and minus 5% rating range. Therefore, the less expensive electronic parts can be used safely in this design, since the looser tolerance will have no degrading effect on the voltage output.

You may use the ANOVA formulas from chapter 9 on a Taguchi design. Such analysis will give you statistical tests for the significance of each factor's effect. However, when the effect is clear-cut, as in our example, further analysis is optional.

Additional Features of the Taguchi Method

One of the key benefits of the orthogonal array is its flexibility in handling a variety of experimental situations. Consider the example of experimental error. In a factorial experiment with analysis for interactions, we need replications to measure for error due to factors we do not test. In the orthogonal array, this error can be found directly by leaving one column or more of the array empty.

Take repeated samples in any experiment to assure that various sources of experimental error are accounted for by the results. The amount of variation occurring within each of these samples is called secondary error, and it, too, can be calculated and placed on the ANOVA table. If the variance of this error becomes significant, it tells the experimenter that sampling consistency is too poor to support the experimental results. It could also mean that the variation in the process is not under statistical control and that it needs correcting.

Another advantage of the orthogonal array is that interactions can be assigned to array columns as easily as factors. There is no need to create new columns just for the interactions. For example, if you wanted to study the interaction of factors *A* and *B* in our preceding experiment, the third column would be assigned to the interaction. This is the line connecting the dots for columns 1 and 2 in the linear graph below an orthogonal array (see Figure 10-1).

A final advantage of the orthogonal array is that it can be modified to fit a larger number of experimental situations. Although it is beyond the discussion of this chapter, two columns in a two-level experiment can be combined to create a four-level factor column. Also, it is possible to mix two- and three-level factors within the same experiment. The result is that the experimenter is able to let the situation under investigation control the design of the experiment with greater ease.

Conclusions Drawn from the First Experiment

When faced with many factors to study in an industrial situation, and when you have a firm understanding of any interactions occurring, the orthogonal array is superb for quickly analyzing which factors are essential.

This first example highlights how quickly and easily an experiment can be set up to study several factors. We did not need to use extensive statistical analysis. In fact, we would normally use software to speed that task. Instead, the intention of Taguchi experimentation is that it should be fast, easy, and standardized. Notice how you were able to go from a list of factors, to testing your design, to analysis using just the orthogonal array. A basic understanding of this method will give you the ability to set up, review, or coordinate industrial experiments with ease.

Highlighting Taguchi's Philosophy of Robust Design Through Parameter Design Experiments: Studying the Customer's Use of a Power Adaptor

In our first example, the intention of the experiment was to find the most economical settings for insignificant factors and the best settings for factors that have a real effect on the output voltage of the power adaptor. However, we should also be interested in producing a product that is robust against the variations experienced by a customer.

The power adaptor is an excellent example of a product that is exposed to many variations in the field. The designers of the power adaptor designed the product to produce 9 volts of DC output when 120 volts of AC is applied. However, the average household in America can have actual outlet voltages

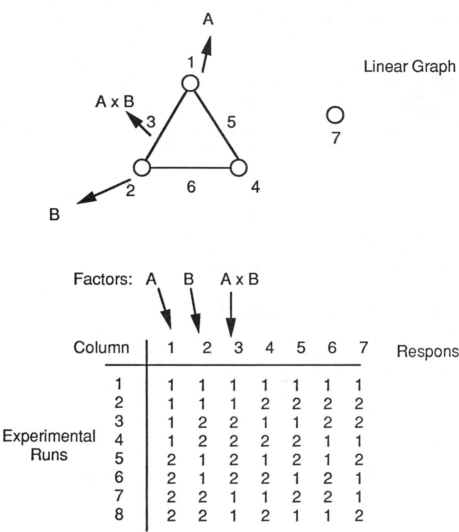

Figure 10-1: Assigning factors and interactions to an L_8 array.

that vary from 110 to 130 volts AC. Therefore, the variations in actual house-hold electrical outlet voltages can adversely alter the output voltage of the power adaptor.

Therefore, in this example, we will examine a way to make the power adaptor design robust against these changes in electric outlet voltages. The technique used is called a *parameter design*. As we have discussed previously, a strong experiment replicates the experimental runs to estimate experimental error. Taguchi has proposed the idea of using these replications to test the effect of what he calls "outside noise factors." These are generally uncontrollable factors in the environment that could upset the quality of your product or process.

For example, heat and humidity in your production area may have an adverse effect on your products. Yet heat and humidity are very expensive to control within a manufacturing site. Thus, Taguchi recommends that the more economical path is to design the products and processes to be robust against these outside factors.

In the case of the power adaptor, we have identified electrical output variations as a noise factor.

Step 1: How to create a parameter design.

The actual design of this experiment is very similar to the one used in the first experiment. Again, you begin with the six electrical parts that you wish to test as controllable factors.

(Factor *A*, level 1) resistor 1 = 237.5 ohms

(Factor *B*, level 2) resistor 2 = 525 ohms

(Factor *C*, level 2) resistor 3 = 1,050 ohms

(Factor *D*, level 1) resistor 4 = 95 ohms

(Factor *E*, level 1) capacitor 1 = 47.5 microfarads

(Factor *F*, level 2) capacitor 2 = 315 microfarads

Again, for the sake of illustration, we place these factors into the first six columns of an L_8 orthogonal array. The seventh column is left open to check for missing significant factors. This frees us to use the replications to test for the effect of voltage variation. In this case, you decide to test the incoming voltage at three different levels, the normal 120 volts AC, a high of 130 volts, and a low of 110 volts. The resulting design is as follows.

Run	Columns										
	1	2	3	4	5	6	7				
			Factors							Voltage	
	A	B	C	D	E	F	e	110	120	130 V AC	
1	1	1	1	1	1	1	1				
2	1	1	1	2	2	2	2				
3	1	2	2	1	1	2	2				
4	1	2	2	2	2	1	1				
5	2	1	2	1	2	1	2				
6	2	1	2	2	1	2	1				
7	2	2	1	1	2	2	1				
8	2	2	1	2	1	1	2				

The experiment is conducted in a slightly different fashion than before. The eight combinations of adaptor designs are built. You then hook each one to a power source producing 110 volts AC and measure their output. Then the power source is increased to 120 volts and again the designs are tested. Finally, the power is increased to 130 volts and the designs are tested. The results are written after the corresponding design combination and beneath the correct voltage being applied at the time.

The resulting data grid would look like the following example.

Run	Columns										
	1	2	3	4	5	6	7				
			Factors							Voltage	
	A	B	C	D	E	F	e	110	120	130 V AC	
1	1	1	1	1	1	1	1	9.1	9.2	9.4 V DC	
2	1	1	1	2	2	2	2	9.0	8.9	9.1	
3	1	2	2	1	1	2	2	8.5	8.4	8.4	
4	1	2	2	2	2	1	1	8.4	8.2	8.9	
5	2	1	2	1	2	1	2	9.3	9.1	9.0	
6	2	1	2	2	1	2	1	9.1	9.0	9.5	
7	2	2	1	1	2	2	1	8.2	8.5	8.6	
8	2	2	1	2	1	1	2	8.1	8.2	8.5	

Step 2: Analyze the data quickly.

As before, a level sum table would be a way to analyze this data quickly. The results are paired with the levels for each factor.

Let us use factor A (resistor 1) as an example. The level 1 settings in column 1 are matched to the results.

Factor A Column 1	Results		
1	9.1	9.2	9.4
1	9.0	8.9	9.1
1	8.5	8.4	8.4
1	8.4	8.2	8.9
2	9.3	9.1	9.0
2	9.1	9.0	9.5
2	8.2	8.5	8.6
2	8.1	8.2	8.5

Thus, the total for level 1 of factor A is

$$A_{low} = 9.1 + 9.2 + 9.4 + 9.0 + \ldots + 8.9 = 105.5$$

and for level 2, the high settings,

$$A_{high} = 9.3 + 9.1 + 9.0 + 9.1 + \ldots + 8.5 = 105.1$$

This is repeated for each of the factors assigned to the orthogonal array.

	Factor						
	A	B	C	D	E	F	e
Level 1	105.5	109.7	104.8	105.7	105.4	105.4	106.1
Level 2	105.1	100.9	105.8	104.9	105.2	105.2	104.5
Range	0.4	8.8	1.0	0.8	0.2	0.2	1.6

A quick glance at the sums tells you that factor B (resistor 2) has the greatest effect on output voltage.

Step 3: How to design for robustness.

The final step in your analysis is to look at the effect of factor B over the range of voltage inputs used in the experiment. This will tell you whether a particular setting for resistor 2 was robust across the range of input voltages.

Returning to the raw data, you would total the levels for factor B at each of the three voltage settings.

Run				Columns						
	1	2	3	4	5	6	7			
				Factors					Voltage	
	A	B	C	D	E	F	e	110	120	130 V AC
1	1	1	1	1	1	1	1	9.1	9.2	9.4 V DC
2	1	1	1	2	2	2	2	9.0	8.9	9.1
3	1	2	2	1	1	2	2	8.5	8.4	8.4
4	1	2	2	2	2	1	1	8.4	8.2	8.9
5	2	1	2	1	2	1	2	9.3	9.1	9.0
6	2	1	2	2	1	2	1	9.1	9.0	9.5
7	2	2	1	1	2	2	1	8.2	8.5	8.6
8	2	2	1	2	1	1	2	8.1	8.2	8.5

For example, when factor B was changed from a low setting (runs 1, 2, 5, and 6) to a high setting (runs 3, 4, 7, and 8) and input voltage was 110 volts AC, the following results were obtained:

$$B_{low} \, V_{110} = 9.1 + 9.0 + 9.3 + 9.1 = 36.5$$

and

$$B_{high} \, V_{110} = 8.5 + 8.4 + 8.2 + 8.1 = 33.2$$

By repeating this exercise for each of the voltage input levels, you can create a level sum table that shows the effect of input voltage on factor B.

Factor B	Input Voltage		
	110	120	130 V AC
Level 1	36.5	36.2	37.0
Level 2	33.2	33.3	34.4

A close examination of this table reveals that a level 1 setting for factor B (resistor 2 at 475 ohms) produced a total variation of 0.8 volts DC. In contrast, the level 2 setting created 1.2 volts DC of variation. Thus, the level 1 setting is more robust against the electrical outlet variation found in most homes.

Again, the insignificant factors are set to their most economical settings. In this case, looser tolerances are assigned to each of the remaining components. The resulting power adaptor design is both cheaper to build and of higher quality to the consumer.

If you want to perform an ANOVA on this data, the input voltage factor is treated as just another factor on the ANOVA table.

Further Applications of the Parameter Design

In this example, the L_8 array had a single outside noise factor assigned to replications. This assignment of other factors outside of the primary design is called an *outer array*. The *inner array* is, in this case, the controllable factors assigned to the L_8 design.

In practice, any experimental design array can be assigned to either the inner or the outer array. For example, the 2^3 design in chapter 9 could have an orthogonal array assigned to the outer array to test several outside noise factors.

Naturally, this technique and its complete analysis is best left to someone with formal education in experimental design. As a manufacturing manager, it is important to realize that these methods exist, that they can be quickly analyzed using simple methods, and that robust designs are a key ingredient in ensuring that manufacturing defects are prevented.

Achieving Robust Products by Testing a Design at Three or More Levels: Making a Heat Treatment Oven Robust

While the first experiment in this chapter demonstrated that a lot of information can be drawn from an orthogonal array, it also pointed out a major problem. With two levels tested, only a linear relationship can be shown on the effect diagram. Unfortunately, many factors tested in an experiment have a dynamic relationship to the response variable. That is, the plotting of the effect diagram can produce a curve (see Figure 10-3).

To discover if a factor has a curvilinear relationship to the response variable, the factor must be tested at three or more levels. Therefore, the orthogonal arrays for testing factors at three levels are very popular. The simplest of these is the L_9 array and it illustrates the testing for nonlinear relationships very well.

Step 1: Select the factors.

The following example shows how the L_9 array can test up to four factors at three levels each. Suppose that a heat treatment line within a metal stamping plant is testing for the optimal setting for the heat treatment oven. You decide to test four factors at three levels each. You choose the L_9 array since it requires only nine experimental runs instead of the 81 required by a factorial design (3^4).

Factor A Line Speed
Low setting = 10 feet/min.
Medium setting = 12 feet/min.
High setting = 14 feet/min.

Factor B Oven Temperature
Low setting = 600 degrees
Medium setting = 650 degrees
High setting = 700 degrees

Factor C Percent Oxygen Present
Low setting = 10%
Medium setting = 11%
High setting = 12%

Factor D Space Between Parts
Low setting = 1 inch
Medium setting = 3 inches
High setting = 5 inches

The response variable is the Rockwell hardness of the parts at three different points. The hardness of the three points is averaged and reported as a single number.

Step 2: Design the three-level experiment.

Figure 10-2 shows an L_9 array and its associated linear graph. The four factors under study can be assigned to the four columns in order. Note that the array is now made up of the numerals one, two, and three. These represent the low, medium, and high settings of a factor, respectively. For example, the factor A column looks like this:

Run	Factor A (Line Speed)
1	1
2	1
3	1
4	2
5	2
6	2
7	3
8	3
9	3

$$L_9(3^4) \text{ Array}$$

	1	2	3	4	Columns
1	1	1	1	1	
2	1	2	2	2	
3	1	3	3	3	
Experimental Runs 4	2	1	2	3	
5	2	2	3	1	
6	2	3	1	2	
7	3	1	3	2	
8	3	2	1	3	
9	3	3	2	1	

Figure 10-2: The L_9 orthogonal array.

When the results are added you can quickly see that any analysis is going to involve creating three-level totals for each factor, instead of the two used in the L_8 examples.

Run	Factor A (Line Speed)	Response
1	1	5.0
2	1	5.5
3	1	4.0
4	2	7.5
5	2	8.7
6	2	8.6
7	3	5.1
8	3	6.3
9	3	6.3

Step 3: How to perform the analysis.

If you grouped the responses according to their respective levels, you would get the following.

Total for $A_{low} = 5.0 + 5.5 + 4.0 = 14.5$

Total for $A_{medium} = 7.5 + 8.7 + 8.6 = 24.8$

Total for $A_{high} = 5.1 + 6.3 + 6.3 = 17.7$

You could use these totals to complete an ANOVA table. The formulas for the effect of each factor are just slightly modified from before to create the sums of squares. For example, the sum of squares for factor A would be

$$SSA = \frac{A_{low}^2 + A_{medium}^2 + A_{high}^2}{n} - CF$$

where n = number of data points at a single level

Thus the sum of squares for factor A is 18.53. Repeating this same formula for the other factors would start the following ANOVA table.

Source	Sum of Square	Degrees of freedom	Variance
A	18.53	2	9.265
B	1.41	2	0.705
C	0.78	2	0.390
D	0.83	2	0.415
Total	21.55	8	

At this point, we could pool the insignificant factors and complete the ANOVA table. However, note that each factor has two degrees of freedom (one less than the three levels). This means that we can further decompose the information contained within each factor into two sets of data—one for the linear effect of the factor and one for the nonlinear effect.

You can find these relationships more easily by drawing out the effect diagram. For example, factor *A* (line speed) is a significant factor in this experiment. If we draw the average response for each level of factor *A* on an effect diagram, we will find a dynamic response relationship (see Figure 10-3). By dividing the level totals for factor *A* by 3, we can find the average hardness at each level.

$$\text{low average} = \frac{14.5}{3} = 4.8$$

$$\text{med. average} = \frac{24.8}{3} = 8.3$$

$$\text{high average} = \frac{17.7}{3} = 5.9$$

As is shown in Figure 10-3, there is a quadratic curve that passes through the three averages. This tells us that the line speed can be optimized by setting it to the maximum of the curve. A simple way to do this is to use the medium line speed setting to get the maximum hardness from the parts.

Dynamic curves, such as this one, are advantageous to manufacturers. If we draw the variation in normal line speed (caused by factors such as the weight of the parts on the line) on our chart, we can see a second advantage to maximizing this process. At its former setting of 14 feet per minute the variations in line speed create a wide range of final hardness. At its optimal setting of 12 feet per minute, variations in the line have little effect on the hardness. In other words, the problem of consistent hardness has not been eliminated; the process has been made robust against the problem (see Figure 10-4).

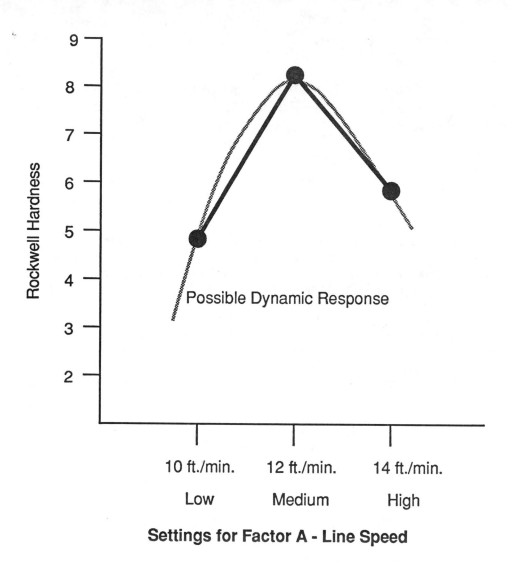

Figure 10-3: The dynamic response of line speed to hardness.

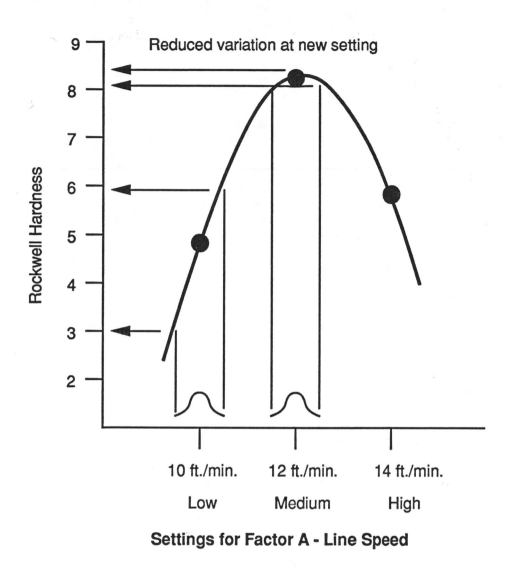

Figure 10-4: Using a dynamic curve to create robustness.

Conclusion

Taguchi has written several books describing his method in detail. Given only a chapter, this discussion has been limited to only the simplest techniques. Still, even the novice can achieve amazing results with these methods.

There are even larger arrays available than those discussed in this chapter. There are arrays up to L_{108} that can test dozens of factors. For example, the L_{27} array can test up to 13 factors at three levels each. In other words, it collects its data in 27 experimental runs instead of the 1,594,323 runs a factorial experiment might require.

In addition to parameter designs to make products and processes more robust, Taguchi has also developed systems of tolerance designing. He recommends that the tolerances be set last, after the manufacturing system has been laid out and the processes optimized.

Finally, Taguchi translates all quality characteristics into a formula called the loss-function (see chapter 14). It expresses the effect of process or product changes in real dollars. This enables experimental results to be translated directly into the language management understands—money.

There are several more powerful features of the Taguchi method^{TM} that have not been discussed in this chapter. If you are interested in pursuing this topic further, refer to the recommended reading section.

The Taguchi method^{TM} of experimentation offers an economical alternative to conventional research. It can scan dozens of factors in a few experimental runs and give you preliminary data. However, it can also be integrated into the traditional experimentation process. Orthogonal arrays are very effective for screening factors and performing initial experiments on complex situations.

CHAPTER 11

Using Statistical Techniques to Audit a Supplier and the Quality of Purchased Parts

The relationship between customer and supplier is changing rapidly. In the past, the relationship was adversarial. Today, many companies are making their suppliers a partner in their operations. Information, people, and other resources are freely exchanged. The supplier is first approved using rigorous standards, and then trusted. The days of sending supplier quality assurance people to vendor locations on a monthly basis are quickly fading.

This chapter outlines the statistical techniques used to monitor a supplier that has been approved as a source company. These techniques are the largest part of a monitoring system. They examine the cost, delivery, and quality performance of a vendor. However, other considerations play a part in the maintenance of vendor relationships. For example, effective communication between the vendor's salesperson and your purchasing agent is vitally important but difficult to quantify.

The overall purpose of the techniques discussed in this chapter is to detect continuous improvement on the part of the supplier. It is no longer enough to meet all requirements for supplied parts. A competitive company must seek out suppliers that will continuously improve their quality and prices. This will enable the company to improve its own market position as a world-class manufacturer. The data collected is not intended to be used to punish a supplier.

How to Measure and Track the Cost Performance of a Vendor

Contracts for supplied material involve cost figures that are basically estimates of the final price of the material. Predicted costs and final costs are frequently two different amounts. The difference between these figures is the cost performance of the supplier. This performance can be examined in both the short term and the long term. However, the first step is to establish a method of evaluating the accuracy of the estimated cost.

$$\text{cost performance} = \frac{\text{final cost} - \text{predicted cost}}{\text{predicted cost}}$$

For example, assume the initial estimate of the cost to produce 10,000 fasteners for the R-Rite Company is $365, but by the time of delivery the cost has risen to $412. The cost performance would be + 0.129.

$$\text{cost performance} = \frac{\$412 - \$365}{\$365} = 0.129$$

The positive number indicates a cost overrun. A negative result would indicate a cost reduction.

Tracking the Short-term Performance of a Vendor Using a Pareto Chart

A Pareto chart is used to examine these costs between vendors in the short term. A Pareto chart sorts out the cost performance of each vendor in order of its magnitude. Figure 11-1 shows what a Pareto chart may look like for a set of vendors.

To obtain the cost figures for a Pareto chart, you must balance the cost performance of each vendor against the volume of material being shipped. Otherwise, a small vendor shipping very few parts could score a higher cost performance than a major vendor struggling to fill hundreds of orders. The easiest way to do this is to report the actual cost over/underruns.

Consider the example of two suppliers providing goods to your company. The first is the aforementioned supplier that provided the fasteners. The difference between predicted costs and actual costs is

$$\text{cost difference} = \text{final cost} - \text{predicted cost}$$

or

$$\text{cost difference} = \$412 - \$365 = \$47$$

A second vendor supplied 1,000 parts at $13.00 each. The predicted cost was originally $12,000 for the entire shipment. Therefore, the cost difference is a cost overrun of $1,000.

$$\text{cost difference} = \$13,000 - \$12,000 = \$1,000$$

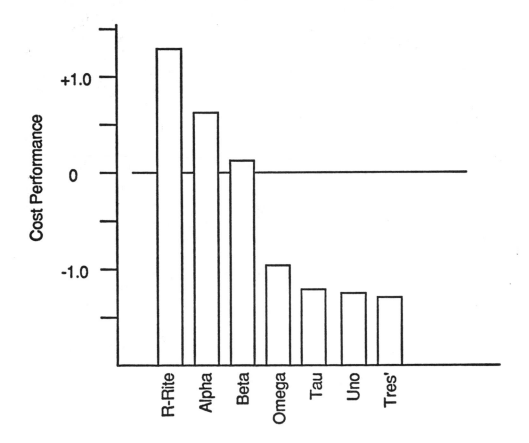

Figure 11-1: A Pareto chart of cost performance by vendor.

On a Pareto chart, the second supplier would be rated higher on the cost overrun scale than the first supplier, even though the second supplier provided a smaller number of finished parts. The actual dollars spent over the target were much higher for the second supplier.

Tracking Long-term Vendor Performance Trends Using a Line Chart

Although costs can be examined over the short term with a Pareto chart, the true performance of a supply company should also be examined over the long term. A supplier with a history of cost overruns that is improving dramatically is preferred over a supplier with a barely acceptable record that never improves.

To examine long-term cost trends, the cost performance of the company can be plotted on a chart. Time would be plotted along the horizontal axis and cost performance along the vertical axis (see Figure 11-2). A company that is improving creates a distinctive downward trend on the chart.

The magnitude of the trend can be quantified using the correlational techniques outlined in chapter 8. The slope of the regression line is negative when a cost improvement is detected. The magnitude of the slope factor is the magnitude of the improvement.

Methods for Evaluating Delivery Accuracy

Timely delivery is absolutely critical to some modern manufacturing and inventory systems, such as Kanban and just-in-time. Even in older systems, timeliness of delivery is very important; therefore both early and late deliveries can have an adverse effect. Late deliveries create shortages, and early deliveries place strain on an inventory system while adding to storage costs.

An easy way to score the accuracy of deliveries is to assess points against deliveries that are either late or early. The best way to do this is to develop a window of delivery. A typical time window in a JIT situation is a few hours in size. For companies beginning a stricter program of delivery, the first windows can be as much as five days in size. The size of the window depends on your particular situation and goals.

For our example, we will assume that a supplied material time window for delivery is one day. If purchased material is due next Tuesday, it can arrive anytime on Tuesday. For every day before or after that date, a point is assessed against the supplier. The records of the last 10 purchase orders from a supplier reveal the following delivery performance.

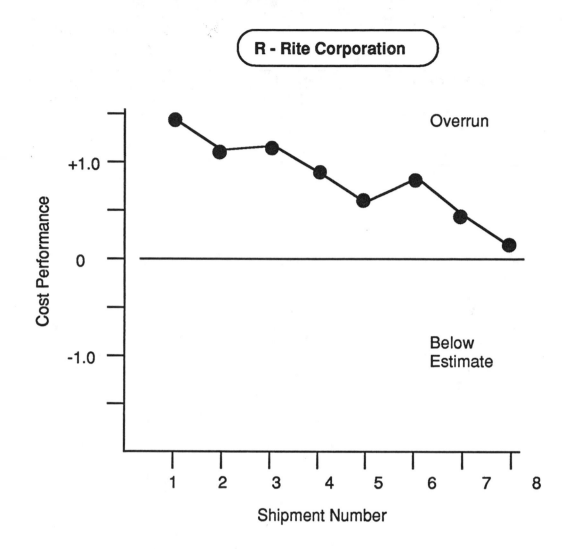

Figure 11-2: Cost performance history chart.

Date Expected	Date Arrived	Points
10-18	10-19	1
10-20	10-20	0
10-21	10-23	2
10-25	10-23	2
10-26	10-27	1
10-26	10-26	0
10-30	10-29	1
11-1	11-1	0
11-3	11-5	2
11-5	11-8	3
	Total	12

This table forms the basis of evaluating delivery performance. To make this point system fair, the importance of each shipment must be factored into the equation. There are many ways to do this, such as multiplying each point by the cost of the shipment or by a factor of importance. We will use the size of the shipment as the factor. The resulting table is as follows.

Points	Shipment Size	Final Score
1	10,000	10,000
0	5,000	0
2	100,000	200,000
2	15,000	30,000
1	7,500	7,500
0	13,000	0
1	12,000	12,000
0	25,000	0
2	10,000	20,000
3	10,000	30,000
	Total	309,500

This method is called *weighted scores*. Notice that shipments three and four both had an initial delivery score of two, but the size of each shipment created vastly different final scores. Also note that the last two shipments were of the same size, but their initial scores changed their final scores.

A Pareto chart of delivery performance can be used to compare suppliers of similar products. Also, you can divide each final score total by the number of shipments to get an average performance by supplier. This will balance the effect of a large supplier against the occasional shipment from a very small supplier.

How to Conduct a Quality Audit of a Shipment of Supplied Goods: Auditing the Quality of Gas Shock Absorbers

The quality of the delivered goods is usually checked for dimensional and attribute conformance. In the case of raw materials, the suppliers might certify the purity of the material. An audit would involve shipping a sample of material to a qualified laboratory for confirmation. This is done infrequently to assure that the supplier's certification program is accurate. In addition, the supplier should have its own internal system for constantly checking the accuracy of the laboratory equipment.

For dimensional data, a sample of the incoming shipment is compared against the specifications. Consider the example of a cylinder for a gas shock absorber. The design prints call for a cylinder that is 5 inches in length. The tolerance is plus or minus 0.02 inches. Assume that a large shipment of the cylinders arrives and that you sample 30 randomly chosen parts. Your sample has an average length of 5.01 inches and a standard deviation of 0.001 inches. Does the average you found show that this lot is significantly off target to be rejected?

Step 1: Calculate the average and standard deviation.

The first test would be to see if your average and standard deviation were statistically different from the standards established in the part drawings. To test for a difference, a *t*-test is used for averages and a chi-square calculation for the standard deviations.

Step 2: Compare the sample average to blueprint specifications by performing a t-test.

Let us begin with the *t*-tests for averages. The formula is as follows. If we add the information obtained through sampling, we can calculate a *t*-value.

$$t = \frac{\bar{x} - \mu}{\frac{s}{\sqrt{n}}}$$

where $\bar{x}$ = sample average
μ = average specified on the prints
s = sample standard deviation
n = number of numbers

Thus

$$t = \frac{5.01 - 5.00}{\frac{0.001}{\sqrt{30}}} = 54.77$$

To find out whether this *t*-value represents a significant difference, we must refer to Appendix B, the table of critical *t*-values. Should the *t*-value obtained in our test be greater than the critical *t*-value in Appendix B, we know that the gas shock absorbers are statistically different from specifications.

The sample had 30 data points, so the *t*-test would have one fewer degrees of freedom ($df = n - 1 = 29$). In most industrial situations, the test is set to the 95% confidence limit. The 95% column at 29 degrees of freedom has a value of 2.045. It can be quickly seen that our results are higher than this number and thus represent a significant difference in the average.

Step 3: Compare the sample standard deviation against the variation allowed on the blueprints.

At this point, we know that the incoming shipment has cylinders that are longer on average than what is called for in the prints. Our next test is to see if the variation we found in the sample is higher than what the prints could tolerate. This requires the use of the chi-square test.

$$\chi^2 = \frac{(n - 1)s^2}{\sigma^2}$$

where χ^2 = chi-square
n = number of parts drawn in the sample
s = sample standard deviation
σ = maximum standard deviation suggested by the prints

To find the maximum standard deviations suggested by the prints, we must make an assumption. Six standard deviations describe the spread of a distribution. Thus, to find the largest acceptable standard deviation, we divide the tolerance spread by 6.

$$\sigma = \frac{\text{tolerance spread}}{6}$$

or

$$\sigma = \frac{0.04}{6} = 0.0067 \, \text{inches}$$

Adding this data to the information obtained from the sample, we obtain the following chi-square.

$$\chi^2 = \frac{(30 - 1) \times 0.001^2}{0.0067^2} = 0.646$$

Since 30 parts were sampled, this test still has 29 degrees of freedom. Looking up the critical chi-value in Appendix C for 95% confidence at 29 degrees of freedom, we find 42.56. Our figure of 0.646 is lower than this figure, so the standard deviation in the sample is said to be equivalent to the maximum standard deviation possible.

Step 4: Calculate the Cpk Ratio for the Shipment

We can put the preceding results into perspective by calculating a *Cpk* ratio for the incoming shipment. With an average of 5.01 and a standard deviation of 0.001, you will obtain the following *Cpk* ratio.

$$Cpk = \frac{\overline{x} - \text{lower spec.}}{3 \times s}$$

where $\overline{x}$ = sample's average
       s = sample's standard deviation

Thus

$$Cpk = \frac{5.01 - 5.00}{3 \times 0.001} = 3.33$$

Therefore, the conclusion we draw from the *t*-test, chi-square, and the *Cpk* index is that these cylinders were produced off optimal target for length, but they have very little variation and they meet capability requirements. We are also firm in the knowledge that the longer average size is a real phenomenon and should be accounted for if dimensions are critical to the final assembly.

How to Conduct a Product Quality Audit When Attribute Data Is Involved: Auditing the Quality of a Shipment of Bottle Caps

Attribute information presents a different problem for a product quality audit. The major problem is that the attribute data is not assignable to the aforementioned tests. Therefore, rules of probability must be used to evaluate whether a change in a product attribute qualities is significant.

Consider the example of an incoming shipment of bottle caps. The quality requirements say that the caps must be free of defects, such as missing print, dents, scratches, and burrs. Counting how many of these bottle caps are defective because of these defects is the attribute information an auditor would obtain.

Assume that the supplier of these bottle caps says that they design their quality control system around a 1.0% acceptable quality level (AQL). Essentially, the supplier is saying that most shipments of their caps should be at or below 1.0% defective. You have sampled 100 of the caps and found three that should be rejected because of quality problems. To find out if that is too high a number of rejects, you can use the Poisson distribution. A Poisson distribution works best for finding the probability of unlikely events. Since most companies want few or no defectives shipped to their plant, the occurrence of unacceptable goods should be relatively rare.

Step 1: Calculate the number of defectives.

The first step is to calculate the average number defective (*np*) expected in your sample.

$$np = n \times p$$

where, n = sample size
p = percent defective expected

In our example, the supplier should have 1-in-a-100 defective, or 0.01. With 100 caps sampled, the *np* is 1.0.

$$np = 100 \times 0.01$$

Step 2: Look up the Poisson probabilities.

The number found to be defective is represented by x; in this case x equals three. Turning to Appendix D (cumulative Poisson probabilities), we look up an *np* equal to 1.0. We find the following table.

x	np = 1.0
0	0.368
1	0.736
2	0.920
3	0.981
4	0.996
5	0.999

The x column represents the chance of x or fewer occurrences of an event when the *np* is equal to 1.0. Applying the 95% confidence rule, we would see if there is less than a 5% chance of three or fewer defectives being found in a given shipment.

Step 3: Compare the desired results with the probability table.

We must examine the meaning of the table carefully. There is a 92% chance (0.920) of two or fewer events occurring. Subtracting the 92% from the 98.1% chance at the $x = 3$ level, we find approximately a 6.1% chance of three defective caps being found.

For our example, this tells us that finding three defective caps in a sample of 100 is not so unlikely as to prompt the rejection of the entire lot. Therefore, we would accept these bottle caps as being, probably, about 1.0% defective.

Examining a Supplier's SPC System to Ensure Continuous Improvement

Today, many companies require their suppliers to have SPC systems and to submit control charts and capability studies along with their respective parts. This leaves it up to the receiving company to audit this data for accuracy and to determine how well the information reflects the quality of the parts.

Consider the example of a supply company that produces bearing seals for use in an axle assembly. The specifications call for a bearing seal that is 1.50 inches in diameter, plus or minus 0.01 inches. With each shipment of seals the supplier includes an average and range chart kept during that lot's production.

A simple method for auditing the shipment quickly would be to pull five random seals and measure their diameter. The average and range of that sample could be compared to the control limits on the SPC chart. If both the average and the range of the sample are within the control limits, then the parts would be accepted.

A better method would be to compare the capability report for the parts with a larger sample of parts taken from the shipment. For example, suppose that the supply company began making these seals after it had submitted capability studies on the part's diameter that showed their processes to be very capable of maintaining the tolerance range. Assume that the capability study was based on 30 parts and that it obtained an average of 1.50 inches and a standard deviation of 0.003 inches.

By sampling 30 pieces at random from any shipment, we can determine if the average or standard deviation for the shipment has deviated significantly from the capability figures. To accomplish this, you use a different t-test and a new test called the F-test. The F-test is performed first to see if the standard deviations in the capability study and the shipment sample are equivalent. If they are different, then the t-test cannot be performed accurately.

The formula for the F-test is

$$F = \frac{s^2{}_1}{s^2{}_2}$$

where s_1 = larger of the two standard deviations
        s_2 = smaller of the two standard deviations

In our example of the bearing seals, suppose that a sample of 30 seals in a recent shipment had an average diameter of 1.495 and a standard deviation of 0.005 inches. To conduct the F-test, the standard deviation from the original capability study would be placed in the denominator of the equation.

$$F = \frac{0.005^2}{0.003^2} = 2.78$$

To find if this F-value is significant, you turn to the table of critical F-values at the 95% confidence level in Appendix E. The degrees of freedom for each standard deviation are one less than the sample size. For example, the standard deviation in the numerator of the preceding F-test was obtained from a sample of 30 parts. Thus

$$df_1 = n_1 - 1$$

or

$$df_1 = 30 - 1 = 29$$

Thirty parts were also sampled to calculate the standard deviation in the denominator. Therefore, the numerator and denominator both have 29 degrees of freedom.

The column for 29 degrees of freedom is not listed in Appendix E, so we trace down the nearest value (30) until it intersects the nearest row to 29 degrees of freedom (also 30). The matching critical value is about 1.84. The value calculated is above this critical figure, so the standard deviations are considered not to be equivalent.

How to Compare Two Sample Averages to See If Product Quality Varies Widely Between Shipments

The t-test used previously calculated the difference between the average found in a sample against a standard. Another version of the t-test can compare two sample averages, such as the average in a capability study versus the average taken from a shipment. By creating a pool sample standard deviation this formula can perform a t-test where the variances are unequal.

Using the same data from the bearing seal example, we can calculate a t-value. The formula for the t-test is

$$t = \frac{\bar{x}_1 - \bar{x}_2}{Sp \cdot \sqrt{\frac{1}{n_1} + \frac{1}{n_2}}}$$

where $\bar{x}_1$ = first sample's average

Sp = pooled sample standard deviation

n_1 = size of the first sample

$\bar{x}_2$ = second sample's average

n_2 = size of the second sample

The pooled standard deviation is first calculated using the following formula:

$$Sp = \sqrt{\frac{(n_1-1)\, s_1^2 + (n_2-1)\, s_2^2}{n_1 + n_2 - 2}}$$

Using the data from our example, you can calculate the following pooled standard deviation.

$$Sp = \sqrt{\frac{(29 \times 0.005^2) + (29 \times 0.003^2)}{30 + 30 - 2}}$$

Using the results from the preceding equation, you can complete the calculation.

$$t = \frac{1.5 - 1.495}{0.00412 \sqrt{\frac{1}{30} + \frac{1}{30}}}$$

Thus

$$t = 4.70$$

Turning to the table of critical t-values in Appendix B, we would look in the 95% confidence column for the value corresponding to 58 degrees of freedom ($df = 30 + 30 - 2$). That critical value is found by going to the closest lower value on the chart, in other words, fifty degrees of freedom, for a critical value of 2.009. Clearly, the calculated t-value exceeds this critical value, thus the averages are significantly different. The recent shipment of seals are different than what the capability study suggested.

To confirm these results, you calculate a *Cpk* ratio for the incoming shipment of seals.

$$Cpk = \frac{1.495 - 1.490}{3 \times 0.005} = 0.33$$

This is a *Cpk* index that is far below the 1.33 minimum specified by most manufacturers. This incoming shipment of seals is unacceptable for use.

Tracking Continuous Improvement of Shipments from a Single Supplier Using the *Cpk* Chart

In many cases, suppliers will send a manufacturer continuous shipments of goods. You can track the quality of each shipment and detect continuous improvement using a *Cpk* chart. This is a chart of the *Cpk* ratio of incoming material over time. For attribute information a parts-per-million chart is used.

To see how the *Cpk* chart is created and used, let us extend the previous example to look at other incoming shipments of the same seals. In the shipment recently examined, we found an average of 1.495 inches and a standard deviation of 0.005. The *Cpk* index was 0.33. To create the *Cpk* chart, we draw the optimal size and tolerance limits horizontally on a piece of graph paper. The next step is to plot a circle where the average for a shipment occurs and a whisker bar for the range of variation of the part sizes. This is found using the following formula.

$$\text{range of variation} = 6 \times \text{standard deviation}$$

For the first sample the theoretical spread equals 0.030 inches (6 x 0.005). Assuming a normal distribution of parts, half of this variation should be above the average and half below. Thus, this is drawn as one-half of this spread above the average, and one-half below (see Figure 11-3).

As each new shipment comes in, 30 or more pieces are sampled and their averages and theoretical spreads are plotted on the chart. In addition, the *Cpk* index is calculated for each incoming shipment and noted at the bottom of the chart. The back of the chart can be used to make notes on any exceptional occurrences during monitoring. In other words, this could be considered another form of SPC chart.

Assume that the following information was gathered over the next five shipments.

Average	Standard Deviation	Cpk
1.499	0.002	1.50
1.502	0.003	0.89
1.500	0.003	1.11
1.500	0.002	1.67
1.499	0.001	3.00

With these plotted on the graph in Figure 11-3, we can see both the quality of each shipment and if there is a trend toward constantly better shipments. The most recent shipment also has the highest *Cpk*, and the average is well centered on the specifications. The trend to look for over time is the shrinkage

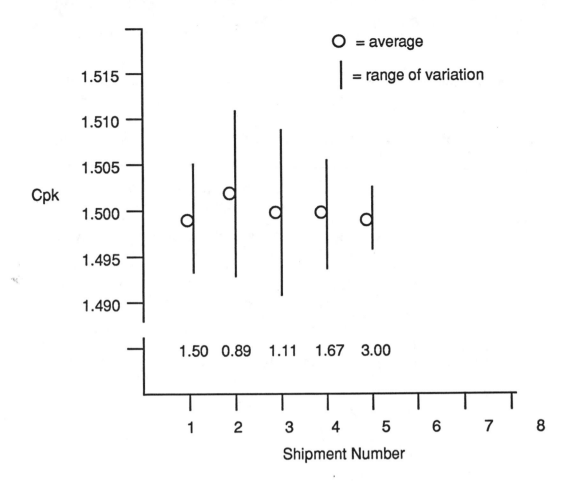

Figure 11-3: A *Cpk* chart for incoming shipments.

of the width of the theoretical spread. This indicates a supplier that is finding new ways to reduce variation in the process.

How to Track Continuous Improvement When Attribute Data Is Collected Using the Parts-per-Million Chart

Attribute information obviously cannot be used to calculate *Cpk* ratios. Therefore, a different type of tracking chart is used for auditing the performance of a vendor. The most popular method is the parts-per-million chart. This chart is created by comparing how many parts had to be rejected by the manufacturer against how many million parts the supplier sent.

The best way to obtain this information is to inspect all products 100%. However, that is usually costly and time consuming. Therefore, the preferred alternative is to take frequent, small, random samples of the product and count the number of defectives encountered.

The parts-per-million calculation averages out a bad lot of parts across the total number of parts received. For example, if a supplier normally sends very good parts but slips up and sends one shipment of bad parts, the effect is diluted. However, a supplier that constantly sends a few bad parts will show up on the chart clearly.

The formula for the calculation is

$$PPM = \frac{No. \ of \ Rejected \ Parts}{Total \ of \ All \ Parts \ Sent \ or \ Sampled} \times 1{,}000{,}000$$

The following examples illustrate how this formula works for both large and small suppliers.

Calculating defective parts from a large supplier.

Let us begin with the large supplier that sends millions of parts every year.

At regular intervals, perhaps monthly or quarterly, you would add up the number of parts that had to be rejected on the line or sent back to the supplier. Assume that you found 30,000 parts to be unusable. This figure is divided by the total number of parts sent to you by the supplier in this time period.

Assume that they sent 15,000,000 parts.

$$PPM = \frac{30{,}000}{15{,}000{,}000} \times 1{,}000{,}000 = 2{,}000$$

In other words, the supplier sent you an average of 2,000 bad parts for every 1 million shipped. This also represents 0.2% defective.

Calculating Defective Parts from an Infrequent Supplier

Now let us look at how the calculation would work for a supplier that only occasionally sends goods. Assume that another supplier sent you a total of 5,000 parts during the last quarter. Of these parts, 17 were rejected on the line and none were sent back after inspection by receiving.

$$PPM = \frac{17}{5,000} \times 1,000,000 = 3,400$$

This represents a higher proportion of defective material than the larger supplier. Not only does the parts-per-million calculation create a fairly representative standard for measuring defective materials, it also is effective for evaluating suppliers that create very infrequent rejections of goods.

To give you some comparisons to work with, it is not unusual in the electronics industry to find a microchip manufacturer that is experiencing less than 200 defective chips per million in production. The customers of some chips have reported parts-per-million figures near zero. A carburetor manufacturer in Japan reported a one part-per-million rejection rate by its customers. Even a stamping plant in the United States reduced its scrap rate so far below its typical 10% that parts-per-million calculations were necessary.

The parts-per-million figures can be plotted on a chart to detect continuous improvement by a supplier. The chart is even easier to create than the *Cpk* chart. A simple two-axis chart is created with the horizontal scale representing time and the vertical scale representing parts per million. After each audit of attribute quality performance, a supplier's score is recorded on the chart. The best companies will have a low parts-per-million score, a descending trend, or both.

How to Detect a Falsified Control Chart: Testing for Randomness in SPC Chart Data

The SPC chart shows the performance of the process over time. You must be alert for trends, runs, and falsified data. The simplest way to look for such problems is to apply the one-third/two-third rule. The zone between the control limits on a chart is divided into thirds. The central third of the zone, that nearest the process average, should have two-thirds of all the plotted points. If not, a trend, run, or nonrandom pattern could be present.

A trend can be spotted by looking for any seven plotted points that either rise or fall on the chart. A run is when seven or more points are together above or below the process average. Seven points is not chosen arbitrarily. Each point on a control chart has a 50/50 chance of landing either above or below the process average. The probability of seven points grouping together is the simple probability of multiplying 0.50 times itself, seven times.

$$P = 0.50 \times 0.50 \times 0.50 \times 0.50 \times 0.50 \times 0.50 \times 0.50 = 0.0078$$

In other words, this is the smallest number for a run that occurs less than once in 100 times by chance. Thus, we have 99% confidence that the run or trend is real.

A statistical test can be applied to an SPC chart to check the randomness of the data. This method is called the *run test*. A run test counts how many data points are grouped together either above or below the process average. However, this method requires at least 40 plotted points to be effective. Therefore, you should use at least two pages of the SPC chart kept for a process.

To conduct the test, you would circle the groups of data points above or below the process average on a control chart. The following chart illustrates how this is done.

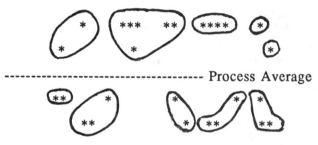

Each circled group represents a run. The preceding figure has 10 runs. There are 14 points above the average and 13 below. Thus

n_1 = number of data points above the process average

n_2 = number of data points below the process average

r = number of runs

For example, assume that you examine some SPC charts and that you find 29 runs, with 34 data points above the process average and 25 below the process average. To test if this pattern is random, apply the following formula:

$$z = \frac{r - \mu + \frac{1}{2}}{\sigma_r}$$

where z = magnitude of the difference
r = the number of runs
μ = the average number of runs expected
σ_r = the standard error of the estimate

To calculate the average number of runs expected, first calculate the following formula:

$$\mu = \frac{2 \times n_1 \times n_2}{n_1 + n_2} + 1$$

Substitute the information from our example to obtain

$$\mu = \frac{2 \times 34 \times 25}{34 + 25} + 1 = 29.8 \text{ runs}$$

Next, you would have to calculate the standard error for this estimate of this number of runs.

$$\sigma_r = \sqrt{\frac{2n_1 n_2 (2n_1 n_2 - n_1 - n_2)}{(n_1 + n_2)^2 \cdot (n_1 + n_2 - 1)}}$$

Substituting the information already obtained,

$$\sigma_r = \sqrt{\frac{2 \cdot 34 \cdot 25 \, (2 \cdot 34 \cdot 25 - 34 - 25)}{(34 + 25)^2 \cdot (34 + 25 - 1)}}$$

$$= 3.717$$

These two calculations give you the information necessary to complete the original formula for the run test.

$$z = \frac{29 - 29.8 + \frac{1}{2}}{3.717} = -0.08$$

When data is in a nonrandom order, the Z value will exceed +/- 1.96. As can be seen in the example, this data is assumed to be random. Falsified information on a control chart will tend to form nonrandom patterns. Therefore, had this test found nonrandomness, a further investigation into the honesty of the control chart is required.

This is not proof that the chart is falsified. Instead, you may have detected an identifiable pattern created by an assignable cause the supplier has not detected. However, if further investigations reveal nonrandom patterns in several control charts, then the suspicion for falsification grows.

How to Use Probability Plotting and Histograms as Supplier Quality Audit Tools

In chapter 3 we discussed the use of probability plotting paper and histograms to show the distribution of the data in a capability study. These same tools can be used as an audit tool. Consider the example of auditing material at a supplier's location to confirm its quality.

Figure 11-4 shows some of the nonnormal distributions that indicate trouble in a process. Suppose that you have sampled 30 pieces from a lot of parts the supplier claims to be capable. A histogram is drawn based on the

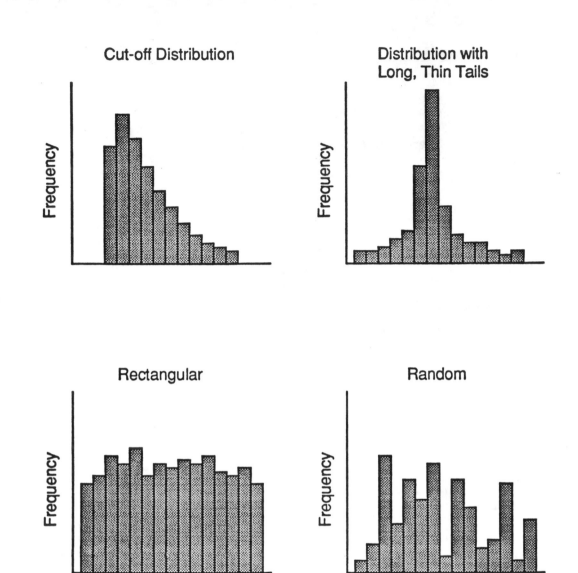

Figure 11-4: Some distributions that indicate trouble during an audit.

data. The frequency of each data reading is shown as a bar on a bar chart, thus creating a histogram. The *Cpk* index you calculate is over the minimal 1.33, but the histogram has a very rectangular shape. This indicates that the product may have been reworked after production.

When a normal distribution is created by a process and the tails land outside of the specifications, reworking the parts out of specification moves them into the middle of the distribution. The tails are literally folded onto the distribution. The resulting effect is a rectangular distribution.

Another distribution to cause alarm is a random distribution. No industrial process creates completely random measurements. Therefore, the random distribution is most likely an artificial creation. This could indicate error or fraud.

When one tail of a distribution is cut off, this could be the result of a mechanical sorter or weight-check device rejecting parts above or below a certain limit. This condition and the aforementioned ones represent processes that are experiencing constant interference. Since the idea of statistical control is to find the natural performance of a process, the detection of these nonnormal patterns indicates that further auditing will only be biased by a process without statistical control.

Conclusion

In addition to the statistical techniques mentioned in this chapter, a good auditor will also seek out the nonstatistical systems that contribute to the performance of a supplier. Finances, management style, housekeeping, safety, and strategic planning are also important aspects to examine when auditing either your own or someone else's SPC system. All of these other areas should be using information from their statistical system to complement their decision-making process.

CHAPTER 12

How to Use Statistical Analyses to Measure Customer Requirements and Improve Manufacturing Decisions

Intelligence gathering is a vital, but often overlooked, function of manufacturing. Most of the methods presented in this book are directed at the internal functions of manufacturing. However, a company cannot survive for long if it ignores the external environment. Paramount among these external factors is the needs of the customers.

As manufacturing manager, you must translate customer requirements into the designs of finished products. Techniques, such as quality function deployment, begin with a list of customer requirements and end with a set of manufacturing instructions. Therefore, it is important that you know how market survey data is collected and how to recognize data that has been properly analyzed.

How to Identify Your Customers

Every company is both a consumer and a supplier. For example, if your company produces metal screws for the appliance industry, then its customer is the appliance manufacturer that buys its product. At the same time, your company is a customer of metal rods used to form the screws. The supplier of the metal rods sees your company as a customer. The appliance maker, in turn, sees your company as a supply company.

A supplier's main concern is the requirements of its purchasing companies. Consider the example of an automotive industry supply company. Perhaps they make something as mundane as a door lock button, but they still face ever-changing specifications, purchasing requirements, and quality assurance procedures. Like any supply company, they must seek out the most important requirements and make sure that they are met.

Intelligence gathering is the process of gleaning the "noise" of communications between the companies and extracting usable information. Usually this begins with an examination of the purchasing agreement. A customer of the supply company usually issues a purchase contract that states the requirements for the goods being purchased. This includes information on quantity, price, and delivery time. However, it frequently specifies quality levels, packing instructions, correction procedures, and other conditions of the contract.

A supplier is usually overwhelmed with the information sent by the purchaser. Therefore, statistical techniques are needed to summarize the incoming data into a more usable form. The most important part of this summary is to detect the few vital requirements of the contract from the myriad of contractual conditions.

Finding the Important Information Using Content Analysis

Content analysis involves examining all communications between two parties and counting which topics are discussed most frequently. This technique is used to monitor periodicals to detect new trends or changing attitudes. In industry, it can be used to detect which topic the purchasers seem most interested in discussing.

To conduct content analysis, you must begin by drawing up a clear set of rules about what will be counted, how it will be counted, and how decisions will be made in questionable cases. The following example illustrates how this is done. Suppose that a zinc die casting company is selling goods to dozens of customers. The management of the company wants to know if the larger accounts are getting more attention than small accounts. You have been assigned the job of assuring that the customers have been receiving appropriate feedback from the manufacturing department.

The first step is to define what to monitor and how it will be counted. You decide that there are three basic forms of communication occurring: phone calls, letters, and face-to-face meetings. Phone calls and face-to-face meetings are easy to measure; for each topic discussed, the number of minutes spent on the topic is recorded. In addition, the number of meetings and phone calls is also noted. For example, a quarterly meeting between the manufacturing department and the customer might be two hours long. In that time the following might be discussed.

Quality	30 min.
Delivery	20
Cost	45
Coordination	15
Misc.	10
Total	120

Notice that the costs of the product dominate the meeting. By recording the time spent on each topic, you begin to get a picture of the chief concerns of the customer.

Letters can be scored by assigning a minutes-per-page rule to the contents. For example, a single page may count for 30 minutes of communications. Therefore, a one-page letter on why the quality of the last shipment was questionable would count for 30 minutes in the quality category.

You can either separate the accumulated data into incoming and outgoing communications, or lump them together. In our example, we will combine both incoming and outgoing communications. In addition, we will form other scales to measure the importance of each piece of communication. For example, the actual importance of a communication can vary, so each piece is given a weight.

Each weight is first defined in detail, such as:

1. *Demerit*: A written manufacturing correction notice has been received.

2. *Warning*: The customer has written or phoned in concerns about our product but no formal complaint form is filed.

3. *Just Talking*: An employee of our firm notes that a customer has made a no comment about our product.

4. *Confirmation*: A letter or phone call has been received confirming that we have met or exceeded the requirements for a product.

5. *Award*: The company receives official recognition for a job well done.

Each of these categories is given a score by which to weight each piece of communication received.

Level of Importance	Score
Demerit	−2
Warning	−1
Just talking	0
Confirmation	1
Award	2

Thus, the letter on why the quality was questionable would be 30 minutes of communications, but -1 on the importance scale because it constitutes a warning. For this method of scoring to work well, the aforementioned rigid set of classification rules is needed.

Another possible level of concern is the source of the communication. A call from the president of the purchasing company to the supplier is probably more important than a call from the purchasing agent to a quality control manager. Therefore, you could create another scale for measuring the importance of the source of the communication.

Source	Score
President	5
Vice-president	4
Production manager	3
Agent	2
Other	1

You can continue to construct the scales needed to measure the vital characteristics of the communications being monitored. Keep the number of scales small so that recording the results is much easier to calculate.

In our example, you would instruct all of your staff members to keep a log of all communications they make with purchasing companies. Besides noting the time, date, and company involved, they would also record the number of minutes on each topic and the scores of importance. This data would then be summarized by totaling the scores by purchasing companies.

To give the summary relevance, the last item is the volume of business sold to that particular supplier. Later, we will use a statistical test to see if the amount and importance of the communication matches the volume of business.

The final tally for the six most frequently contacted customers may look like this:

Company	Communica-tion Time	Total Impor-tance	Source Score	Volume ($100,000)
Ajax	430 min	100 pts.	60	$4.5
Beanpole	420	85	45	3.9
Cruthers	310	90	15	2.5
Divid	120	90	15	1.9
Excell	90	15	15	0.8
Faide	80	25	10	2.0

By examining one line of the table, you can see how these scores were created. Let us examine the data for the Excell company. Excell sent five letters and made 14 phone calls to your manufacturing staff during the period of this study. The total communication time was recorded as 90 minutes. Each source of communication was ranked on the scale of importance (ranging from -2 to 2). Most of the phone calls were either neutral or slightly positive; thus they scored either one or zero points for importance. Most of the letters scored a positive point for importance. When added together, the score of importance was 15.

The source of each letter and phone call was also scored using the source scoring method described earlier. All of the phone calls and letters were from purchasing agents or concerned line workers. Thus, the source score is a low 15.

How to Conduct Further Analysis of Communication Content Using Kendall's Coefficient of Concordance

The summary could end at this point. You could scan the raw data and decide whether the amount and importance of communications is matching the volume of business. The alternative is to rank each of the purchasers according to their scores and perform statistical tests.

To rank each of the companies, the data is ranked 1 for the highest amount or importance, 2 for the second highest, and so on. When there is a tie, the ranks are averaged. For example, the numeral 90 appears twice in the "Total Importance" column, competing for second and third place. Therefore, we average these ranks and assign them to each company.

$$2\text{nd place} + 3\text{rd place} = 2 + 3 = 5$$

So

$$\frac{5}{2} = 2.5$$

Thus, the completed table of rankings becomes

Company	Communica-tion Time	Total Impor-tance	Source Score	Volume
Ajax	1	1	2	1
Beanpole	2	4	1	2
Cruthers	3	2.5	3	3
Divid	4	2.5	4.5	5
Excell	5	6	4.5	6
Faide	6	5	6	4

You can analyze these rankings using a statistical test called the Kendall Coefficient of Concordance. Concordance is how well the rankings between companies match. When concordance is high, each company is receiving an almost equal number of total rankings.

In our case, we do not want concordance. We want the higher-volume purchasers to receive higher rankings than the other suppliers. To see if this is true, we can add together the rankings for each supplier. For example, the Ajax company had three first-place rankings and one second-place ranking.

$$1 + 1 + 2 + 1 = 5$$

Thus, the total of the rankings for Ajax is five. Repeating this same procedure for the other companies reveals the concordance. The Kendall Coefficient test is used to see if the concordance is significantly high. It can range from zero to one. A score of zero represents perfect concordance.

Company	Rank Total
Ajax	5
Beanpole	9
Cruthers	11.5
Divid	16
Excell	21.5
Faide	21

To calculate the amount of concordance, the Kendall formula is

$$W = \left(\frac{12 \cdot \Sigma R \text{ totals}^2}{k^2 \cdot N(N^2 - 1)} \right) - \frac{3(N + 1)}{N - 1}$$

where ΣR totals^2 = sum of total rankings by company, squared
k = number of scales used
N = number of companies being measured
W = concordance

To find the sum of the square of rank totals, you have to create another column of data.

Company	Rank Total	Totals Squared
Ajax	5	25
Beanpole	9	81
Cruthers	11.5	132.25
Divid	16	256
Excell	21.5	462.25
Faide	21	441
Total		1,397.5

By placing this information into the Kendall formula, you obtain the following.

$$W = \left(\frac{12 \cdot 1{,}397.5}{4^2 \cdot 6(36 - 1)} \right) - \frac{3(6 + 1)}{6 - 1}$$

Thus

$$W = 0.791$$

This is close to the perfect disconcordance of 1. Therefore, this is the result we were seeking. Companies with high volumes received higher rankings of communications.

Another Way to Examine Content Analysis: Spearman's Correlation Coefficient (rho)

Spearman's test for correlation between two factors was developed especially for data that has been ranked. The correlation coefficient is called *rho*. The formula is

$$rho = 1 - \frac{6 \cdot \Sigma d^2}{N^3 - N}$$

where Σd^2 = sum of deviations between rankings, squared
N = the number of data pairs

An example of how the Spearman formula is calculated can be taken from our original zinc die casting problem. One possible test is whether the total communication time correlates to the volume of business. Again, you use the rankings established in the preceding example.

Company	Communication Time	Business Volume
Ajax	1	1
Beanpole	2	2
Cruthers	3	3
Divid	4	5
Excell	5	6
Faide	6	4

As you can see, the rankings for these two factors are very close to one another. To calculate a Spearman correlation, you will need to subtract rankings across the rows to find the deviation of rankings for each company. These deviations will then be squared.

Company	Comm. Time	Volume	(d) Deviation	d^2
Ajax	1	1	0	0
Beanpole	2	2	0	0
Cruthers	3	3	0	0
Divid	4	5	−1	1
Excell	5	6	+1	1
Faide	6	4	+2	4
			Total	6

With six pairs of numbers, you can now complete the correlation calculation.

$$rho = 1 - \frac{6 \times 6}{6^3 - 6}$$

$$rho = 0.829$$

Looking at Appendix F for critical Spearman coefficients, we find that this is a significant correlation at the 95% confidence level. Thus, we have found that there is a strong correlation between the amount of communication occurring and the volume of business.

This same calculation could be repeated for the importance ratings and the source score. The resulting summary table and statistical tests provide valuable information to the management of the supply company. For example, the data collected this year by topic could be compared to data from past years.

Suppose our die cast company had General Motors as a customer. Back in 1985, the bulk of communication would have centered around quality issues. By 1988, this would have changed to topics such as delivery, pricing, and design. By comparing these past trends to today's data, the company could see the direction General Motors is heading with its supply network. Then the management of the zinc die casting company could anticipate future trends and plan accordingly.

Conversely, if a topic of communication from a customer is very high and the responses by your company are very low, perhaps a critical concern is not being properly addressed. Thus, you can see how content analysis can serve as a valuable intelligence gathering tool for any company.

How to Examine the Final Customer's Needs Using Focus Groups and Other Customer Survey Methods

For a world-class manufacturer, attention to the voice of the customer is critical to success. For example, suppose that you are the manufacturing manager for a company that produces the hinge mechanism for car doors. Using one of the following survey methods, you learn that car buyers are upset if a door closes too easily or too hard.

From this general complaint you can establish manufacturing controls on the hinge to ensure customer satisfaction. For example, further studies and experiments may find that door closure is ideal when it requires between 7 and 15 pounds of effort. Below 7 pounds of closing effort the door will be blown shut by wind unexpectedly. Above 15 pounds of force customers report difficulty in shutting the door completely.

From this finding you break down the customer's requirement into specific performance specifications. In other words, the ideal closing force is 11 pounds with a tolerance range of plus or minus 5 pounds. This performance specification is then broken down into engineering specifications for the part. For example, the hinge assembly bolt has to be held to a torque of 70 foot-pounds, plus or minus 5 foot-pounds, to achieve correct closing force in the finished door. In turn, the engineering specifications are then translated into shop floor instructions, such as a control chart at the site of the hinge bolt assembly area to check torque.

This simple example shows that discovering customer needs is critical to the planning and implementation of a successful total quality manufacturing environment.

How to Gather Data from a Focus Group

A focus group occurs when you bring together several customers to discuss various attributes of your product. It is an intensive form of interviewing where you use a series of neutral questions to glean the preferences of the customer. The following example illustrates how this is done. Later, the data is analyzed with statistical methods to enhance its value.

To gather information from several customers, you must write down a structured set of questions. Then at each meeting with a group of customers, you ask the same set of questions. This allows you to make direct comparisons of the answers between companies. Where similarities exist, you can incorporate common requirements into your manufacturing plan.

For example, the question of product quality frequently arises in a purchasing meeting. You may ask, "If we send you 1,000 parts, how will you assure their quality?"

> Company 1: "We will inspect by attributes and MIL-STD-105D."
>
> Company 2: "We require you to have SPC."
>
> Company 3: "We want you to certify the quality of the parts before shipment."

Although these three answers look different, you can design a system of statistical process control that would meet all three requirements.

To quantify the data collected, you could discreetly time the responses given to each question. The more important responses will usually involve the longest discussions. Alternatively, you could keep a count of the times a particular issue is discussed.

It is particularly important to record the mentioning of a subject outside of the realm of the original question. For example, in discussing quality with the customer, you might note that the customer repeatedly mentioned the subject of delivery times. This is an indication of another important topic to note for later attention.

How to Confirm Survey Data with Other Written Information

Of course, market survey methods are never used by themselves for evaluating the customer requirements. A careful reading of the purchase contract, cooperation in customer audits, review of material disposition reports, and an examination of the trade literature is highly recommended as a complementary activity.

The review of literature is a good example. You can collect all of the content analysis you want, but without checking for announcements of policy changes at your customers, you leave yourself open to being caught unprepared. For example, if your largest customer has rarely mentioned delivery scheduling but the local newspaper notes that this same company is hiring just-in-time specialists, it may be time to start planning for change.

How to Conduct a Market Survey

If your company produces goods for immediate sale, it should be keenly interested in the market demands for its products. You must be aware of your customers' feelings about your product, and you must identify potential new customers. The traditional method for gathering this information is the market survey.

A market survey is a technology unto itself. Creating, giving, and evaluating survey information is part art and part science. It usually takes a skilled professional to coordinate the work. However, the analysis of the survey and the results can be accomplished by following a few simple techniques.

A survey can take many forms. In an obvious survey the customer is aware of being asked for information by the company. An obvious survey can be done by asking questions through the mail, on the phone, or face to face. A hidden survey can be conducted by disguising the survey as something else. For example, the warranty cards included with each appliance purchased contain questions about you, where you bought the appliance, and why you chose that particular brand. The warranty card makes the survey seem to be part of applying for the warranty, but in reality it is gathering valuable market information.

The construction of a survey revolves around a set of goals the company has established. These goals specify the type of information a company needs from the survey. Ideally, these goals are the minimal amount of information needed to make critical marketing and internal operation decisions.

For example, suppose that your company makes clock radios. There are plenty of clock radio makers in the world, so the market is saturated. In addition, several brands are produced by companies with strong brand name recognition by consumers. Therefore, you will need to detect an unmet need of the marketplace to create a market share for your product.

To find this need, you decide to construct a survey for potential customers. Naturally, proper sample selection is critical for the validity of the survey. This step requires the services of an expert. In this case, you buy a list of names of current clock radio owners. A representative sample is drawn from the list.

The survey itself can be formed from three types of questions: nominal, ordinal, and open.

1. *Nominal*: Nominal data is information that can be placed into a distinct category. Examples include a person's gender, age, education, and company. Usually, nominal questions establish the background and classification of the person answering the survey. This allows the surveyor to group results by specific categories, such as region of the country, age group, or income.

2. *Ordinal:* An ordinal question asks respondents to rank their feelings toward a particular subject. The rankings can then be summarized and analyzed statistically. An example of an ordinal question is "When setting the time on your current clock radio, do you find the procedure to be

Difficult   1   2   3   4   5   Easy

By choosing a ranking for the degree of difficulty, the respondent is quantifying his or her feelings about a particular model of clock radio.

3. *Open:* An open question allows the respondent to freely express an answer. For example, "What I like best about my clock radio is _____." Such a question is used sparingly, since the consistency of answers will probably vary widely. However, the answers can still be classified using a method called the *Q-sort.* In Q-sorting a panel of judges reads each answer and selects an appropriate category, such as "ease of use," "convenient," or "decorative." By comparing how well several judges match the sorting of the responses, you can be assured of the validity of classifications.

How to Use Statistical Methods
for Reporting Survey Results

All survey results produce raw data. As stated previously, raw data by itself is not an efficient use of numbers. Statistical summaries and analysis enhance understanding of the data.

Step 1: Tabulate the survey data.

A simple summary of the tabulated survey data is the first step in analyzing any survey. Consider the example of the clock radio manufacturer. Assume that this is your company and it produced a survey of existing clock radio owners, obtaining the following results concerning the quality of the competing clocks.

Quality of the Product

	No. Responding	%
Very good	43	39.1
Good	32	29.1
Average	12	10.9
Bad	9	8.2
Very bad	3	2.7
Don't know	11	10.0
	Total	100%

Notice that the survey's ordinal scale for quality also includes a category for "don't know." This allows people without an opinion to be counted.

Even with this simple summary it is interesting to note that about as many people were unsure of the quality as those that rated their current clock radios below average in quality. The majority of current clock owners find their clocks of good quality. This tells you that your product will have to be of high quality just to compete with the other clock radio makers.

Step 2: Analyze a summary of customer survey data using chi-square.

As a further step in analysis, you could compare internal information against the results of the survey. For example, suppose that the clock radio maker had been collecting warranty cards from its own customers that asked questions similar to those in the market survey. Specifically, assume that the same quality question is also on the warranty card. Then a direct comparison could be made between the two sets of information.

	Original Survey	Warranty Information
Very good	39.1%	42%
Good	29.1	22
Average	10.9	14
Bad	8.2	12
Very bad	2.7	5
Don't know	10.0	5

On the surface, the answers appear to agree. However, there is a statistical test to see if the pattern of answers for the first survey matches the pattern for the second survey. This test is called the chi-square, and it tests for differences between patterns.

The formula for the chi-square is

$$\chi^2 = \sum \frac{(F_o - F_e)^2}{F_e}$$

where F_o = frequency observed
F_e = frequency expected
χ^2 = chi-square

The results of the first survey would be the pattern we would have observed. The warranty survey was collected first, so it represents the expected pattern of response.

	F_o	F_e	F_o-F_e	$(F_o$-$F_e)^2$
Very good	39.1%	42%	−2.9	8.41
Good	29.1	22	7.1	50.41
Average	10.9	14	−3.1	9.61
Bad	8.2	12	−3.8	14.44
Very bad	2.7	5	−2.3	5.29
Don't know	10.0	5	5.0	25.00

The chi-square works by subtracting the expected frequency from the observed frequency. The results are the differences between the two patterns of numbers. These differences are then squared, creating the fourth column. These numbers are then divided by the original expected frequency for each row.

$(F_o$-$F_e)2/F_e$
0.20
2.29
0.69
1.20
1.06
5.00

10.44   Total = χ^2 (chi)

The total of these calculations is the chi-square. All that remains is to look up the critical value at a 90% confidence level in Appendix C for the degrees of freedom involved. The degrees of freedom for this version of the chi-square test are

$$df = k - 1$$

where k = the number of categories

Therefore

$$df = 6 - 1 = 5$$

The 90% confidence limit is used in most survey work because of the high variations that are typical when a large group of people respond to a question. Looking in Appendix C for critical chi-square values for this problem reveals a critical value of 9.24. Since our chi-square was 10.44, the critical value is exceeded and we assume that the two patterns do not match. Had the results been less than the critical value, we would assume that the two patterns in the two surveys matched statistically. In either case, we say that we have 90% confidence in these results.

Examining the original data reveals interesting comparisons, such as that 64% of the warranty respondents found the clock radio quality to be above average, while 68.2% of the owners of other clock radios rated them above average. Your conclusion might be that your company has strong competition because your product is not seen as having superior quality over other brands.

How to Summarize Raw Survey Data More Effectively Using a Contingency Table

A frequent criticism of surveys is that they do not adequately represent the general population. In other words, the sample of respondents is not representative of the market. A contingency table is a powerful tool of statistics to portray representation.

The first step is to list the socioeconomic factors that define the population of interest. For the clock radio maker, we will assume that they decided that gender and age are important factors involved in the purchasing of clock radios. Perhaps a general market survey published in a trade magazine indicates that more women than men buy clock radios. Further, the company may have information that older people prefer clock radios over other appliance purchases. Therefore, you would want to make sure that the age and gender of the people in the sample match the general population.

The second step is to form a contingency table. A contingency table is a comparison of two or more factors through crosstabulation. The following example illustrates how a contingency table is formed. By looking up census data on the population you are interested in, you can find the proportion of people in various groups. We will assume that the population of the region being sampled has the following distribution.

Male's age:	Under 18	9%
	18–64	30%
	65+	10%
Female's age:	Under 18	9%
	18–64	30%
	65+	12%

Crosstabulating this data creates a contingency table.

		Age			
		Under 18	**18–64**	**65+**	**Total**
Sex	Male	9%	30%	10%	48%
	Female	9%	30%	12%	52%
	Total	18%	60%	22%	100%

Notice that the crosstabulation of the two factors allows you to find new information, such as the fact that 60% of the population is between 18 and 64 years of age or that over half of the population is female.

The preceding contingency table creates the pattern to expect in the population. To test the validity of the survey sample, the same groups are crosstabulated to create the observed pattern. In the survey by the clock radio maker, the following number of respondents was counted in each group.

Male:	Under 18	45
	18–64	140
	65+	7
Female:	Under 18	56
	18–64	67
	65+	8
Total:		323

Naturally, these numbers will have to be converted into percentages for comparison to the population's contingency table.

$$\text{percentage} = \left(\frac{\text{number}}{\text{total}}\right) \times 100$$

The resulting percentages are

Group		Number	Percent
Male:	Under 18	45	13.9
	18–64	140	43.3
	65+	7	2.3
Female:	Under 18	56	17.3
	18–64	67	20.7
	65+	8	2.5

How to Ensure That Customer Survey Data Reflects Reality: Using a Chi-Square Analysis

To conduct the chi-square analysis, the column of percentages just calculated is used as the observed column. The population's proportions are the expected column. The rest of the chi-square calculation proceeds as before.

F_o	F_e	F_o-F_e	$(F_o-F_e)^2$	$\dfrac{F_o - F_e}{F_e}$
13.9	9	4.9	24.01	2.67
43.3	30	13.3	176.89	5.90
2.3	10	−7.7	59.29	5.93
17.3	9	8.3	68.89	7.65
20.7	30	−9.3	86.49	2.88
2.5	12	−9.5	90.25	7.52
			Total	32.55

The degrees of freedom for a chi-square between contingency tables are calculated differently.

$$df = (\text{rows} - 1) \times (\text{columns} - 1)$$

In other words, it is one less than the number of rows in the contingency table times one less the number of columns. Since we had two rows and three columns in our table, the degrees of freedom are 2.

$$df = (2 - 1) \times (3 - 1) = 2$$

Looking up the critical chi-square for two degrees of freedom at 90% confidence in Appendix C, we find a value of 4.60. Our chi-square total was 32.55, which easily exceeds the critical value. Clearly, the two contingency tables do not match. Thus, the sample does not represent the general population from which it was drawn. This means that the validity of the survey data can be questioned.

Conclusion

As we have seen in this chapter, a company can easily collect quantitative data on the needs and requirements of customers. However, this is only a brief introduction into the possibilities of surveying. Companies that are more interested in gathering intelligence on the external environment should hire experts in this field. The manufacturing professionals within the company should know about the techniques of surveying so that such a person can discriminate between valid and sloppy data.

CHAPTER 13

How to Increase the Safety of Your Products and Manufacturing Processes Using Statistical Methods

Safety is usually handled by departments such as industrial safety, product assurance, safety systems engineering, and product liability. Despite the impression this leaves that safety has many facets, safety is the same issue no matter who is in charge. The possibility of harm to employees from unsafe manufacturing processes is the same competitive risk as the possible harm to a customer from an unsafe product. Thus, the same statistically based methods of risk assessment/risk reduction can be used by any safety-related function. Plant safety and product liability are separated in this chapter for illustrative purposes only.

How to Judge the Safety of Your Plant

Typically, industrial safety departments are responsible for making sure that common-sense practices and the safety practices mandated by law are implemented in the manufacturing area. This could include functions such as ensuring the proper disposal of wastes, the wearing of safety glasses, and the installment of shields on machinery. It also includes worker and management education to make safety awareness a high priority of any job. Therefore, the industrial safety department usually collects statistics on the rate and types of accidents at the plant and in the industry as a whole.

This traditional practice of the industrial safety department looking back at what has happened and trying to prevent its recurrence is the mistaken stereotype of safety departments. It is more important for a safety professional to study upcoming products, practices, and processes to suggest ways to prevent accidents.

Safety engineering works like a backward version of reliability engineering. A reliability engineer examines each component of a product and evaluates its reliability. Then these are added together to estimate the reliability of the entire product. A safety engineer would look at a product as a collection of risks and then try to trace each risk back to its source. Later we will show how this process works.

A safety engineer performs a thankless task. Unlike the other engineering functions discussed so far, it is very difficult for a safety engineer to document the cost reduction of an accident that never occurred because of the safety measures that were adopted. Furthermore, when accidents do occur and the safety engineer has to trace and eliminate the causes, the entire process is extremely expensive.

How to Collect and Summarize Safety Statistics: Using Accident and Injury Reports

We will only briefly describe how statistics are gathered, analyzed, and presented after the fact. Anyone that has worked in a manufacturing plant is familiar with the posted accident reports and the signs that say how many days since the last accident. These are supposedly present to increase safety awareness. However, this is only a minor function of the safety department and will be covered accordingly.

The typical system of collecting safety statistics is to require the reporting of all accidents and injuries at work. These can range from minor cuts and pulled muscles to fatal injuries or disabilities. The traditional method for giving each injury its appropriate magnitude was to report the type of injury and the number of labor hours lost as a result.

For example, a cut finger might take 15 minutes out of a worker's day to get a bandage from the industrial nurse. Thus, the labor hour loss is only 0.25. In contrast, a broken leg could remove a worker from the job for six weeks. Six times the 40-hour work week represents a labor hour loss of 240.

Sometimes the accident and injury report in a plant is posted by type of accident, cause, and loss of labor hours.

Injury	Cause	Lost Labor Hours
Hurt back	Improper lifting	10
Hurt back	Fell on ice	10
Cut fingers	Caught on conveyer rollers	2
Broken leg	Fell off lift truck	100

Such a summary is fine for tracking what has already occurred, but these statistics must be analyzed for their root causes. This is done through the use of crosstabulation tables. Crosstabulation tables compare two or more factors on a single grid, as shown in chapter 12.

The first step in creating a crosstabulation table for accident statistics is to make the raw data relevant to the situations involved. Consider the example of investigating whether the shift or department accident rates are equal. If they are unequal, you know that as manufacturing manager you need to schedule further training and safety awareness programs on the affected shift.

The first step is to form an accident rate based on the lost labor hours versus the total labor hours of work involved. For example, a small department may only assign a total of 2,000 labor hours per month. The accident rate would then be a proportion of labor hours lost to accidents divided by the total labor hours in the department.

$$\text{accident rate} = \frac{\text{lost labor hours}}{\text{total labor hours}}$$

Suppose that the small department with 2,000 labor hours per month has a single accident during that month that results in 20 lost labor hours. The accident rate is 0.01.

$$\text{accident rate} = \frac{20}{2,000} = 0.01$$

A second department with 10,000 monthly labor hours has several accidents that result in 400 lost labor hours. Its rate is 0.04. To compare the departments by shift, you create a three-by-four array with the accident rates of each department's shift recorded in the appropriate location.

| | Shift | | |
Department	First	Second	Third
Press room	0.02	0.05	0.01
Paint	0.00	0.01	0.00
Assembly	0.20	0.30	0.20
Machine shop	0.10	0.10	0.12

Using this method, you can see quickly that second-shift assembly has the highest accident rate. Naturally, preventive investigations would begin there. In addition, it is possible to compute totals for each shift and each department. You need only the labor hours and lost hours for each group.

For example, the machine shop has 10,000 labor hours first shift, 5,000 second shift, and 2,000 third shift. The lost hours for the same shifts are 1,000, 500, and 240 respectively. Therefore the total accident rate for the machine shop is

$$\text{accident rate} = \frac{(1{,}000 + 500 + 240)}{(10{,}000 + 5{,}000 + 2{,}000)} = 0.102$$

Calculating such totals would indicate departments with unusually high accident rates. A two-way analysis of variance could also complete the analysis of larger crosstabulation tables.

Additional crosstabulation tables could be created to investigate other possible associations with accident rates. For example, you could compare the hours performing a job before an accident occurred to the severity of the accident, the time of day, and the accident rate, or the seniority of the workers versus the accident rate.

How to Calculate the Rate of Accident Incidence

The Occupational Safety and Health Act (OSHA) sets forth a standard method for reporting the incidence of accidents on the job.

$$\text{incidence rate} = \frac{(\text{total of all accidents} \times 200{,}000)}{\text{total hours}}$$

The 200,000 figure represents a standard of 100 employees working full time for one year. The total hours represent the total number of work hours for all employees over a one-year period. The total of all accidents includes those that did not result in a loss of work hours. Therefore, the incidence rate will be different than the accident rates calculated earlier.

For example, assume that a company suffered 18 accidents over a one year period and it had 250 full-time employees. The average full-time employee works about 2,000 hours a year. This represents total labor hours for the plant as 500,000. Thus, the incidence rate is calculated as

$$\text{incidence rate} = \frac{(18 \times 200{,}000)}{500{,}000} = 7.2$$

This means that there were 7.2 accidents per every 100 employees during the year. The 200,000 in the numerator of the equation converts the rate into a per-100-employees standard. Naturally, this rate can also be calculated for shorter or longer periods of time to match other nonsafety statistics. In either case, this is the rate that a company reports to OSHA. Other methods of calculating safety for internal improvement plans are equally valid for internal use.

Using Statistical Methods to Discover Possible Routes Toward Accident Prevention

Whether within the plant or in the customer's home, accident prevention is the number-one job of any safety related function. Preventive measures can involve several different tasks, such as education, design review, audits, labor negotiations, and accident investigations.

How to Find the Potential Source of an Accident Using Fault-Tree Analysis

The most common statistical method used is called *fault-tree analysis.* Fault-tree analysis involves the tracing of a potential accident back to its root causes.

The following example illustrates how the procedure works. Consider the case of the product review of a proposed design for a motor scooter. Motor scooters are popular transportation products, but they have many of the safety hazards of any two-wheel vehicle. For example, riders of two-wheel vehicles have been injured when wheels lose stability. There are various possible causes for this loss of stability, such as the rider hitting a patch of sand on a curve.

Step 1: List the potential hazards.

The first step in fault-tree analysis is to list every potential hazard of the current motor scooter design. These are broken down by the basic systems that make up the scooter.

> Engine
> Steering
> Brakes
> Electrical
> Cargo
> Styling

Step 2: Break down each hazard into components.

For our example, we will look at the braking system. Each part of the braking system is listed, such as cables, springs, pads, calipers, drums, and discs. For each of these parts another list is made of the potential hazards that could result.

Braking System

                    Brake Pads

                                      Failure from wear
                                        Failure from oil leak
                                        Failure from wetness
                                        Seizure from cracks
                                        Failure because of
                                              other parts failing

---

The more complex the product, the longer the final list.

Step 3: Establish specific hazard rates for each potential cause.

Now your job is to investigate the potential hazards that are most likely to happen. This information is partially based on reliability reports and partially on accident reports for similar products. Consider the example of the brakes failing because of wetness. This could occur because the rider forded a body of water, because it was raining, or because the scooter had just been washed. Logic dictates that most often the brakes become wet because of rain.

Step 4: Estimate the occurrence of specific accidents by using fault-tree data.

To determine the chance that rain will eventually cause an accident, the probability of each step towards an accident is drawn out on a fault tree chart. For example, the first step is to measure how often it is raining and then the chance that someone will ride in the rain, need the brakes, and experience a failure that causes an accident.

% Days it Rains

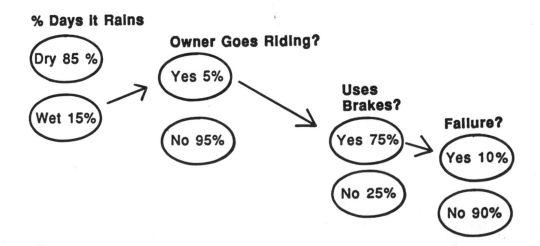

To experience an accident during a rainy day, the rider must decide to go riding, need the brakes, and experience a failure. The probability of this occurring is the product of each step probability.

$$\text{accident} = 0.15 \times 0.05 \times 0.75 \times 0.10 = 0.0005625$$

This may seem like a very low chance of an accident, but it must be multiplied by the number of riders that would own the scooter. If the manufacturer assumes that 10,000 people will own the scooter during the first year of production, then 5.625 riders (actually rounded to 6) will experience an accident due to wet brakes. It is now up to the liability people to determine whether this is a tolerable risk. Studies have shown that the public will willingly accept a risk as high as a once-in-one-million chance. This example's 6 in 10,000 chance is well above an assume tolerance.

Step 5: Improve the design of the product.

If your company's management decides that the scooter will have to be improved before production, the same fault-tree chart can point to opportunities for improvement. Each step can be evaluated to see if the manufacturer can decrease the risks. For example, there is nothing the manufacturer can do about the weather, so there will always be the 15% chance of rain. A rider education program telling owners not to ride in the rain would be very expensive and of limited effectiveness. However, sealing the brake area against moisture is a comparatively inexpensive design change. If the failure rate due to wetness was cut in half because of the design change, then the overall accident rate, in this case, would also drop by half.

$$\text{accident} = 0.15 \times 0.05 \times 0.75 \times 0.05 = 0.0002812$$

This represents about three accidents due to wet brakes for every 10,000 riders. This risk is still too high for the company. Therefore, engineering must be consulted to find a better design that presents less risk—for example, the use of a dual rear wheel to minimize skids during wet conditions.

How to Reduce the Risk of an Accident Using Hazard Analysis

Specific hazards can be investigated independently of the entire system. This is called *hazard analysis*, and it is different from fault-tree analysis. Fault-tree analysis is used when a series of events must occur for a hazard to be present. Hazard analysis looks at conditions that are constantly at risk. For our example, we will investigate the hazards associated with the engine on a scooter. Because a two-cycle engine uses flammable liquids and high pressures with many moving parts, several hazards are always present.

Step 1: Rank the hazard by severity.

Each hazard is not of equal potential severity. For example, the engine stalling out may cause an inconvenience, but it is unlikely to cause an accident. However, an engine fire could burn the rider. Therefore, there is a need to weight each hazard according to its severity. The traditional scale of hazards is

Negligible: annoying, but no real hazard to the consumer
Marginal: might cause injury or damage but can be controlled
Critical: will cause injury or damage
Catastrophic: will cause severe injury, damage, or death

The magnitude of each of these can be weighted by a sliding scale that best matches the particular situation. In our example, the following scale is used.

Negligible = 1 point
Marginal = 2 points
Critical = 5 points
Catastrophic = 10 points

The resulting hazard analysis may look like this.

Component	Hazard	Hazard Weight
Engine	Gasoline explosion	10
	Gasoline fire	5
	Burn from hot parts	5
	Engine kick-back	2
	General failure	1
	Stalling	1

Step 2: Calculate the hazard of a particular situation.

These weighted problems can then be used to calculate the actual hazard a potential customer may experience. The formula is the product of the severity of the hazard, the frequency of occurrence, and the life of the product.

$$hazard = Kft$$

where K = severity rating of the hazard
f = frequency the hazard occurs
t = average life span of the product

In our example, we can evaluate the hazard of an engine fire by assuming that the average scooter is ridden for 500 hours and that there is a one-in-a-million chance of an engine fire.

$$\text{hazard} = 5 \times \frac{1}{1,000,000} \times 500 = 0.0025$$

Step 3: Evaluate the risk to the population of consumers.

Multiplying this by the expected 10,000 riders for the first year yields a total hazard of an engine fire of 25 riders. Again, this would have to be evaluated by the company's management for the acceptability of the risk. In this case, the risk is too high because the possibility of serious injury and damages to the company is all but certain.

How to Find the Root Cause of Accidents Using Correlation Analysis

One of the main philosophies of safety engineering is that you can prevent a safety problem by eliminating its causes. For example, the safety of the workplace depends on a countless number of factors. However, some of these factors are known or can be easily discovered. Simple correlation analysis can uncover an association between an existing condition and a safety problem.

A classic safety question provides an excellent illustration. Many plant supervisors believe that employees are least alert after break time. They have relaxed their bodies and senses, and they are usually still digesting their food. Therefore, the overall alertness of the work force is diminished slightly. The question is whether this assumed drop in alertness results in more accidents.

To test for the association, you begin by forming a frequency distribution of accidents by time of occurrence. By examining past accident reports, you record how long after the most recent break time each accident occurred. For example, if lunch is from 12:00 to 12:30, and an accident occurred at 12:45, then it occurred 15 minutes after the last break.

If there is little association between break time and an accident, the distribution of the times should be fairly even. Assume that the following numbers were recorded.

Time after Break	Number of Accidents
0 to 15 min.	17
15 to 30	11
30 to 45	3
45 to 60	2
60 to 75	0
75 to 90	5
	Total 38

This frequency distribution would quickly show that most accidents occur within 30 minutes of break time. In fact, nearly three-quarters of all accidents have occurred in that time span. Therefore, you and the safety department need to deploy countermeasures to ensure that employees are alert after break times.

How to Determine Your Company's Liability for Your Products Using Statistical Methods

Measuring potential risk against possible financial loss is the responsibility of the production liability staff. The major task of such a group is to reduce the vulnerability of a company to lawsuits. This involves the documentation of safety testing and engineering changes, the improvement of operating instructions, and the evaluation of lawsuits on similar products.

In addition, product liability personnel have found that statistical analysis can be a cost-reducing ally in preventing liability problems. By the time a lawsuit is seen by the liability group, the picture of risk has become cloudy. For every lawsuit filed, there are usually dozens of complaints made by customers who do not sue, and hundreds of other pieces of information related to the risk that are reported to other departments. Therefore, when many lawsuits have been filed and a liability person sees a problem, the problem is severe and atypical.

Therefore, liability-sensitive managers are turning their attention to prevention by studying the same data used for hazard analysis. Consider the motor scooter example again to examine engine fire hazard. Suppose that the engineering department wanted to know what hazard rates for various components would be the highest tolerable to prevent lawsuits.

Step 1: Collect historic data.

Using the motor scooter data collected earlier, you begin by collecting data on the number of lawsuits filed by cause. Such data could form the following table.

Cause of Suit	Number	Awards
Brake failure	2	$ 59,000
Engine fire	1	$100,000
Falling from scooter	5	$125,000
Personal injury (not falls)	1	$ 30,000

The first piece of interesting information obtained is that engine fire suits result in the highest damages awarded. This information will be used later.

Step 2: Relate the data to the frequency of complaints.

The next step is to search for any data related to people complaining about the same problems that resulted in these lawsuits. The assumption is that more people complain than actually file lawsuits. Hopefully, the number of complaints will roughly match the incidence of hazards. If you know how often a problem actually occurs and how many complaints will turn into lawsuits, you can set the hazard rate specification.

To find the needed information, you can compile warranty data, repair records from the dealers, and complaints submitted to the company. Next, the duplicate reports are eliminated. The resulting information is added to the lawsuit table.

Step 3: Calculate the proportion of lawsuits to complaints.

The proportion of complaints resulting in a lawsuit is calculated using the following formula.

$$\text{proportion} = \frac{\text{number of lawsuits}}{\text{number of complaints}}$$

Thus, the following table is created.

Cause of Suit	No. of Suits	No. of Complaints	Proportion
Brake failure	2	212	0.0094
Engine fire	1	19	0.0526
Falling from scooter	5	89	0.0562
Personal injury (not falls)	1	14	0.0714

These proportions of lawsuits to complaints are then used to calculate specifications for hazard rates. Management must decide on the maximum number of lawsuits it can tolerate. Zero is not an answer, because there is no way to eliminate the possibility of a lawsuit.

Therefore, suits with potentially high damage awards are usually set to a low number.

Step 4: Establish your tolerance to liability exposure.

Consider the risk of an engine fire. If management decides that only one lawsuit per year can be tolerated, then the following formula can be used to set the hazard rate specification:

$$\text{hazard rate} = \frac{\text{lawsuit tolerance}}{\text{population} \times \text{proportion}}$$

where the population represents the total customer base (in this case the number of riders) and proportion is the ratio of lawsuits to complaints.

Using the foregoing data,

$$\text{hazard rate (engine fires)} = \frac{1}{10,000 \times 0.0526} = 0.0019$$

We are assuming a riding population of 10,000. As we discovered in the hazard analysis conducted earlier, the probability of an engine fire was 0.0025. Thus, this risk is still too high if the target is to restrict the number of lawsuits to one. The same formula can be repeated for the other potential hazards, such as riders falling off the scooters and injuring themselves.

$$\text{hazard rate (falls)} = \frac{2}{10,000 \times 0.0562} = 0.0036$$

In this example, we are assuming that the company can tolerate up to two lawsuits per year. Therefore, the total of hazard rates for malfunctions that can result in a fall should be less than 0.0036.

Other tests liability specialists can conduct to prevent lawsuits include reliability testing until failure, examining the use of a product, testing the product for potential misuse, and measuring the effectiveness of the operating instructions.

How to Evaluate Product Safety Improvements by Using Chi-Square Calculations

The following example illustrates how any of these tests can be conducted. Suppose you are the manufacturing manager of a company that makes a children's swing set and wants to test the product for safety problems before it is placed on the market. The company would give product testers prototypes of the swing set and tell them to record even the slightest problems with assembly or use.

You would then compile a table of recorded problems.

Problem	Frequency Reported
Swing chain breaks	22
Pinched fingers	19
Difficulty in assembly	5
Collapses	3
Tips over	1
Hard to oil	1

You would then interview each of the participants to learn in greater detail the circumstances surrounding each complaint. For example, the participants may discover that the breaking chains on the swing are a result of misuse, such as several children trying to swing at the same time. This information is fed back to the engineers so that the potential problems are designed out of the swing set.

A new group of product testers is selected and given the modified swing set. Again, the same information is gathered and compared to the previous frequencies.

Problem	Frequency Old Design	New Design
Swing chain breaks	22	12
Pinched fingers	19	3
Difficulty in assembly	5	1
Collapses	3	0
Tips over	1	1
Hard to oil	1	0

A simple chi-square calculation (see chapter 12) can be used to see if the change in the frequency of problems is statistically significant. The old design would be the expected frequency. The new design would be the frequency observed.

F_o	F_e	$F_o - F_e$	$(F_o - F_e)^2$	$\dfrac{(F_o - F_e)^2}{F_e}$
12	22	−10	100	4.54
3	19	−16	256	13.47
1	5	−4	16	3.20
0	3	−3	9	3.00
1	1	0	0	0.00
0	1	−1	1	1.00
			Total	25.21

The degrees of freedom for this test are five ($df = n - 1$). Using the values in Appendix C and assuming a 95% confidence level, the critical chi-square value is 11.07. Clearly, our chi-square total of 25.21 exceeds this amount. Therefore, the improvements in the swing set have significantly changed the incidence of problems. The next step would be to determine whether the new predicted accident rates were too high. If so, then further redesign and testing would be conducted.

The records of these tests and the redesigns are retained. They have enormous value in the defense against a product liability lawsuit. When properly conducted, statistical tests such as these demonstrate that the company took elaborate precautions to find, eliminate, and warn customers of potential dangers.

Conclusion

Neither safety nor liability professionals are helpless to prevent safety-related problems. Besides the methods learned through experience, statistics can play a role in predicting possible problems and helping a company to design better products and processes. By understanding these techniques and participating in their usage, a manufacturing manager can play an active role in assuring the safety of both workers and consumers.

CHAPTER 14

Problem-Solving Work Teams: How to Join Human Skills and Statistical Methods to Become a World-Class Manufacturer

To become a world-class manufacturer, you must encourage all employees to work together in teams dedicated to solving specific problems while searching for competitive opportunities. For the purpose of simplicity, we will call these groups *problem-solving work teams.*

In general, any statistical method can be used as a tool for problem solving. However, there are simple techniques that make the use of statistical techniques as applied by groups more efficient. These techniques are designed to focus thinking and communication on the problem at hand. This chapter reviews those methods. Many of the complementary statistical techniques have already been discussed in this book. The methods are now a part of the problem-solving process.

The methods presented have two primary benefits. First, they improve the ability of team members to communicate among themselves using standard tools of analysis. Second, they allow a team to evaluate both the problems at hand and the effectiveness of their proposed solutions. This ability to both communicate and evaluate is invaluable for convincing management that change is necessary in the manufacturing area.

The Problem-Solving Cycle: The Key to Merging Statistics with Team Efforts

Although there are several schools of thought on the actual steps taken in problem solving, most fall into the pattern presented here. Once a problem-solving work team is formed, it is critical that clear communication about the task at hand be established, that specific goals be set, that information about the situation be collected, that success be tested for its effectiveness, and that solutions be exploited for their potential. The following six-step method puts these activities into a logical and progressive order.

Step 1: Identify the problem.

Suppose that you have been selected to lead a team of workers from the welding area of a bicycle manufacturing plant. You have been assigned the task of examining the environment of the welding area and drawing up a list of potential problems to solve. Your team would then be responsible for working with management to locate potential solutions to problems and opportunities for manufacturing improvements.

Your team would first obtain from management a list of the criteria to follow when selecting potential projects. These criteria help the team to avoid attacking problems beyond their means, such as labor complaints, and to avoid wasting time on trivial activities. The team lists and clarifies the remaining range of appropriate projects. Once a final list of potential projects is created, the team votes on the first problem to attack. For illustrative purposes, assume that they selected bad welds as their project. In some companies, management might form these teams and assign specific problems for improvement efforts.

Step 2: Evaluate the problem.

The next step is to define the selected project in more detail. In our example, bad welds does not tell us the magnitude or nature of the problem. Therefore, the team would identify, gather, and present data about the problem. For example, they could measure and report that the largest part of the problem is that almost a third of the welds made are rejected in later testing.

Part of this evaluation process is to quantify a baseline of the current situation. A baseline is the key statistic that identifies the current level of the problem. For example, one-third of the welds being defective could be used as a baseline of the problem. The variations in the daily quality of welds would complement the baseline information. Thus, the team would have a standard to compare improvements against.

Step 3: Select possible solutions.

At this point, your problem-solving team lists potential causes of the problems and their possible solutions. Further statistical analysis and other technical investigations help the team to better identify those potential solutions that would have a meaningful effect. Then the team elects which solution to try first, second, third, and so on. This is their action list—a list of actions the team will implement in an attempt to correct the selected problem.

Step 4: Take action.

Suppose that the welding group chooses to issue a welding standard for all welders. The welders would be briefly trained on the appearance of a proper weld, and several examples of such a weld would be posted around the area. After this action is implemented, it is up to the problem-solving team to track the reaction of their baseline data to the new method. Therefore, the team continues to collect weld rejection data before, during, and after the new welding standard is implemented.

Step 5: Evaluate the results.

The team summarizes the situation after each action is tried, and it is then compared to the baseline. In the case of the welders, the percentage of welds rejected a few weeks after the new welding standard was implemented is compared to the percentage at the time the team was formed. If the percentage has dropped significantly, then the action is seen as an improvement. If no improvement is detected, this still represents important information. The team now knows that a welding standard has little effect on the quality of welds.

Step 6: Pursue continuous improvement.

No matter what the results of the action taken by the team, the results are noted and the next action is attempted. Thus, the team slowly builds up knowledge of which methods work and which do not. Typically, the original problem is slowly improved until further attention by the team is not needed. Thus, the next most important problem is selected and attacked. In short, the problem-solving cycle never ends. The teams continue to find and attack problems. To date, no team in manufacturing has reported running out of problems to solve.

How to Identify, Quantify, Compare, and Evaluate a Problem Using Statistical Problem-Solving Tools

Traditional problem-solving methods include Pareto analysis, flowcharts, histograms, control charts, scattergrams, and cost/benefit analysis. Combined with nonstatistical methods, such as cause-and-effect charts, these methods represent a toolbox for identifying, quantifying, comparing, and evaluating selected problems. The following examples show how these simple methods are used over an extended period of time as the eyes and ears of the problem-solving teams.

How to Rank the Causes of Appearance Problems of Newly Delivered Cars Using Pareto Analysis

Pareto analysis is based on an idea called the Pareto principle. That principle states that any set of problems will have a large number of trivial elements and a few critical elements. In other words, two or three problems in a manufacturing company usually account for the majority of the losses the company suffers.

There are two types of Pareto analysis. The first attempt to finds the most frequently occurring problems in a company, departments or for a specific product. The second type, called true Pareto, examines each problem and ranks problems according to their economic impact. The difference between the two methods can be illustrated easily.

Consider the example of an automobile manufacturer that is receiving many complaints from car dealers about the quality of the cars when they arrive at the showroom. To quantify the complaint, the automotive maker would send audit teams to the showrooms to examine the actual quality problems. Defects such as dirt, scratches, dents, rust, and so on would be noted.

The count of the defects would be translated into a frequency distribution and a bar chart of the frequency of each problem. For example, suppose that the automotive audit teams found the following number of defects.

Type of Defect	Number of Defects
Dirt	340
Scratches	129
Dents	48
Rust	11
Oil marks	7
Paint fades	6
Bad stripes	3
Fit & finish of doors	1
Paint chips	1

Notice that the first two defects are the vital few we discussed earlier. The remaining defects occur less frequently. The Pareto chart is just a bar chart of these same frequencies (see Figure 14-1).

An economic Pareto analysis would look at the economy of these same defects. For example, the company may wish to know the economic loss from each defect. That is, dirt is easily removed, but scratches costs much more to fix. Therefore, a second column is formed to judge the cost for fixing the defects listed.

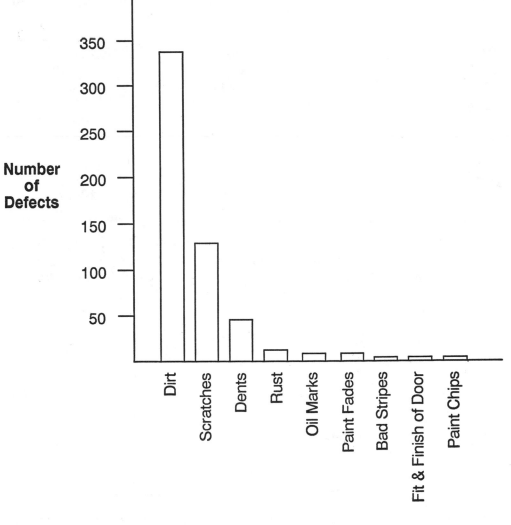

Figure 14-1: Pareto chart of the defects found on new cars.

Defect	Number	Cost/Defects
Dirt	340	$0.25
Scratches	129	4.00
Dents	48	6.00
Rust	11	10.00
Oil marks	7	0.45
Paint fades	6	9.00
Bad stripes	3	5.00
Fit & finish of doors	1	100.00
Paint chips	1	5.00

By multiplying the cost to correct the defect by the number of defects found, you establish the economy of the problem. Note that performing this multiplication for each of the defects, you have created a different order of magnitude.

Defect	Total Cost
Scratches	$516.00
Dents	288.00
Rust	110.00
Fit & finish of doors	100.00
Dirt	85.00
Paint fades	54.00
Bad stripes	15.00
Paint chips	5.00
Oil marks	3.15

Dirt, the former top defect, is now pushed down to fifth place because it is easily corrected. This same approach could be expanded by continuing to multiply the results by other factors, such as the severity of the defect.

Pareto analysis in either form is good for evaluating the number and magnitude of defects, or other factors, causing a specific problem. With the information from a Pareto chart, the problem-solving team could select a source of trouble to attack first. In our example, it might be scratches, the most expensive and one of the most frequent problems.

How to Investigate Consumer Dissatisfaction with Color TV Sets Using Pareto Analysis

A manufacturer of electronic consumer products had long used employee-based problem-solving work teams. One of these teams decided to examine the cause of consumer dissatisfaction with their largest selling product, a color TV set.

The work team began by examining complaints from the customer service records, warranty cards, and market research data. A Pareto chart was drawn of the defects that were reported. Interestingly, the highest frequency defect was one that the company did not consider important: small scratches in the plastic cabinet. Since black was a popular color for the cabinet, the scratches were easy for the consumers to detect.

The work team used this information to take corrective action at the point of manufacture. It discovered that most of these scratches were a result of the normal handling and packaging of the TV sets. The team members decided that it was beyond their authority to make major changes in the manufacturing process to reduce the number of times a TV was handled. Therefore, they tried a different idea. They asked purchasing to require the suppliers of the molded cabinets to wrap them in a protective plastic covering.

The plastic clings to the cabinet by static attraction and is removed only by the customer after purchase. Six months after management implemented this change, the new Pareto chart of customer dissatisfaction showed that scratches had dropped from first to tenth place. Clearly, the Pareto chart had identified a problem and recorded the amount of success the team had accomplished in reducing the problem.

How to Find the Cause of a Problem Using Scattergrams

Correlation coefficients and regression analysis are powerful tools for finding associations between two events. However, the statistics involved are usually overwhelming to use, explain, and understand for a work group interested in only a simple investigation of a problem. In contrast, a scattergram can be used as a simple tool for finding associations without leading to statistical analysis (as in chapter 5).

Let us return to the automotive maker as an example. If we look at the two most frequent defects again, scratches and dirt, we see a possible association between the two. Wouldn't a dirty car scratch easier than a clean one?

To find out, the work team could use a scattergram. A scattergram is a simple plotting tool to show the amount of association between two events or factors. In our example, we want to see if dirty cars have more scratches. The work team would have to develop a scale of dirtiness.

Clean car	1
Some dirt	2
Light covering	3
Very dirty	4

First, you would select and examine a sample of cars. If the team could not physically be sent to where the cars are delivered, then your criteria could be sent to selected dealerships for the delivery people to record the quality of the appearance of the cars. Each car would be rated for how dirty it is and the number of scratches it has. Each of these sets of two data points is recorded on a piece of graph paper. The horizontal axis is the dirtiness of the car, and the vertical axis is the number of scratches found (see Figure 14-2). The first car checked was rated a 2 on the dirtiness scale and had three scratches. Therefore, a point is drawn corresponding to 2,3. This is repeated for the other cars in the sample.

Analysis of the chart is simple. If there is no relationship between the two factors, then the points should appear almost randomly on the chart. If an association is present, the points will begin to form a pattern. In our chart, the groups of dots seem to rise as the car gets dirtier. The more dirt there is on a car, the greater the number of scratches.

This type of study was done by a major automotive maker. The company's team studied the relationship between dirty cars and scratches. They, too, found that dirty cars had more scratches. The most likely cause was the result of railroad and automotive dealer employees squeezing alongside the cars while they were on flatcars. The people rubbing up against the cars were grinding any dirt present into the finish.

The corrective action selected was to wash the cars before and after shipment by rail or container ship. A second Pareto chart showed that cleaning the cars resulted in an almost complete elimination of the dirt and scratch problems.

How Evaluate the Extent of a Problem Using a Histogram

As we discussed in chapter 3 and later in chapter 11, the histogram is an important part of a capability study. Its shape and size can determine whether a process is operating as efficiently as possible. It is also possible to use the histogram as a simple tool of communication for evaluating the performance of a manufacturing process. By showing the variation within an existing process visually using a histogram, you, as team leader, can quickly communicate process capability. This also gives you a baseline for measuring improvements. Your goal is to reduce the amount of variation.

Suppose that a work team is looking at the stamping of electrical contacts that are used in switching equipment. The specifications for the contact say that the contact point must be 0.20 inches in diameter, plus or minus 0.02 inches. Naturally, a capability study with *Cpk* ratios could tell us whether the specifications were being met. However, only the histogram would be needed to communicate the capability of this process to a large audience.

Assuming that the work team investigates the contact points by conducting a capability study on 100 parts, they might find the following distribution of measurements.

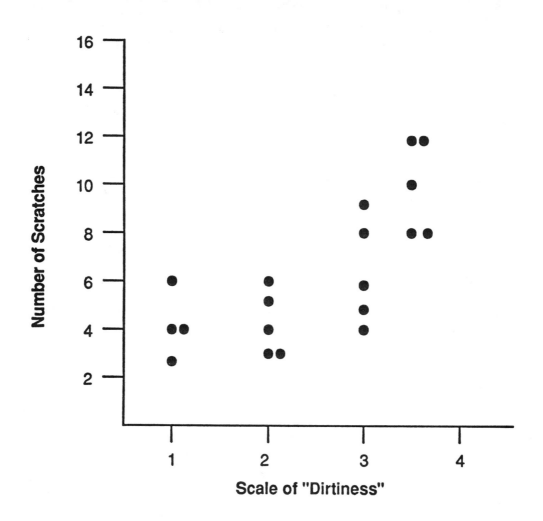

Figure 14-2: Scattergram showing relation between dirt and scratches.

Diameter	Frequency
0.17	3
0.18	11
0.19	19
0.20	43
0.21	23
0.22	1
0.23	0

As you can see, they have measurements both in and out of the specification range of 0.18 to 0.22 inches. However, the first step would be to create a histogram of the process. Figure 14-3 is the resulting histogram, and it shows a distribution with too much variation: that is, some of the diameters are outside of specification. The ideal histogram would approximate a normal curve with all of the measurements well within the tolerances. This variation tells the problem-solving team that capability of the process must be improved. Nonstatistical problem-solving tools such as a cause-and-effect chart or visual inspection of the process logs may be required to trace down the cause of the variation. In this example, we will assume that the team found that the stamping operator would occasionally adjust the stroke height of the stamping press to correct problems with burrs. These changes were both toward longer and shorter stroke height. Thus, not only were burrs eliminated, but undersized contact points resulted from this source of increased variation in the process.

The problem-solving team might have to request an experimental study by engineering to find the stroke height that produced minimum burring and correct point sizes. If such a combination is found and implemented, the problem-solving team can then conduct another capability study and compare the new histogram to the old one. The change in shape and spread in the histogram will indicate the amount of improvement the team has accomplished.

How to Locate Problems and Discover Their Cause Using Defect Maps

A defect map is exactly what it sounds like, a map of where defects occur. It is one of the simplest statistical methods for accumulating and organizing raw data that also can provide instant interpretation. For example, a medical company was once recording where leaks occurred on a pump diaphragm. The leaks all accumulated in one area, thus lending a strong clue as to the cause of the leak.

As another example, assume that the maker of electric stoves has found that several types of visual defects can occur during shipment. Because defects tend to cluster by location due to a common cause, a map of the type and number of defects is the perfect tool of investigation.

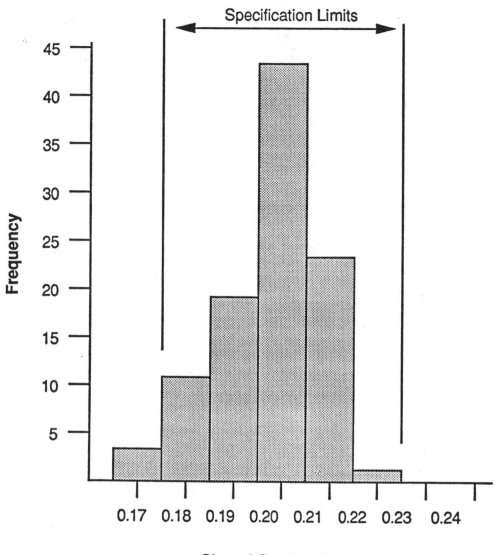

Figure 14-3: Histogram of contact point size capability study.

The problem-solving work team for such a situation would most likely be made up of quality assurance personnel and salespeople. They would be most interested in making sure that the electric stoves reached the customers as free of visual defects as possible.

To accomplish their task, such a work team would have to create a defect checklist that lists defects along with a description of the defect and the severity factor. For example, a scratch is not such a simple defect as it may first appear. Small scratches on hidden surfaces or that are invisible from more than 3 feet away might be called minor scratches. A large scratch across the front of an appliance might be called a major scratch. Thus, even scratches have levels of severity.

To create the map of the defects, the team would audit electric stoves in a randomly selected sample of stores as the units are unpacked from the factory. A simple line drawing of the stove serves as the defect map. A number and a letter are placed at the location of each defect found on the units. The letter identifies the type and severity of the defect. The number represents how many defects were found at this location. After several stoves are inspected, the data from the map is used to draw a finished summary illustration of the resulting data (see Figure 14-4).

Looking at our final map, we can quickly see the power in this technique. To begin with, the team is interested in the location and types of defects from shipping problems. To make their study more valid, they would begin by selecting a sample of stoves at the factory and examining them closely before they are packed and shipped. Then by conducting the same inspection after they are received by a dealer, the team can count the number of additional defects that occurred during the shipping phase.

Assume that they select 30 stoves at random and decide to follow them to their dealer destinations. At the factory, they draw a defect map based on the defects found on the 30 units. The map shows only a few minor defects with none clustering in any particular location. This represents a fairly random occurrence of defects.

However, once they check again at the dealers and subtract the defects already known to exist, they discover a different pattern. The number of defects has climbed to an average of five per unit. The most frequent of the these defects are dents, and they cluster near the lower corners of the appliance. Because of this clustering of dents near corners and the bottom of the units, the problem-solving team has a solid lead on the cause. Because the dents are in one location, the cause should be easy to identify.

Tracing the shipping process backwards, the team quickly finds something that causes contact with the appliance on the corners: a lift truck. After the stoves are packed, a lift truck carries them to a waiting railroad car. The driver of the lift truck cannot see when the stoves are tightly packed together, so he coasts forward in the rail car until the sound of stoves

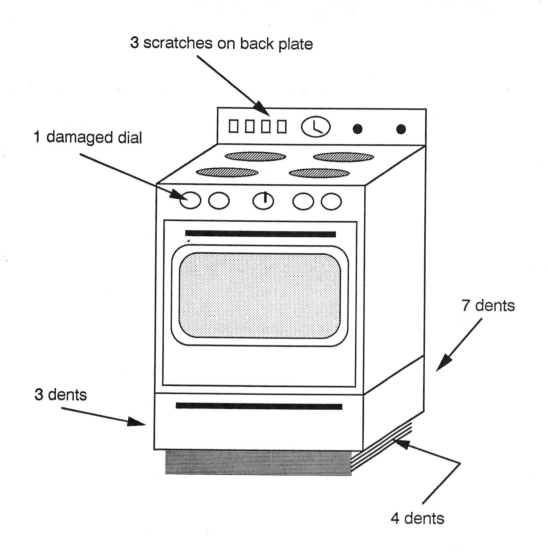

3 scratches on back plate

1 damaged dial

7 dents

3 dents

4 dents

Figure 14-4: Defect map of an electric stove.

being pushed together tells him that the units are tightly packed. This impact causes the dents.

The team eliminates the source of the dents by changing the type of packaging used on the stoves. A wooden rail is attached to the pallet under the stove so that the pallets collide on the rail car instead of the stoves. The reduction in dents can be documented by drawing a new defect map after the implementation of the new pallet design.

How to Describe the Flow of a Manufacturing Process Using Flowcharts

A flowchart is a simple diagram of the production stages of a manufacturing process. It is used as a tool of communication for a problem-solving team. In many cases, a team will be discussing a manufacturing problem without first drawing out the actual steps of production. Thus, some team members are not aware of the relationships of one process to another.

To make the flowchart fully effective, statistics are added. These can range from probability of success to defect rates to capability ratios. The following example illustrates how a flowchart is created and used.

Suppose that a company's turning department has had difficulty meeting the specifications for a flow control nozzle. Several turning operations result in the finished nozzle. However, if any of the operations create unnecessary variation, the final product usually suffers. To see the relationships between operations and variation, a flowchart can be a handy problem-solving tool (see Figure 14-5).

Let us examine the chart more closely to see the source of problems. In the first step of the process, the needle is turned. The correct flow through the nozzle requires that the end of the needle be 0.95 inches in diameter or smaller. The inside diameter of the nozzle must be 1.00 inches or larger. By knowing the capability for each stage of the process, comparisons for potential success can be calculated.

For example, assume that the following capability figures are obtained for the needle and the nozzle.

> *Needle:*
> Average = 0.94 inches
> Standard deviation = 0.02 inches
>
> *Nozzle* (inside diameter):
> Average = 1.01 inches
> Standard deviation = 0.01 inches

By calculating Z-scores for the variation above 0.95 inches for the needle and below 1.00 inches for the nozzle, we can obtain a probability of either part being too large or too small. Remember, the Z-score is

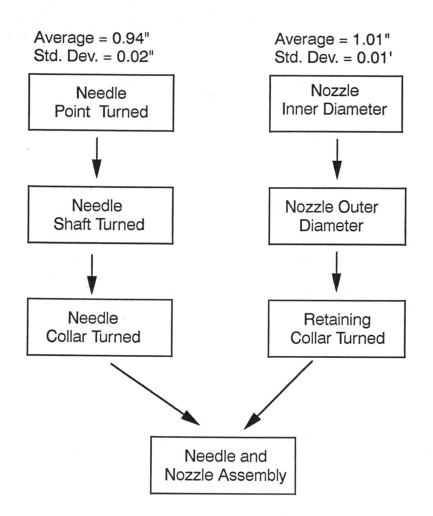

Figure 14-5: Flowchart with some statistical information added.

$$Z = \frac{\text{average} - \text{score of interest}}{\text{standard deviation}}$$

Therefore

$$\text{Z-score (needle)} = \frac{0.95 - 0.94}{0.02} = 0.50$$

$$\text{Z-score (nozzle)} = \frac{1.01 - 1.00}{0.01} = 1.00$$

Looking up the area under the curve from the average to these Z-scores in Appendix A yields 0.1985 and 0.3413, respectively. However, our interest is in the probability that a part could fall in the region beyond the Z-score. Therefore, the areas under the curve are subtracted from 0.50, or the area under one-half of the curve.

$$0.50 - 0.1985 = 0.3015$$

and

$$0.50 - 0.3413 = 0.1587$$

These two numbers are more than just the area under the curve beyond the calculated Z-scores; they are also the probability of a part occurring in this region. Thus, you can calculate directly the probability of a needle that is too large being placed in a nozzle that is too small merely by multiplying the two probabilities.

$$0.3015 \times 0.1587 = 0.048$$

In other words, with the current flowchart and the capabilities of just these two steps in the process, there will be about 4.8% of the total production with flow control units producing too little flow.

If the problem-solving team finds a way to improve the capability of either or both of the processes involved, the improvement can be obtained by repeating the foregoing calculations.

Examining Scrap Rates Using a Flowchart

A small manufacturing plant decides to investigate the true cost of scrap rates across the steps of production. In this particular situation, the product being manufactured is unimportant. What is important is the scrap rate at each step of the process. In this case, the production of the product requires three production steps, each with a 1% scrap rate.

The flowchart is a good tool for demonstrating to a group the cost of scrap as it moves through the production process. For example, if this example requires a final production of 50,000 units, then the production rate at each step of the process must be increased to account for the scrap. If the final production is meant to be 50,000 units, then the number of units produced in the last stage of production must be large enough that when 1% is scrapped, 50,000 units remain. The solution to this is a simple proportion.

$$\frac{50,000\,\text{units}}{x} = \frac{99\%}{100\%}$$

Converting this proportion algebraically results in the following formula.

$$50,000 \times 100 = 99x$$

or

$$x = 50,505 \text{ units}$$

Therefore, the last production step must produce 50,505 units to make the 50,000 production goal. The step before the last stage also has a 1% scrap rate. Therefore, the same formula applies, but this time, this step of production must supply the 50,505 parts needed for the last step.

$$50,505 \times 100 = 99x$$

or

$$x = 51,015 \text{ units}$$

Repeating this calculation for the first step yields the following.

$$51,015 \times 100 = 99x$$

or

$$x = 52,056 \text{ units}$$

In other words, the first step of the process must produce 2,056 extra units of production to meet the final production goal. The second step must produce an additional 1,015 units and the final step 505 units. Notice how the third step back produces 1,551 units more to meet a 1% scrap rate than the 505 units needed to meet a 1% scrap rate at the last step of the production process. Therefore, the reduction of scrap rates earlier in the process passes its benefits along the rest of the process. In addition, a problem-solving team can quickly see how a constant scrap rate within the plant translates to larger and larger production rates needed earlier in the process.

If the first step's scrap rate was reduced to zero because of problem-solving team methods, the additional 1,041 units of production would be unnecessary. This would represent a considerable reduction in the cost of production.

How to Justify Team-Suggested Actions
Using Cost/Benefit Analysis

In many cases the problem-solving team also must cost-justify some of the actions they have taken or are proposing. In such a case, a cost versus benefit analysis is usually required. However, there is no single form or technique that is universal to all companies. Therefore, the best approach is to ask management for a format to follow. If one is not available, the following is suggested.

Cost/benefit analysis is actually very simple. In one column you list the potential costs of implementing your suggestion and in another column you list the potential benefits. The bottom line of the analysis is whether the suggested improvement will reduce costs, improve quality, and/or increase the productivity of the plant. To obtain some of the information, a few short calculations may be required. As before, an example will be used to illustrate.

Consider the example of a problem-solving team working in an electronics factory. The normal activity for this team is to operate the soldering machine. This machine solders terminals to the ends of a cable. In all, 16 wires are soldered to the terminal. Currently, the machine has a scrap chart that indicates a scrap rate of 3%. With 125,000 terminals worth of production per year, that represents 3,750 terminals that must be scrapped.

The team has suggested that a new solder chamber be purchased for the machine, based on a study that showed that the temperature consistency of the solder directly affected the quality of the finished unit. The new unit will cost $5,000 and is expected to drop the scrap rate to 0.5%.

The team begins calculating the cost side of the analysis. To begin with, there is the $5,000 of capital expenditure to purchase the unit. Then there will be a one-week changeover period when production will be shut down for installation and training. With an annual production of 125,000 units, one week would represent 2,500 units of production lost.

$$\text{weekly production} = \frac{125,000}{50 \text{ weeks}} = 2,500$$

For each unit not made, the sales loss is $4.50. Therefore, the loss from a week's shutdown would be $11,250. Thus, the cost for the new chamber is actually $16,250 (lost production + capital cost).

On the benefit side of the equation, the new scrap rate that is anticipated should cut the scrap rate to 625 parts defective out of 125,000 parts of production. This is a significant reduction from the current average of 3,750 defective parts per 125,000 parts of production. Therefore, the cost to scrap 3,125 pieces is eliminated from the production process. Assuming a cost of $2.50 to scrap a unit, the potential cost reduction would be $7,812.50.

However, this is not the only benefit. The reduced scrap rate also gives the company 3,125 more units to sell. Assuming that the market can absorb the extra production, this represents an increased sales potential of $14,062.50 ($4.50 profit per piece times 3,125 more pieces). Combined with the scrap savings, the benefit is $21,875.

The ratio of costs to benefits can be expressed in conventional managerial finance terms, such as return on investment or payback. For example, the number of months until payback would be

$$\text{payback} = \frac{\text{cost}}{\text{benefits}} \times 12 \text{ months}$$

or

$$\text{payback} = \frac{\$16,260}{\$21,875} \times 12 \text{ months} = 8.9 \text{ months}$$

In other words, the improvement should pay for itself within nine months.

Evaluating the Success of Manufacturing Solutions by Calculating a Loss Function

An alternative to cost/benefit and capability indexes is the loss function. It translates deviations from specifications in terms of dollars lost. The loss function is controversial because the dollars it reports are really a form of "funny money." In other words, hypothetical amounts of money. The actual amount of loss would be difficult to establish. However, the loss function is specifically designed for continuous improvement and is finding a widening field of acceptance by companies. These companies use the loss function for everything from experimentation to managerial decision making.

The basis of the loss function is that products should be produced to their specified targets. These targets can be the optimal dimensions, delivery time, or other measurable data. In contrast, the *Cpk* index discussed in chapter 3 emphasizes the reduction of process variation as the primary goal of the manufacturing department. The loss function encourages such a reduction in variation only after a process is on target.

For example, if the dust cover for a gear box must have a 4-inch inside diameter, then 4 inches is the target dimension. When the cover is produced at the lower or upper specification, it will not fit properly and a loss is experienced by the company in reworking or scrapping the part. When the cover is exactly 4 inches in diameter, it should function properly and the company suffers little or no loss.

The traditional view of the tolerance range around an optimal size is that parts made within specification are equally good. The loss function states that as the size of a part deviates from the target value, the loss becomes greater. In other words, tolerances serve only as guidelines, with the true goal being the target size.

Figure 14-6 shows this relationship. The formula for the loss function connects the aforementioned points with a quadratic curve. Therefore, if you wish to calculate the loss for a production process, the formula is

$$\text{loss} = k\,[s^2 + (y - m)^2]$$

where $k = \dfrac{A}{\Delta^2}$

  A = cost of the countermeasure (scrap or rework)
  Δ = square of distance from target to one of the specification limits
  s = standard deviation
  y = actual part size
  m = target value

The following example illustrates how this formula is calculated. Suppose that an electronics manufacturer produces a power supply used in its line of home entertainment systems. The final output of this power supply is supposed to be 50 volts DC. The tolerance for the final output is plus or minus 5 volts DC. The manufacturer has determined that it costs $6.00 to repair or adjust a power supply out of specification. A sample of power supplies shows that the process is slightly off target with an average output of 49.8 volts DC. The standard deviation of the sample is 1.5 volts DC.

Step 1: Calculate the k value from the cost of repair.

The first step is to calculate k. The cost of the countermeasure is $6.00 and the distance from the target of 50 volts DC to the specification limits is 5 volts DC. Therefore,

$$k = \frac{\$6.00}{5 \text{ volts}^2} = \$0.24$$

To complete the calculation, k is inserted into the formula.

Step 2: Complete the loss formula.

Using the data for the power supplies, we can complete this calculation.

$$\text{loss} = \$0.24\,[1.5^2 + (49.8 \text{ volts} - 50 \text{ volts})^2] = \$0.5496$$

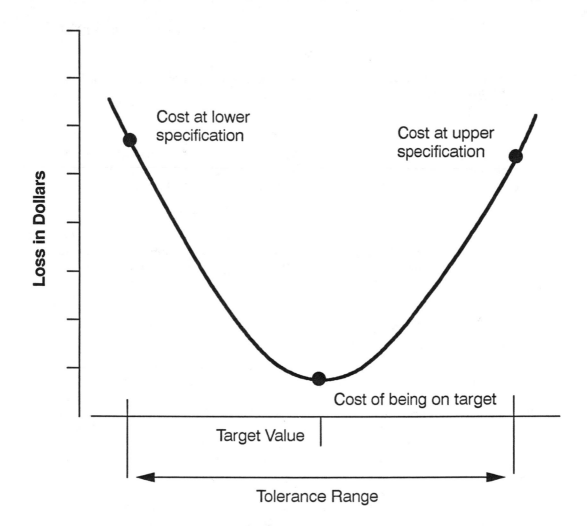

Figure 14-6: Graphic representation of the loss function.

In other words, the power supply capability experiences about a 55-cent loss per unit due to the capability of the process.

Step 3: Interpret the potential for improvement.

Assume that a supplier of the power supplies has a process average of 47 volts but a smaller standard deviation of 1.0 volts. Assuming that the *k* factor is the same, the outcome of the formula is quite different.

$$\text{loss} = \$0.24 \left[1.0^2 + (47 - 50)^2 \right] = \$2.40$$

The loss is well over four times the loss experienced at the electronics plant. Despite the reduction in variation, the formula reacts more strongly to a process being off target. Thus, you would not use the supplied part even though it would look more attractive because of its lower part-to-part variation.

How to Improve Process Capability Using Either Loss Function or the *Cpk* Index

The loss function is sometimes used by experimenters and as part of a process capability study. However, it is more effectively used as a tool of evaluation for problem-solving groups. Consider the example of an automatic screw machine process that is producing all of its parts within specification. A standard capability report would show a strong *Cpk* index, and the process would probably be ignored for improvements. However, a loss function would detect any deviations from target. This would lead a problem-solving team to investigate improvements for the process.

After each suggestion is implemented, another loss function can be calculated to detect the amount of improvement. For example, assume that the screw machine process was producing a small part that had to be 5.00 mm in length. The tolerance range was plus or minus 0.05 mm. The current process produced parts that averaged 5.01 mm in size with a standard deviation of 0.01 mm. If we first calculate a *Cpk* index (see chapter 3), we can see how strong the capability appears to be.

$$Cpk = \frac{5.05 - 5.01}{3 \times 0.01} = 1.33$$

This is a good *Cpk* index, recalling the requirement for processes to be at least 1.00. However, if we assume that it costs 50 cents to scrap a part out of specification, we can begin to see the loss experienced by this process. Using the *k* calculation from the loss function, we obtain

$$k = \frac{\$0.50}{(0.05)^2} = \$200$$

Thus

$$\text{loss} = \$200 \ [0.01^2 + (5.01 - 5.00)^2 \ ] = \$0.04$$

So the process is experiencing a four-cent-per-part loss because of its current capability. If the process produces 1 million of these parts per year, the total loss would be \$40,000. This is occurring within a process that is fully capable according to the *Cpk* index.

If the process is brought onto the target of 5.00 mm, the loss drops.

$$\text{loss} = \$200 \ [0.01^2 + (5.00 - 5.00)^2 \ ] = \$0.02$$

The centering of the process on the target value of 5.00 mm results in a 50% reduction in the loss.

If used religiously, the loss function drives processes toward low variations and process averages that are on target. The result is a manufacturing system that is predictable. If handled correctly, this system would have high success rates for mating parts and completing assemblies with little scrap or wasted time.

Case Study: How a Problem-Solving Work Team Improved the Manufacturability of an Office Desk

Assume that you are the manufacturing manager for a office furniture company. The fastest selling product this year is an all wooden office desk for executives. Unfortunately, the number of complaints about this desk is also growing at a fast rate. The president of the company has assigned you the task of finding and correcting the problems in the desk.

As a first step, you would form a problem-solving work team comprised of engineers, first line supervisors, quality assurance personnel, and operators. The methods introduced in this chapter can be used to improve communications and to evaluate both problems and the benefits of proposed solutions.

Perhaps the first tool you would deploy would be a Pareto chart of the problems reported by the customers. Assume that the most frequently reported problem was warpage of the desk top. This warpage now becomes your primary target as a problem-solving team.

To further understand the situation, your team draws a flowchart of the office desk manufacturing process. Then they brainstorm for ideas on where the warpage is occurring. The quality assurance personnel add statistical information on the degree of warpage discovered during final inspection versus warpage in the field. Their findings show that the warpage occurs during manufacturing.

A fish-bone diagram is drawn to show possible cause-and-effect relationships. From this chart your team identifies several possible causes of the warpage. Taking a quick vote, the team decides to check the stacking of cut pieces of desktop. Their examinations find nothing in the way the boards are stacked that could cause the warpage.

The next idea is then tested. The manufacturing engineers measure the degree of warpage before and after the boards are cut. They discover that the generally flat raw boards start to warp dramatically after they are cut. Further investigation discovers that the sawing of the ends of the boards is allowing too much moisture into the wood and thus starting the warping process.

The team recommends to management that the production process be changed so that each desktop is stained as quickly as possible after it is cut. The cost to the company for the change will be about $10,000. The team calculates that the new process will cut about $125,000 from the warranty costs each year. The new process is approved, and the improvements are documented by the team.

This example shows that statistical techniques can be blended into a structured approach to problem solving. The statistics help to describe and evaluate the team's efforts. The structured approach makes the team more efficient by creating several tools of communication that spread understanding more quickly and generate more ideas. Competitiveness is defined by the company that can innovate most effectively.

Conclusion

Problem solving is a complex process involving people, data, and machinery. Statistics can provide intelligence on a situation. With such information, the problem-solving teams are easy to lead by following the logical path toward a solution. By counting, comparing, and summarizing, most industrial problems become self-evident. By establishing a baseline early, the results of suggested improvements can be tested directly. In short, statistical reasoning forms the backbone of the problem-solving process.

CHAPTER 15

How to Use Statistical Methods to Plan and Control Production in an Uncertain Operating Environment

"If only I was certain," is the lament of any manager forced to make a decision where the facts are not clear-cut. So far, we have emphasized that ideas can be tested and evaluated for their effectiveness. However, every manufacturing manager will face situations where the outcome of a decision cannot be known until after an action is taken. For example, the decision to automate a plant is usually made after thorough studies of the situation. However, the impact of automation on the work force and the quality of production is unknown until the plant is automated. Therefore, you are uncertain of the outcome and you must minimize the risk of being wrong. This chapter reviews a few simple techniques for evaluating the impact of your decision, right or wrong.

How to Make a Decision under Uncertainty Using the Payoff Table: Deciding Whether to Increase Production in Anticipation of a Growing Market

The primary tool of decisionmaking under uncertainty is the payoff table. The payoff table is a crosstabulation of the options at your disposal and a set of possible future events. The following example illustrates how the payoff table is constructed.

Suppose that you are the production manager for a manufacturer of a line of clothing. The company is faced with a decision whether to increase production this year or reduce it to save money. These choices represent the two options you must decide between. The results of each decision will depend on how the clothing market does over the next 12 months. The market could increase, decrease, or remain fairly stable. The market research people report that the market is growing, but at the same time you notice an overall slowdown in the nation's economy. The future is uncertain.

To assist in making this decision, you draw up a payoff table that compares each choice against each possible outcome. In this case, there are two possible decisions and three possible outcomes. These are laid out on a cross-tabulation design of corresponding blocks.

	Outcomes of the Market		
Strategies	**Growth**	**Reduction**	**No Change**
(A) Increase production			
(B) Decrease production			

For each block in the table, you make an estimate of the effect of the combination of choice to market response. For example, strategy A (making more clothes) and an increase in the market means that the extra clothing will sell well and bring extra profits to the company. Therefore, based on past sales performance figures, you estimate that 1 million dollars in profits could be realized. This amount of profit is written into the first block.

	Outcomes of the Market		
Strategies	**Growth**	**Reduction**	**No Change**
(A) Increase production	1,000		
(B) Decrease production			

(figures in thousands of dollars)

However, if strategy A is chosen and the market decreases, then the company will be stuck with unsold clothing that will have to be liquidated at drastically lower prices. Even with fast action and the disposal of all of the clothing, the company would still realize no profits at all. This zero profit outcome is recorded in the next block.

Each outcome is evaluated to fill in all of the blocks on the payoff table. For example, if you decide to produce less, then you face a different set of outcomes. The decision to produce less clothing means less people are hired and fewer machine hours used; thus production costs are reduced. Yet the price of the clothing remains the same so that if the market stays stable or grows, your company still increases its profits.

Strategies	Outcomes of the Market		
	Growth	Reduction	No Change
(A) Increase production	1,000	0	350
(B) Decrease production	250	100	500

Once the table is completed, it can be examined and tested for the best decision.

Many decisions are possible with the small amount of information presented in the preceding example. A more typical payoff table would be much larger than this one. However, this small example demonstrates that a set of decision-making rules is necessary.

Evaluating the Payoff Table Using the Maximin Rule

This rule is an abbreviation of "maximize your minimum." In other words, you select the strategy that will give you the best results in the worse case.

Examining the payoff table, strategy B has the highest profits in the worse case. If less clothing is made and the market decreases, there would still be a $100,000 payoff in additional profits. This is seen as the strategy for the conservative decision maker. Risk is minimized, even if it is unknown.

Evaluating the Payoff Table Using the Maximax Rule

This is an abbreviation of "maximize your maximum." That is, choose the strategy that represents the greatest potential gain.

Examining the payoff table, strategy A would be the best decision. It has the highest potential payoff. This type of decision rule is used by the aggressive decision maker who is seeking maximum reward despite the risks.

Statistically Evaluating the Payoff Table Using Hurwicz's Alpha

The aforementioned decision rules are quick and easy to use. Unfortunately, they do not take into account the other possible outcomes. In most decision making, these rules are used sparingly. Instead, some of the law of probability and other statistical theories are used to analyze the payoff table.

The Hurwicz method allows the decision maker to weight possible outcomes to match his or her own personal feelings. For example, the president of the clothing company might be fairly conservative with a little bit of aggressiveness when it comes to business. Therefore, he might weight an aggressive outcome with a factor of 0.25 and the conservative outcome at 0.75.

These weights are multiplied into the highest and lowest outcomes for each strategy on the payoff table and the results are compared.

$$\text{strategy A} = (1{,}000 \times 0.25) + (0 \times 0.75) = 250$$

$$\text{strategy B} = (600 \times 0.25) + (100 \times 0.75) = 225$$

Strategy A produces the highest possible outcome. Therefore, it is selected based on the balance between a conservative and an aggressive decision-making tactic. However, if you still feel that the difference between the two results is too close, you may want to try the following method.

Evaluating a Payoff Table Using Bayes's Method

The method based on the works of the famous pioneer of the mathematics of probability, Thomas Bayes, takes into account all of the possible outcomes at the same time. When working under uncertainty, the likelihood of any of the outcomes is given equal length. For example, in the payoff table we have been examining, there are three possible outcomes. Therefore, each is given a one-third (0.333) chance of occurring. Applying these arbitrary probabilities to the payoff table creates the following.

$$\text{strategy A} = (1{,}000 \times 0.333) + (350 \times 0.333) + (0 \times 0.333) = 450$$

$$\text{strategy B} = (250 \times 0.333) + (500 \times 0.333) + (100 \times 0.333) = 283$$

Clearly, strategy A has the highest potential for the company because the odds of a highly profitable outcome outweigh the safer outcomes of strategy B.

How to Plan Production When the Risk Involved Can Be Estimated

In many instances of using statistical knowledge, the risks of the possible outcomes will be known. The payoff table is still used as the primary approach to decision making, but the probability of an event occurring takes on a much more important role.

Let us continue with our clothing manufacturer example. Assume that you are seeking further information about the possible outcomes. You have investigated the past performance of the marketplace. Through such research, you find that during 30% of the years investigated the market rose and 20% of the time it decreased. During the remaining 50% of the years there was no change in the size of the clothing market.

The probabilities are multiplied into the payoff table from the preceding example.

Strategies	Outcomes of the Market		
	Growth	Reduction	No Change
(A) Increase production	1,000	0	350
(B) Decrease production	250	100	500

When the probabilities are factored into each corresponding block, the following table is created.

Strategies	Outcomes		
	Growth	Reduction	No Change
A	(1,000 x 0.30)	(0 x 0.20)	(350 x 0.50)
B	(250 x 0.30)	(100 x 0.20)	(500 x 0.50)

Thus

Strategies	Outcomes		
	Growth	Reduction	No Change
A	300	0	175
B	75	20	250

(figures are in thousands of dollars)

Now the maximin and maximax rules can be applied to make the final decision. For example, under the maximin rule, strategy B would be selected. The worse case still creates $20,000 in probability adjusted profits. The maximax rule would choose strategy A since it has a potential payoff of $300,000.

How to Form a Strong Picture of Possible Production Scenarios Using Simulations and the Monte Carlo Technique

Probabilities and other related decision-making methods have a weakness. They can only predict the general outcome of a situation. Unfortunately, many situations are dynamic over time, such as the amount of work-in-progress (WIP) occurring within a production process. The flow diagram on the following page details the manufacturing process of a valve. Consider the example of turned parts in a box waiting to be threaded. During the course of a single day, the number of parts waiting for the threading operation will rise and fall. Under a just-in-time system of production, you would want the WIP to be as close to zero as possible. At the same time, you do not want machines going idle too long while they wait for a slower process to supply them with parts.

To examine the potential effect of a decision on a process over time, a simulation is often performed. The simulation sets up the situation on a mathematical model and then feeds it randomly chosen events and records the outcome. For example, the machine waiting to thread parts can thread 50 parts per hour. However, the machine that turns the part produces from 1 to 100 parts per hour due to variations in the machine, the occurrence of break times, and so on. A simulation would feed a math model random digits between 80 and 120 to see how robust the threading machine is in coping with such a fluctuation in available parts.

Flow chart:

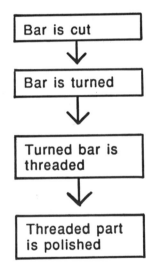

An Example of the Simulation of Parts Queuing in a Production Process

Let us continue with the supply of parts to the threading machine. Suppose that you are the production planner for the threading machine. You want to schedule just enough time on the threading machine to make sure that all parts are threaded without creating too much of a backlog of parts waiting to be processed.

Unfortunately, each hour will have various numbers of parts being sent from the turning department. This will create both busy days and slack hours. During the busy hours, some parts will have to wait until the next hour to be threaded. What you need to know is whether this backlog will pile up to a point where machines are running for several more hours than needed to catch up with the turning department.

Testing the Current Flow of Work-In-Progress Using the Monte Carlo Method

The Monte Carlo method is a simple technique of simulation that can be programmed into most computers and some advanced pocket calculators. The idea is to simulate the hourly number of parts expected by randomly choosing a number between 1 and 100. The backlog or underusage of the threading machine is calculated for each hour by subtracting the 50-parts-per hour ability of the threading machine from the current reserve of turned parts. If a backlog occurs, it is added to the next hour's number of parts. If the backlog is going to get out of hand in reality, the simulation should create the same effect.

Let us set up a Monte Carlo simulation and test the efficiency of having a single threading machine processing 50 parts per hour. First, we randomly choose numbers between 1 and 100. Because this is an illustration, we will limit the simulation to a 20-hour period. If this was a full simulation, at least a month of data would be created.

Each occurrence of a reserve of over 50 parts in one hour will be called a backlog and added into the next hour's total. If fewer than 50 parts are in the reserve, the difference will be called underutilization. For example, using a computer program to select random numbers creates the first three hours of data as

Hour	Parts Available
1	15
2	82
3	56

The first hour creates no backlog because the threading machine can easily process the 15 parts sent up from the turning department. In other words, the machine would spend most of the hour waiting for parts. However, during the second hour 82 parts are received. Fifty of these parts can be handled that hour, but the remaining 32 carry over to the next hour's reserve. During the third hour, the 32 parts are processed, but 56 more parts arrive. That is a total of 88 parts in the reserve during the third hour. After 50 parts are threaded, a backlog of 38 parts is created for the fourth hour, and so on.

Completing this brief simulation for 20 hours creates the following results.

Hour	Parts	Backlog	Underutilization
1	15	0	35
2	82	32	0
3	56	38	0
4	68	56	0
5	58	64	0
6	40	54	0
7	41	45	0
8	11	6	0
9	34	0	10
10	25	0	25
11	66	16	0
12	17	0	17
13	79	29	0
14	58	37	0
15	67	54	0
16	42	46	0
17	38	34	0
18	86	70	0
19	85	105	0
20	12	67	0

The simulation results allow you to make several observations about how well five support people can handle the incoming calls. For example, about 80% of the hours ended in backlogs. A careful examination of the number of backlogs each hour indicated that once over 100 parts were waiting.

In addition, slow hours were fairly rare. Only about 9% of the hours involved the machine being underutilized. Most of the time, the operator spent seven or eight hectic hours trying to keep up with incoming parts. This could also give you some idea how often an extra machine would have to be used to help with the backlog.

In short, the simulation of a situation over time provides you with multiple dimensions of data to use in the decision-making process.

How to Decide Whether to Add Equipment
Using the Monte Carlo Method

Suppose that you are thinking about adding a second threading machine to the process to reduce the backlog. Looking only at the average number of parts coming in, the second machine would seem to be a waste. However, by running the same simulation as before, but with a second machine, you can evaluate the effect on backlogs, slack times, and the stress of the job.

Taking the same random sequence of parts, but assuming that two smaller and less expensive machines can thread 60 parts per hour, the following results are observed.

Hour	Parts	Backlog	Underutilization
1	15	0	45
2	82	22	0
3	56	18	0
4	68	26	0
5	58	24	0
6	40	4	0
7	41	0	15
8	11	0	49
9	34	0	26
10	25	0	35
11	66	6	0
12	17	0	37
13	79	19	0
14	58	17	0
15	67	24	0
16	42	6	0
17	38	0	16
18	86	26	0
19	85	51	0
20	12	3	0
Totals	980	246	223

Using two less expensive (and less productive) machines, the change becomes obvious. First, the number of backlogged parts and underutilized parts balance. Second, only about two-thirds of the days involve backlogs. These backlog periods also last a much shorter time, around four or five hours.

In contrast, the length and magnitude of slack time increases with a second machine. Therefore, you would have to balance the cost to change to two smaller machines against the expanded number of slack production hours. If other tasks were available for these slack days, then two small machines may provide the ideal size for the threading department.

How to Simulate Normally Distributed Occurrences of an Event Using the Monte Carlo Method: Testing the Dispatching of Trucks

In our previous example, the number of parts coming in occurred at random. However, in most real-life situations the response of the environment will follow some sort of distribution. For example, we have seen in previous chapters how reliabilities follow an exponential distribution and that small samples of manufacturing processes usually follow the *t* distribution.

For this example, assume that the data is distributed under the normal curve. A trucking firm is responsible for the delivery of small packages within a medium-sized city. The exact miles each truck travels each day to deliver the packages vary. However, the distribution of these distances over a one-year period forms a normal distribution. The average distance was 55 miles with a standard deviation of 10 miles.

The dispatcher at this company must decide how many trucks to assign to the small package delivery service. The average driver can cover 20 miles in a day. The logical choice would be to assign three drivers that could cover a combined drive of 60 miles. This would be more than enough to meet the 55-mile average. However, how will the three drivers cope with the daily variations in the miles required?

We begin by assuming that any requirement of over 60 miles a day will have to be covered the following day. This is the same as the backlog of phone calls in the first example. The next step is to lay out a simulation of the distances required each day. Since the distribution of these distances follows the normal distribution, about two-thirds of the requirements will be within one standard deviation of the average.

The randomly chosen miles will have to conform to the normal distribution probabilities. Using Appendix A, you can look up the area under the curve for each standard deviation from the average—the Z-score of the number of standard deviations in question. For example, the area at three standard deviations is 49.86%. Therefore, there is little chance of mileage beyond plus or minus three standard deviations.

Continuing this exercise finds the following.

Between Standard Deviations	Probability
−3 and −2	2%
−2 and −1	14%
−1 and average	34%
average and +1	34%
+1 and +2	14%
+2 and +3	2%

Therefore, the randomly chosen miles must conform to this model. This is accomplished in a computer program by generating a random digit between 1 and 100, then assigning the number of miles required using the following table.

Random Digit	Miles Required
1–2	30
3–16	40
17–50	50
51–84	60
85–98	70
99–100	80

Each mile required corresponds to the center of the range between standard deviations. The distribution of number categories matches the distribution of area under the normal curve.

Thus, the simulation selects a random digit, assigns the proper number of miles, and then calculates the effect on the three-driver system.

Day	Random Digit	Miles	Backlog
1	19	50	0
2	3	40	0
3	79	60	0
4	56	60	0
5	70	60	0
6	92	70	10
7	77	60	10
8	65	60	10
9	13	40	−10
10	20	50	−10
11	39	50	−10
12	30	50	−10
13	11	40	−20
14	93	70	10
15	45	50	0
16	29	50	−10
17	41	50	−10
18	30	50	−10
19	79	60	0
20	94	70	10
Totals		1,090	−70

By examining the simulation, the dispatcher can begin to see patterns in the data. For example, the drivers seem to be slightly underutilized even though the simulation produces close to the 55 miles per day average. In addition, backlogs are infrequent and short. A package never has to wait more than a day for delivery.

Conclusion

Although good decision making is not a matter of statistics alone, statistical techniques can provide excellent information about a situation, its outcomes, and payoffs. When used with mathematical techniques, such as simulations of the future, you can evaluate the effectiveness of your decisions before they are made.

CHAPTER 16

How to Create and Deliver a Professional Presentation of Statistical Information

The ability to work with statistical methods to solve manufacturing problems is sufficient for the professional working alone. Eventually, however, you must present your statistical findings to others. Your purpose might be to change opinions, inform management, or to address a public group. Whatever purpose is involved, you should be able to make a professional presentation. Lacking this ability, you will quickly be labeled another boring statistician.

The techniques to make a statistical presentation interesting and effective are simple.

The Golden Rule of any Presentation: Think of the Audience

Most people view statistics as a page full of boring numbers and a statistician as a professor-type slowly reading meaningless facts and figures to an audience. These stereotypes can be abolished by a professional who adapts a presentation to fit the interests of the audience. The following examples show how the different levels of statistical knowledge in each audience are accounted for in the presentation.

Suppose you are the manufacturing engineer at a plant that produces piston rings for automobile engines. For over a month you have been studying the critical characteristics of the rings. The most important of these is the gap at the ring split after the ring is installed into a piston cylinder. That gap has to be no more than 0.04 millimeters in size. Your capability studies on finished engines reveal that all gaps are estimated to be within 0.01 millimeter.

Presentation 1: To the stockholders

You must make a five-minute presentation to the stockholders on the quality of the piston rings. It is assumed that no one in the audience has any statistical training.

The Presentation: Thanking the Chairman of the Board, you turn toward the audience, hold up a giant model of a piston ring, and say, "I have been asked to comment on the quality of our primary product, the piston ring. Let me just say that the quality is excellent. How excellent? Let me give you a brief example. Do you see this model of a piston ring? When a piston ring is mounted into an engine, it is vital that the gap left at the end of the ring is neither too large nor too small. I have personally audited our rings in dozens of finished motors, and that gap is always within one-quarter of the width of a human hair."

After a few more comments, you thank the audience for your chance to speak, and you sit down.

Go back and look at the comments on quality again. Do you see any statistical terms or numbers? There are none. The audience has no statistical training, so the information is presented in plain English. (This is the best way to present any statistical information to most audiences.) Also note the use of an analogy to help the audience identify with the measurement scale being used. People realize that a human hair is thin and that one-quarter of that thickness is very thin indeed. If the presenter had said the gaps were within 0.01 millimeter, most of the audience would have a difficult time envisioning that size.

Presentation 2: To the shop-floor work force

The day after your successful presentation to the stockholders, your boss asks you to present the same information to the work force so that they will know what a great job they are doing. The workers have been trained in statistical process control and have a good grasp of the importance of capability ratios.

The Presentation: Stepping to the front of the cafeteria during the weekly meeting of the employees, you thank the foreman for this opportunity and begin, "I want to report on the great job all of you have been doing to increase the quality of our piston rings. Take a look at this chart showing the capability ratios for ring gaps over the past two years. Two years ago we were struggling to reach a *Cpk* of 1.00. Of course, SPC was new then and we were still learning. A year ago we got that *Cpk* up to the required 1.33. Now look at this year's results. We have reached a *Cpk* of 3.00. That's the highest in the industry. In fact, we should be able to win a bigger ring contract from GM because of this."

After taking a few questions, you sit down.

Even though the information is the same, the first two presentations differ dramatically. Note that the talk to the employees revolves around the established objectives of the SPC system. You should make the information relevant to the work requirements of the audience. The use of the word *we* is frequent to reinforce the concept of teamwork. Both the style of the presentation and the terminology reflect the goals and skills of the group.

Presentation 3: To Senior Management

Impressed by your first two presentations, your boss now wants you to tell management about the success of the piston rings. Some managers have no statistical training, while others have been to many seminars.

The Presentation: Stepping to the front of the meeting room, you thank your boss for the introduction and greet the managers of the company.

"Ladies and gentlemen," you begin, "the constantly improving quality of our company's piston rings will represent a cost reduction of $100,000 during this fiscal year. Two years ago we were having a difficult time keeping our major ring customers because the ring gap in about 10% of the assembled engines was out of specification. For two years we have applied statistical process control, work teams, and heavy management involvement to solve this problem. Last year we reached our goal of meeting the customer specifications. This year, I am proud to announce, we have far exceeded the customer requirements.

"In fact, the ring gaps are so consistent now that our own internal scrap rate has fallen from 5% to zero. Because of that improvement, our manufacturing throughput is able to increase 5%. We simply aren't spending the time and money to scrap rings anymore. Thus, we should realize a $100,000 savings in operations costs."

See how this presentation is again adapted to the audience. The presenter is using the single language of management—money. Quality and progress are both expressed in terms of money. In addition, the tone of the presentation is formal. This is appropriate for any presentation to a higher authority.

The Second Rule: Make Your Case Quickly

The previous presentations to three different groups are all similar in one respect: The presenter made his or her point first. The first sentence in each presentation tells the audience the conclusion of the talk. This technique is critical to capturing and holding an audience's attention. It is used in both written and oral presentations.

When statistical information is going to be presented, most audiences expect a long, dry lecture filled with numbers. Even a hostile audience will listen to your first sentence or two. That is why many professional speech trainers encourage people to open a talk with a joke, to catch the attention of the audience. However, in a statistical presentation you are working on a strictly professional level, so jokes are not recommended. Instead, open with a statement that relates to the interests of the audience.

Consider the example of the stockholders' meeting. The stockholders only know that someone is going to talk for five minutes on the quality of the product. By opening your remarks with the comment that quality is excellent, the audience knows it does not have to wait five minutes to find out how good the piston rings are this year. Then by holding up the model of a piston ring, the already attentive audience is curious about what you will say next.

The Third Rule: Keep Your Presentation Short

Once audience attention is captured, it is vital that their attention be held for the entire presentation. There are two ways to accomplish this: Either make a long presentation so fascinating that no one will dare leave the room, or keep the presentation so short that it is over before anyone's attention span lapses. In the real world, it is easier to make a presentation short than it is to make a statistical presentation fascinating.

The best rule of thumb for a statistical presentation is to keep it under five minutes. Most statistical situations can be boiled down to one central theme. The format of the presentation is to make your conclusions first and then to spend the next four minutes explaining the reasons for your conclusions.

The exception to this rule is when the statistical presentation is made to a group of professionals—for example, the presenting of a research paper to a professional society or the discussion by a group of professionals working on a solution to a manufacturing problem. In both cases, the audience must hear complete statistical summaries to help them fully understand the situation. However, the occasional use of an analogy or anecdote will help relieve the usual boredom of such meetings.

How to Communicate Clearly with a Written Statistical Report

Although the aforementioned rules of presentation seem as if they apply only to oral presentations, they are equally valid for written presentations. The only difference between the two forms of communication is that writing tends to be more formal.

A good written report uses short, descriptive sentences. You should make your point and then back it up with the statistical results. The typical format for a written statistical summary is as follows:

1. State the conclusion first.
2. Review the problem at hand.
3. List the supporting evidence for your conclusion.
4. Call for action.
5. Attach supporting appendixes.

State the Conclusion First

The first paragraph of a statistical report should summarize your conclusions. The idea is to capture the reader's attention as soon as possible, just as with an oral presentation. Most managers will read only the first page of any publication. If you do not make your point early, chances are the reader will go uninformed.

Review the Problem at Hand

The second paragraph should review the question at hand. This may seem like a backwards approach at first, but bear in mind that the typical reader of a statistical report is already informed of the questions and is seeking possible solutions. For example, a company is worried about whether the capability ratios of their machines are high enough to meet a customer's vendor quality assurance standards. The report from quality assurance may read,

> Our recent audit of all production areas here at T Corporation reveals that 95% of the machines are meeting capability requirements for Farley Motor Company. The remaining 5% of machines are near their requirements and have work teams attacking the causes of identifiable variation.
>
> Farley Motor Company requires us to sample at least 30 pieces of production and to calculate *Cpk* ratios for critical characteristics identified on the blueprints. The minimum requirement is a *Cpk* ratio of 1.33.

With only a few sentences the reader aware of the problems knows the outcome of the audits. An uninformed reader can quickly divine the importance of the report within two paragraphs.

List the Supporting Evidence for Your Conclusion

The evidence to support the conclusion follows the first two paragraphs. For our example of capability audits, the author would probably prepare a table that compares specifications against *Cpk*'s, noting sample averages and standard deviations. To make the reading of these figures easier, they would probably be listed from highest to lowest capability, or listed by production departments.

Call for Action

The final narrative of a report is a call for action. As stated throughout this book, statistics do not work by themselves. If the information you gather is not going to be used for making decisions or taking actions, then there is no point in gathering the data. Therefore, any statistical report should end with specific recommended actions.

Our earlier capability report might end with a recommendation that continuous improvement of the incapable machines continue and that documentation of the pursuit of improved capability is presented to management.

Attach Supporting Appendixes

Appendixes, when needed, are attached to a written report. A simple report on machine capabilities would not require any attachments. A detailed research report would demand the use of several appendices. Anytime that the audience might need to read the actual results of statistical tests, an appendix should be employed.

A common appendix is a bibliographic list of resources consulted in the preparation of the report. This type of appendix is needed whenever a special formula has been used, or when references to previous research are cited in the report. The bibliographic appendix allows a reader to trace the background material that went into your report.

A Written Report on the Results of Testing the Capabilities of Two Machines

Imagine that you are the process engineer for a manufacturing firm. Central to the production process of most parts are two 100-ton presses, numbered 34 and 69. Management has asked you to conduct tests on each press to see if one press is capable of higher quality than the other. They have also requested that your results be presented as a formal research paper.

A research report would list the tests performed and comment briefly on the significance of their outcomes. Again, the conclusions are stated first and a call for action last.

For a general audience, any statistical information is usually presented as a narrative. For example, suppose that five pieces from two different presses were compared for differences in variation using the F-test at an alpha error of 5%. To make this information more palatable, the test is reported as, "We sampled five parts from the two presses and found that there was a significant difference in their performance. Specifically, press 34 maintained much lower variation than press 69."

In short, the rule for reporting statistical results is to say what the information tells you as simply as possible. Make it quick and to the point. If one press seems to work better than the one next to it, then say that. There is no need for fancy words or elaborate statistical notations. Those are only appropriate for a formal report to a journal for publication.

After the narrative is completed, you can attach illustrations and appendixes as needed. One appendix would be the neat and orderly presentation of the statistical data related to the report. For example, the comparison of the performance of the two presses would include detailed descriptions of statistical tests used to compare averages and standard deviations.

Report on the Performance of Presses 34 and 69

Each press was allowed to produce 30 parts (angle bracket AD-295). The average overall length of the two samples was compared.

press 34: average = 13.5
standard deviation = 0.05

press 69: average = 13.4
standard deviation = 0.03

t-test for difference between means = 9.39
Significant at the 0.99 level

F-test for difference between standard deviations = 2.78
Not significant

Illustrations are excellent for summarizing complex situations in a simple chart. For example, time series data, such as a company's annual sales rates for the past 20 years, is difficult to understand as a table of numbers, but is clearly interpreted as a line chart (see Figure 16-1).

How to Prepare Illustrations
for a Professional Presentation

The one element of a report that has been abused is the use of illustrations. The two most common mistakes are the overuse of illustrations and the creation of graphics that violate the guidelines of effective communication during a presentation.

Overuse usually occurs in an oral presentation when the presenter flashes quickly from one graph to another. This also occurs in written reports when illustrations make up over one-half of the report. The correct method for a five-minute presentation or a report of up to five pages is to use no more than two illustrations. An ideal situation for a short oral presentation is to use only one illustration.

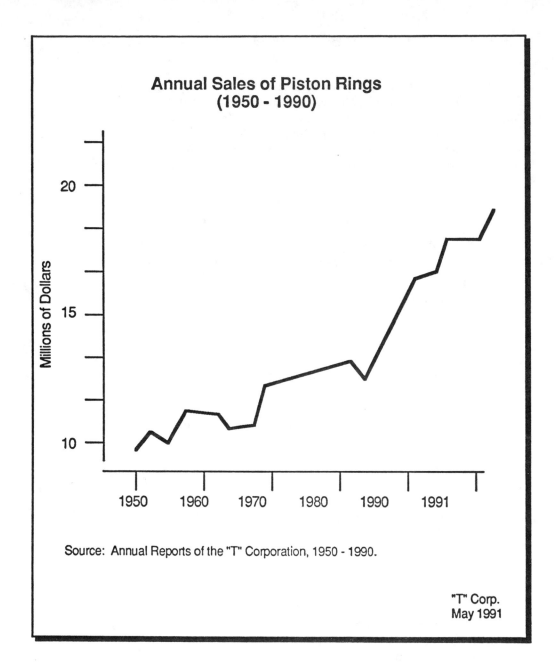

Figure 16-1: A properly prepared illustration.

Use the single most important illustration that reinforces the central theme of a report. In an oral presentation, this single illustration is usually projected onto the wall for easy reading. It remains there for the duration of the presentation to reinforce the theme constantly.

Consider the example of the capability audit presented earlier. The central theme of the presentation is that 5% of the machines tested are not capable. A simple pie chart showing a 5% slice labeled *incapable* will make the point.

As noted earlier, the second most common violation of the rules of illustration is to present the graphic incorrectly. Illustrations should be clear, easy to read, and informative. To achieve this, the preparer of an illustration must strip away every unnecessary element of the illustration. The idea is to present the maximum amount of information with the minimum number of graphic elements. (Refer again to Figure 16-1.)

Of course, for any illustration there are a few elements that are mandatory. Every illustration must have a title that quickly describes what the illustration is about. It must also have the author and date in the lower right-hand corner. (Note that if you made an illustration at work, the company's name is used instead of the author's name.) In the lower left-hand corner is the source of the information. This is usually in a bibliographic form and contains enough information so that the reader is able to locate the source.

Scales, keys, and footnotes are optional in an illustration. In most cases, these are only used where absolutely necessary. For example, a special study on production would note the time, process, and product involved.

Use Personal Computers and Desktop Publishing to Prepare Your Statistical Report

In the past, word processors and graphics programs have been a valuable aid in the creation of written material and audiovisual aids. However, these have been greatly enhanced with the advent of desktop publishing. With a desktop publishing software package and a laser printer, anyone can create documents or visual aids of typeset quality.

Because of this dramatic increase in the quality of output, the attractiveness of a document can also be increased. A reader is more likely to read the contents of an attractively compiled document. In addition, some statistical software programs now have the ability to cut and paste their results into desktop publishing documents. These abilities greatly improve your ability to make a stunning presentation. Therefore, any serious presenter of statistical information should investigate the potentials of desktop publishing.

At the same time, desktop publishing creates two common problems. The software is capable of creating dozens of typefaces and hundreds of graphic effects on a single page. It is remarkably easy to get carried away and create a "muddy" presentation. The best rule to follow is to balance the design of a page and keep all elements to a minimum. The other problem is that an attractive page can be achieved, but you spend so much time on page layout that you neglect the contents of the report. In all applications of desktop publishing, it is vital to develop crisp, clean content before worrying about page layout.

Conclusion

A clean, quick, and to-the-point presentation is not only professional, but it communicates effectively. Use the style of presentation discussed in this chapter and demand it from your staff. Write a one-page procedure for the presentation of information in written reports and oral presentations. This will speed the communication of statistical information.

CHAPTER 17

How to Select
a Statistical Software Package

Although many of the methods presented in this book can be done quickly with a pocket calculator, the demanding realities of the manufacturing environment usually require the purchase of a computer and a software package that can perform statistical functions. Since new software packages are introduced almost daily and existing packages are constantly updated, we will discuss only the method of selecting the correct package for your particular needs. Specific packages will be mentioned only for illustrative purposes.

The steps presented in this chapter should be used whenever you or your company feels that a statistical software package is needed. By following these steps, you may find that you need more than you think, or that you already have a software package that can adequately perform the job. Each of these steps helps you to examine statistical software needs in as many different lights as possible and to look beyond the purchase to actual use and potential problems.

Step 1: Make a list of the statistical functions you need to perform on a computer.

The best first step for selecting computer software is to sit down and list all of the needs you have for statistical analysis. Pay particular attention to those needs that will save time and increase accuracy in reporting to management. These will help you to justify the purchase to the appropriate managers.

Your list of needs will also assist in the software selection process. Consider the case of a quality control department. Its list of statistical functions is as follows:

- descriptive statistics
- some experimental analysis
- gauge repeatability and reproducibility
- capability studies

349

These functions would then be broken down into the specific statistical operations they encompass. For example, "some experimental analysis" might be broken down into

- *t*-test for averages
- *F*-test for variation
- *chi*-square for standard deviations
- *chi*-square for contingency tables
- crosstabulation capability
- linear and nonlinear regressions
- correlation analysis
- one-way ANOVA

Each item should be scored according to need and potential benefits. Many people use a scale that ranks a low need or benefit as 1, the average need or benefit as 2, and an important need or benefit as 3. For example, "crosstabulation ability" might be ranked highly for need and benefit by a department that wants to compare many process factors for possible correlation with process problems.

By ranking the items by their importance, you structure your list of needs into an order from the most important to the least important features to seek in a software package. The packages you examine that fulfill all of the requirements would be considered first. Packages that fulfill almost all of the requirements would be put on an alternative list, in case later testing disqualified the first choices.

Step 2: Make a list of potential future needs

After the checklist of present needs is completed, a list of future needs should also be created. The best way to form such a list is to survey each potential user of the computer software. They should know best about what they may apply in the future. Such a list might look like the following:

- full experimental analysis
- mathematical modeling
- compatibility with the mainframe
- ability to collect data from a spreadsheet

Again, each of these needs would be broken down into a list of specific operations. For example, "mainframe compatibility" might be broken down into the exact mainframe to share files, which protocol would be used in sharing files, and the means of communicating with the mainframe.

If possible, rank order this list of features to assist you in evaluating software. By using this second detailed list in reviewing the potential software packages, you can quickly eliminate those packages that fail to meet most of the requirements.

Step 3: Determine how well the software must work with other packages

The statistical packages available on the market usually feature the ability to share data files with other programs. For example, a basic statistical analysis package might have the ability to read data from a Lotus 1-2-3 spreadsheet or a dBase IV data file. At the same time, this package might be able to write its statistical reports in an ASCII format that your word processor can use.

This ability to share data files with other programs is growing rapidly in the statistical packages now available. In the future, we anticipate new software programs that are easier to use for data sharing and that interact with a larger number of popular application programs.

Spend some time looking at the possible benefits of having a statistical package that shares data. For example, suppose you are the manufacturing manager at a production facility that encourages the concept of Total Quality Management (TQM). As part of your system you need to analyze cost data from the production process. The accounting department currently enters that information on electronic spreadsheets. If your statistical package could read those spreadsheet files, it would save dozens of hours of hand entry of the same information. In addition, your statistical summaries could be saved in ASCII format, sent to your desktop publishing program on the same computer, and printed in near-typeset quality for a management presentation to the workers.

Step 4: Determine your budget for purchasing a package.

One of the main restrictions you may encounter is the budget allocated for the purchase of statistical software. Some packages cost under $100 and perform many statistical functions effectively. However, other statistical packages (especially those made for mainframe and UNIX-based computers) can run into the tens of thousands of dollars to purchase and support.

Your budget information allows you to plan how much to spend on the package and how much might be needed to put the package to work. For example, the purchase price of computer software usually represents less than half of the true cost. For example, a $1,000, off-the-shelf computer package for a personal computer will usually end up costing over $2,000. The extra expenses come from having to train others to use the package, the time to install and maintain the package, the cost of updates, and the price of extra equipment. The extra equipment could be a combination of various pieces of computer equipment to make the software package work more efficiently. This could include a math coprocessor, a larger hard disk, a better quality printer, or added computer memory.

Step 5: Determine how many people will be using the software.

The number of potential users determines the type of computer on which you will want to install the software. One or two people that need statistical analysis all of the time can usually be adequately provided for with a personal computer running the software. Three or more people scattered across the company will need a mainframe, local area network (LAN), or mini-computer. The exact choice will depend on your particular situation.

For example, three or more people in the same department are correctly served with a LAN whenever users need to share common data files. However, a similar number of users spread out over a company with a communication network tied to a mainframe or mini-computer might elect to use the existing terminals to access the software from a single computer.

Another important question is whether the software selected will closely match the type of programs already being used on existing computer equipment. If it does, the users will need less training to learn the operation of the software and they will feel more comfortable using the package. That will save you both time and money in putting the software to effective use.

Step 6: Determine how many times a day the software will be used.

The impact of a software package on existing computer usage will require additional planning for implementation. For example, a LAN-based software package may be used only once a day per person, but each use is estimated to last an hour. If the LAN is already at full capacity, then additional workstations or tighter scheduling may be required. Another possibility is to introduce batch processing of statistical analysis so that the network's time is used more efficiently.

The overall number of users and how many times they will use the package also helps you to plan the security system for the software. A security system involves more than keeping out unauthorized users; it should also ensure that users cannot accidentally destroy their own or another's data. If many people will be using the software frequently, then safeguards should be developed to protect data files.

Plan an active program of data backups to ensure the safety of statistical data stored electronically. The data should be copied to two forms of media and physically separated. For example, a statistical package used from the hard disk of a personal computer should back its data up to floppy disks or magnetic tape for storage in a different building. Then if the personal computer is destroyed, as in a fire, the data backups can be used to restore all data records within a day on a new computer.

Step 7: Determine the maximum number of variables, cases, and records likely to be used within an analysis.

Consider the largest analysis you will ever perform with your statistical package. Some packages will not store more than 100 variables at one time, but you may anticipate analyzing a market survey with over 150 questions. Other packages have a limit on the number of data points that can be entered. If you are entering all of the readings recorded on an SPC chart for one year of production for a specific manufacturing process, you could very easily enter over 50,000 numbers.

There is a two-fold reason for considering these factors. First, the maximum number of records used for a single application will help specify the capability of a software package to select. Some applications in statistics require only a few records (or pieces of data) to be used for each analysis. The capability study is an excellent example. The largest capability study will use 300 or fewer pieces of data. Thus, an inexpensive software program can easily handle the task. In contrast, the development and analysis of a survey instrument for a government contract might require that tens of thousands of records, each with dozens of pieces of information, be accessed and analyzed. These sheer numbers require a large computer with an equally large memory. In addition, the software must be capable of running at very high speeds to complete the task quickly. An 8088 or 68000 processor based computer could take weeks to complete the calculations a mainframe can do in minutes.

The second reason the number of records is important concerns the determination of the need for storage space for the data. A personal computer with a 40-megabyte hard drive can handle the data storage of many capability studies. However, large, complex, and repeated surveys or experimental research studies require mass data storage capabilities. These can be provided by magnetic tape drives, removable hard disks, and optical disks.

Step 8: Determine if special application software will be required.

No single statistical package performs every possible statistical function. Therefore, if special applications become part of the list of needs, you may have to purchase more than one software package or application programs that work with your statistical package. For example, the NCSS package can perform a wide array of statistical functions. However, if you will be performing experiments with replications, then you have to purchase an add-on program for this specific need.

An inexpensive way to meet some simple specialized needs is to use an existing software package. The classic example is the electronic spreadsheet, such as Lotus 1-2-3 or Excel. Special applications, such as probability analysis or accelerated testing models, can be developed on such software. In fact, Appendix D of this book was created in such a manner. Of course, when an application is developed in-house, it should be carefully reviewed, tested, and documented. Such in-house applications are usually expensive to develop and vulnerable to quality problems.

Step 9: Use the assessment of your needs to select and test a statistical package

The preceding steps are to be used as guidelines in selecting which application programs to test. In practice, you should select at least three programs that seem to fit your needs and budget. These selected programs should ideally be brought in-house for testing with your computers and users. If the software cannot be tested at your location, then take some potential users and some example data files and go to a retail store to test the software. Either way, you must answer the following fundamental questions before purchasing software.

- *Will the software that best fits your needs also run on your equipment?* All of the software packages that are selected as best meeting your needs should be taken to your office and run on your equipment. Only by physically seeing the software work on your company's computer equipment can you be sure of its compatibility. Consider the case of the public domain statistical software available that runs under BASIC. A problem occurs when you realize that the software does not specify whose version of the BASIC language it uses. For example, if installed for an IBM PC, it will not run on the supposedly compatible Compaq computer.

  Another situation is that the perfect software package is located, but it runs only on a computer your company does not have—for example, you find an Apple Macintosh program but your company is exclusively equipped with IBM PS/2 systems. The next step would be to determine if it would be practical and cheaper to buy the needed machine, as opposed to merely using a less capable package.

- *Do you need to capture data remotely?* Many statistical tasks require that a technician capture data readings from a remote machine, probe, or instrument. For example, a frequent requirement for a manufacturer is to have the ability to capture the data being collected by the coordinate measuring machine (CMM). If a separate computer could read and store the data, detailed capability studies or experiments would be possible at a far lower cost than entering the same information by hand. However, whenever remote data capture is a requirement, data transfer becomes an issue.

  In many cases, it takes more than a simple cable linking the remote data capture device to the computer to transfer the information. In the most straightforward situations, a communications software package must be present in both machines to effect a transfer. Naturally, both of these packages must be compatible for the transfer to work.

In other situations, a host of other problems are encountered. For example, an automated measuring gauge might send out readings in non-ASCII strings. Unless your computer has a program to recognize the sending signals and the data, the transfer will be unsuccessful. Therefore, a thorough review of software and hardware is required when data capture is a requirement.

- *How many people will have to be trained in the use of the software?* A critical issue related to productivity is the user friendliness of the software packages you are evaluating. In the case of statistical software, user friendliness has two characteristics. The first is that it is easy for the user to learn the operation of the package. Second, the day-to-day operation of the package is easy.

  For example, a package that requires the user to pass through several screens of questions before an analysis can begin is not very user friendly. A second package that allows a user familiar with the package to skip many steps and proceed straight to analysis would be considered friendly.

  No matter which software package you select, some training will be necessary. The obvious direction of training will be in the use of the software package. The price of current packages does not correlate to ease of use. Some inexpensive packages are difficult to learn and use, while some of the most expensive packages are extremely easy to learn and use.

  For a difficult package, new personnel will have to be trained when they are hired and existing personnel will have to be kept up to date on the newest software developments.

  Another less obvious training need is in the area of statistical applications. Statistical software will usually make available unfamiliar types of analysis. For example, ANOVA may have been done by calculator or spreadsheet in the past, but a Taguchi application package may present a new philosophy about ANOVA. Therefore, you will need to be retrained on these new approaches.

  When potential users test the software packages, feel free to ask them how they liked the programs. Make sure to list their likes and dislikes as part of your analysis. These lists might show a particular package as being unpopular with the potential users.

- *Will the type of data you collect and the analysis you perform work with every package?* As stated earlier, no software should be considered until you physically see it running on your own equipment. The final selection of a software package should involve a series of tests involving actual data collected at your company. Ideally, this data should be of two types. The first should be a typical set of data the software will have to analyze. The second should be an extreme case. The following example illustrates the types of data to use.

Assume that you are a production coordinator who plans to use a statistical package to create the SPC charts needed in the manufacturing areas. A typical case would be the 100 to 150 pieces of data collected to form an SPC chart. One part of the set would be variable data and another part would be attribute data. They would be entered into the software as separate files and the resulting SPC chart control limits would be compared to those calculated by hand.

An extreme set of data would be only a few samples from a production process. These would be fed into the computer to see if the software compensated automatically for the small sample size. If the software makes no correction or issues no warning, then the package would be rejected.

You may also want to supplement this test by creating a data file with "bad" data. For example, you may create a data file made up of measurements of a 1-inch diameter shaft. Planted in the data would be, for example, a 3-inch reading. Clearly, that reading would be an error. As part of your test, see if the package has error screening that picks up this problem data point. Without effective error screening, false information could be accidently entered into a data set.

In addition, the software should be judged on its presentation of the statistical information. A package that creates easy-to-read, logical outputs of the analysis is best. A package that also creates charts to summarize the data, trends, and so on is also judged to be superior.

- *What kind of support does the software require?* Software, just like the computer it runs on, can have problems and breakdowns. These are usually called "bugs." Bugs in a software package can run from being so minor you are unaware of their occurrence, to so severe that data is lost or the answers are wrong. Therefore, you should always insist on continuous support of any software package.

  For statistical packages, this should include a toll-free phone number to the software company's support personnel. It should also include updates and corrections to the software to fix bugs and increase the utility of the program. Mainframe packages should include on-site visits from the software company to maintain the software and data file structure, as well as provide some training to your personnel in the correct operation of the software.

Two major pitfalls of buying computer software must be avoided. The first is the software package that will be obsolete within a year of purchase.

SPSS, Inc. and SAS Institute, Inc. are two good examples of companies with software packages that have existed for years without going obsolete. These companies have strived to keep the packages up to date and bug free.

The usual causes for obsolescence involve the following:

1. The software package is not updated to a new operating system.
2. Math coprocessors or other new methods of increasing the speed of calculation are not supported.
3. New statistical techniques are not added to the package.
4. The developer does not improve the package to match user suggestions.
5. The ability of the package to work with other software applications is not exploited.

In addition, never buy the first version of any package. A revised package is more likely to have additional features and fewer bugs.

The second pitfall to avoid is a software company that goes out of business shortly after your purchase. To avoid this problem, a little background research on the company is warranted. Usually, a review of computer trade magazines will reveal the health or problems of a statistics software company. A good company will be one that has been in business for more than three or four years.

Conclusion

The guidelines discussed in this chapter represent the minimum amount of investigating you will want to do before purchasing a package. You may also want to talk to other people at your company or other sites that are currently using a statistical package. Ask them what they like and dislike about their software. If you can, find out what type of data they are analyzing and how it is analyzed. Often, the complaints of users stem from their own practices rather than the capability of the software.

You may also want to read books about the use of statistical software. If possible, get the manual to the statistical software you are reviewing. As you read the manual, ask yourself whether you readily understand how the package works. A well-written manual will save your company in support calls and extra training.

The real revolution in statistical packages is that they are no longer designed only for statisticians. Today's statistical packages are useful to any professional engaged in planning, controlling, designing, or monitoring processes. As manufacturing manager you can use a statistical package to perform quickly the calculations shown in this book. Then you can concentrate on the interpretation and use of your new-found information, instead of being tied down with analysis.

Finally, as stated at the beginning of this book: Statistics do not stand alone. Look carefully at how well the package you are considering will integrate with the software you already own. Will your spreadsheets be easily read by your statistical package? Will your statistical package print to your plotter? Can the output from your statistical package be cut and pasted into your word processor or desktop publishing system? If it can, you can create professional looking, near-typeset quality statistical reports. And, as you will learn in using statistics, presentation is half of the persuasion.

CHAPTER 18

How to Promote Statistical Thinking through Cross-Departmental Problem-Solving Teams

Statistics serve a specific and vital role in manufacturing. The advent of statistical process control, experimentation on the factory floor, and just-in-time delivery systems has increased the need for every professional in a manufacturing company to have some degree of skill in using statistical methods.

As a manufacturing manager you will discover that your job function will frequently require you to cooperate with professionals from other departments within your company. Competitive, world-class companies use teams of employees to attack problems and complete projects. Frequently these groups take the form of cross-departmental work teams. Professionals from several departments within the company work together to achieve a common goal. Usually, these goals are a direct result of the company's total quality management plan.

As a manager, other professionals will look toward you as a leader of a team. You will be expected to specify the statistical tools used to complete the task assigned to your cross-departmental team. For example, you may be matched with people from engineering, purchasing, and customer relations to design a new product. The management of the project and the tracking of both the cost and quality of the product could be your responsibility. However, for a successful team effort, each member must think statistically about the goals you set. Therefore, you must encourage other team members to use statistical methods.

To aid you in promoting statistical thinking, this chapter reviews the primary function of several departments within a manufacturing company. By seeing where each department's interests lie, you can better judge how to encourage specific people to use statistical methods. When many professionals within a company use statistical methods, then a common, objective language of communication through numbers is possible. For example, the charting of machine operator efficiency might be a job for the personnel department. This information can then be shared and understood by other professionals who have learned to think statistically.

How to Use Statistics to Improve Your Daily Operations

Manufacturing is the combining of people, materials, and machines to create a product. This involves planning, controlling, organizing, and monitoring. Both managers and other manufacturing professionals need to utilize a lot of nonstatistical techniques to accomplish daily tasks. Cost accounting, management skills, physics, chemistry, politics, personalities, and personal emotions are just some of the sources of information a person can use to make a decision, solve a problem, or plan future activities. The role of statistics is to fill in cracks between these other sources. Statistics "glue" these other functions together by producing a performance measure for continuous improvements.

Without statistics, the goal of continuous improvement is frequently hampered. It is not unusual to find a production planning meeting brought to a standstill because someone in an important position says that there is too much risk or the company does not know the consequences of a proposed action.

Statistics measure the risks, gather the evidence, and probe the unknown. The estimations provided by statistical reasoning and testing provide decision makers with the information they need.

Another aspect of the use of statistics is the difference between effectiveness and efficiency. Effectiveness is the magnitude of the ability to solve a problem or complete a task. A manager that completes a yearly set of tasks ahead of schedule is said to be effective. Efficiency is completing a task or solving a problem with maximum economy. For example, a highly paid political lobbyist may convince Congress to grant your company immunity from trade legislation and thus save you millions of dollars every year. The money spent on the lobbyist was efficiently used. However, if the same lobbyist worked only one week to accomplish the task and spent the next 51 weeks in Florida, we would say that he may be effective, but he is not efficient.

The secondary role of statistics in manufacturing is to find the best path to a good combination of efficiency and effectiveness. We will examine how that is done using a number of the examples from manufacturing. Study these examples to see how a single statistical method can be applied to several different and disparate situations.

How to Emphasize Which Statistical Methods Can be Applied by Other Departments

For the sake of clarity, we will divide the manufacturing plant into six general departments that represent common interests more than actual departmental divisions.

1. Management and personnel
2. Production
3. Quality
4. Inventory
5. Engineering and technical support
6. Sales and marketing

For each of these six areas we will discuss their primary roles and how statistics play a part. In addition, we will discuss possible applications of statistical methods more commonly used by another department. This should give you a set a guidelines for participating in cross-departmental teams to solve a major problem.

Involving Top Management and the Personnel Department

Management and the personnel department are responsible for the hiring, tracking, development, and control of the people that work within the company.

Management is responsible for establishing the statistical policy of the company. Statistics are no longer an ungovernable method within industry. Instead, company policies must incorporate statistical methods in the strategic plan. The most visible evidence of this in recent years is the widespread use of statistical process control (SPC). The first step in applying SPC is to write a company operations policy that states that the strategic goal of the company is the continuous improvement of operations and customer satisfaction. From this general policy, management further establishes a series of procedures for the use, distribution, and interpretation of statistical methods. One example of these procedures is the management information system. It is critical that the data gathered and summarized within the plant be reported to management so that actions can be taken. Statistics that are gathered for the record are, for the most part, useless. Acting on the intelligence that statistics provide is the opportunity for both improvement and profit.

After the policies and procedures are established, management works with each department to create specific plans as to how statistical methods are incorporated into daily operations. Specifically, statistical methods are woven into current practices or replace obsolete techniques. Adding more tasks to an already overburdened work force is counterproductive.

One example of these plans is the failure mode and effect analysis (FMEA). This is a report on a new product going into manufacturing that states which aspects of the product are most critical to its functional success. For each of these critical areas, the company states which method it will use to monitor the critical characteristics. Usually, statistical methods such as sampling, destructive testing, and process control charts are listed.

The personnel department is responsible for the hiring or training of people capable of working with the statistical methods the company applies. For example, an engineering candidate may be screened for knowledge of experimental methods or a new machine operator may be trained to fill in SPC charts.

In addition, the personnel department may collect statistical summaries of personnel performance. These may include rates of absenteeism, plant productivity, accident rates, sick days claimed, and other measures of work force effectiveness. Any of this information could be charted on simple line charts while both management and personnel work to improve each performance record through new and inventive programs.

Such information can be integrated into manufacturing engineering projects, such as overall manufacturing productivity reports. By having the personnel department collect data related to people, you are free to collect machine-specific information.

How to Coordinate Statistical Activities in the Production Department

The production department involves everyone from the production planning function to the line supervisors to the machine operators. The role of the production department is to route, schedule, and dispatch the materials, people, and tools necessary for manufacturing specific products. In addition, a modern manufacturing plant must monitor the success of its efforts so that continuous improvement of production methods is pursued. Your job as manufacturing manager is to facilitate and lead these efforts.

The production department must monitor dozens of other pieces of information. These include the following:

1. the rate of purchase requisitions released on time;
2. the accuracy of purchase orders;
3. lead-time stress;
4. how many work orders are past due;
5. the average cost to scrap or rework a part;
6. the average number of downtime hours per 1,000 hours of machine operation;
7. the accuracy of the production schedule;
8. percent utilization of equipment; and
9. location and magnitude of the causes of work delays.

Although this is not a complete list of statistics the production department should be monitoring, it covers most of the important areas. Any of these statistics can be gathered and reported using the methods outlined in chapter 1. In most cases, the information is merely charted as the planned occurrence versus the observed performance.

As a manufacturing manager, you should actively review this data from the production department. You should request copies of these reports. Then you will have the essential baseline data needed to make tests, experiment with new methods, and evaluate the improvements in new designs.

In addition to monitoring plant performance, the production department should be actively involved in problem solving and project management. Taken together, we can call these two activities crisis management. Since a production area can be unpredictable, it is wise for a production department to practice methods for coping with the unexpected.

This ongoing crisis management in a production department requires the use of cross-departmental teams. Therefore, you will probably be expected to provide technical leadership within one of these teams. This includes the suggestion of proper statistical techniques to use in a particular situation.

How the Quality Department Uses Statistics to Watch the Quality of the Product and the Cost of Defects

The quality department is still undergoing major changes in many companies. Twenty years ago the department would have been called quality control. Ten years ago the name likely would have been quality assurance. Today the trend is toward the name quality department, quality audit or excellence in manufacturing. These name changes represent the fundamental changes in the role of the quality department.

The inspection function of quality still exists, but it is done much less during production. SPC has taken over that role, and the production department should be responsible for SPC. The need to audit vendors has increased with the switch to just-in-time delivery systems. Without perfect quality a just-in-time system fails. Also, the personnel in quality are taking on more of a support role as they train and consult the production and engineering departments. The newest twist in this consultation trend is the reporting of the cost of quality (COQ) to other departments. This is the cost of any mistakes made during manufacturing.

In addition to these primary functions, the quality department might also become involved with the following activities.

1. Capability studies
2. In-plant audits
3. Make-or-buy decisions
4. Tool wear studies
5. Methods testing

6. Experimentation
7. Problem solving
8. Failure analysis
9. Customer surveys

In a cross-departmental team, the information from the quality department represents the current strength of manufacturing and the voices of both customers and suppliers. This wide range of information is particularly helpful for giving a team the "big picture."

How the Inventory Manager Might Use Statistics

The inventory department is responsible for the flow, control, and storage of the materials involved in manufacturing. This includes the final products. The keystone statistic for inventory is the number of turns per year. This is calculated as

$$\frac{\text{yearly sales}}{\text{inventory value}} = \text{turns}$$

Thus, if a company had $50 million in sales and the average value of the inventory was $10 million, they had five turns of inventory per year. The importance of this statistic is growing as new methods of inventory, such as zero inventories and just-in-time, begin to dominate the field. Under these systems, the turns reach ever higher numbers. It is not difficult today to find a warehouse with a turn of 48 hours or less.

In addition to turns, the managers of the inventory control staff have a wide array of mathematical formulas to calculate, such as minimum inventory, maximum stock on hand, and optimal material levels. These types of calculations are supplemented with statistical estimates and probabilities. In chapter 7, we examined how statistics work in harmony with standard inventory calculations to help design a just-in-time system of delivery and inventory.

In addition to the aforementioned methods, other statistical techniques, such as the following, can assist the planning and monitoring of an inventory system.

1. Monitoring the lead time in requesting materials
2. Monitoring the effectiveness of material transportation within manufacturing
3. Auditing the closeout of paperwork
4. Determining the costs from damage or missing stock
5. Picking and placing accuracy

This type of information can be vital for assisting inventory control personnel in searching out and eliminating delays or other problems in the system. Therefore, the probability is high that a you will become involved in a cross-departmental team that includes inventory control personnel.

How Statistics Aid Engineering Professionals and Technical Support Staff

These departments are responsible for the technology of the manufacturing operation. This technology includes the design of products, processes, and systems. Specifically, it includes tasks such as setting tolerances, establishing machine set-ups, testing of products, calibration of equipment, research and development, and active problem solving. At every step statistics play an important role.

In chapters 9 and 10, we discussed a concept called *factory as laboratory*. This is the idea of continuously testing and improving every aspect of the manufacturing system through the use of experimentation. An experiment is an expensive process of investigation. It would be inefficient to repeat an experiment unnecessarily.

In addition to experimentation, these departments frequently employ other statistical techniques to complement the use of mathematical calculations, such as

1. correlation studies on the effect of selected factors on process performance;
2. estimation and probabilities as part of project management;
3. descriptive statistics to establish the current conditions present in manufacturing;
4. cost estimates for bids;
5. time estimates for work standards;
6. statistical process control to monitor the efficiency of a process;
7. failure and reliability analysis matched against customer requirements.

Actually, the list could include any statistical technique. Engineers and technicians must always keep a battery of available methods at hand to cope with the often unexpected tasks they are assigned. In addition to statistical methods, this can include such divergent techniques as computer programming, linear programming, system dynamics, systems analysis, queuing theory, control theory, physics, chemistry, and industrial engineering.

How the Sales and Marketing Departments Play an Active Role in Manufacturing

The sales and marketing departments are responsible for identifying and pursuing potential customers for the products and services their company produces. This is a unique task today because no product can be sold without an accompanying service. That service is the availability of information about the qualities of the product and how it was made.

This means that you must monitor and report production data to the customer. Which data to collect and how to best present it is a question the sales department must answer through close communications with the customer.

A world-class manufacturer must have close ties with the customer and understand the customer's needs. Listening to the customer's voice is critical. If the customer's needs are met and exceeded, business growth is possible.

Furthermore, a world-class manufacturer must present a quality image in the marketplace. The marketing department can both research customer perceptions and suggest methods of enhancing your company's quality image. Therefore, it is vital to remember that you no longer work in a vacuum. You must communicate constantly with customers through the sales and marketing channels already in existence.

Consider the example of an automotive parts supplier. This type of company would supply parts to one of the major automotive companies, such as Ford or General Motors. However, they can no longer sell just parts; instead, each set of parts is accompanied by statistical reports that assure the quality of the product. In most cases, every production run shipped must have a statistical process control chart included in the standard paperwork. This means that the salespeople must have a working knowledge of simple statistical techniques to be effective with customers.

The chapters on descriptive statistics, quality assurance, and statistical process control can greatly benefit sales and marketing personnel. Marketing personnel must be able to sample and estimate potential customers with accuracy. Worldwide competition is making niche marketing more difficult.

In addition, the marketing and sales departments are responsible for putting together detailed forecasts of future demands for products and services. These are used by the other manufacturing departments for planning activities and material requests. Chapter 8 discussed the basic methods of forecasting.

Other statistical techniques, such as the following, can be used by these departments to find subtle routes toward continuous improvement:

1. testing sales performance by area from different people to determine the optimal sales assignments;
2. correlating forecasts against actual performance to improve the methods of prediction;
3. estimating the cost of a dissatisfied customer;
4. monitoring the responses of manufacturing to demand;

5. developing and testing survey instruments before they are given to the general public;

6. researching more effective sales techniques.

Thus, even the sales and marketing groups within a company have a pressing need to be familiar with statistical methods and reasoning.

Training: The Key to Promoting Statistical Thinking

The best way to promote the widespread use of statistical thinking is to demonstrate the effectiveness of a few statistical methods as part of your team effort. Other team members will be curious to learn more about statistics when they see that statistics can save money and find solutions to difficult problems. To convert this curiosity into enthusiasm, practical and effective training is needed. Having a knowledgeable person teach statistical methods using examples from your own company will develop employees into better workers and professionals. However, training must proceed with caution. You should compile a list of specific statistical tasks the participants will be able to do after receiving training. This helps you to plan a custom-designed training course based on your own needs.

The epidemic of math illiteracy at all levels of employment makes it imperative that you screen people for their math abilities before training begins. People with weaker math skills can receive extra training to strengthen their comprehension of statistics.

Training is also an excellent opportunity to reinforce the total quality message of the company. The training could begin with a statement of the purpose of statistics within your company. This would be the obvious message. However, more subtle messages are transmitted during training. The mere fact that people have been assigned time away from their normal jobs to learn this skill indicates the importance of statistics as a job function. In addition, by using examples from the plant of cost savings through statistical thinking, another message is sent emphasizing statistics as an important tool of management.

Finally, training is an opportunity for people from different work areas and job descriptions to meet and discuss common problems. When upper management is invited to attend such training, it is usually the first time that people from the factory floor are able to listen to management concerns while they express frustrations about working situations. This promotes improved communication throughout the company.

In short, not only is training an excellent way to spread statistical thinking within your company without upsetting political feelings, it also promotes understanding and communicates your company's message of continuous improvement.

Conclusion

When seeking world-class manufacturing techniques, you will almost never work alone. Cross-departmental teams and group problem-solving efforts in your own department will require the intelligent delegation of statistical tasks to others. Therefore, you must first learn your statistical tools and which tools are best used by others. This book can serve as a guide, giving specific examples from many departments. Only when statistical techniques are used as part of continuous improvement among all employees and operations can your company depend on reaping financial benefits.

Recommended Reading

Barker, Thomas B., *Quality by Experimental Design*, New York, Dekker Press and ASQC, 1985. A discussion of the experimental process that combines classic methods with Taguchi's philosophy.

Baumol, William J., *Economic Theory and Operations Analysis*, Englewood Cliffs, NJ, Prentice-Hall, 1977. Discusses the quantitative approach to the operation of a business. Uses both statistical and mathematical techniques in decision making.

Becker, Charles H., *Plant Manager's Manual and Guide*, Englewood Cliffs, NJ, Prentice-Hall, 1987. An overview of the roles and responsibilities of a plant manager.

Besterfield, Dale H., *Quality Control*, Englewood Cliffs, NJ, Prentice-Hall, 1986. An introduction to the quality assurance function.

Blalock, Hubert M., *Social Statistics*, New York, McGraw-Hill, 1972. Discusses the analysis of nonvariable data.

Box, G. E. P., Hunter, W., and Hunter, J. S., *Statistics for Experimenters*, New York, John Wiley & Sons, 1978. The best book to read on how to analyze an experiment.

Brown, Robert T., *Decision Rules for Inventory Management*, New York, Holt, Reinhart and Winston, 1967. A helpful guide to the decisions made in inventory management.

Clements, Richard B., *The Management of Desktop Publishing*, Harrision, NY, MGI Management Institute, 1988. Includes guidelines on using desktop publishing for technical reports.

Clements, Richard R., *Statistical Process Control and Beyond*, Melbourne, FL, Robert E. Krieger Publishing, 1988. An overview of the implementation and management of an SPC system. Also discusses what happens after an SPC system has been implemented.

Department of Defense, *Total Quality Management (DoD 5000.5)*, OASD(P&L) TQM, Washington, DC, Pentagon, 1989. An overview of total quality management as a system of continuous improvement for all organizations.

Emory, C. William, *Business Research Methods*, Homewood, IL, Richard D. Irwin, Inc., 1980. Discusses the method of experimenting and other techniques of research for business.

Hall, Robert W., *Zero Inventories*, Homewood, IL, Dow Jones-Irwin, 1983. Discusses the just-in-time philosophy and method.

Hay, Edward J., *The Just-in-Time Breakthrough*, New York, John Wiley and Sons, 1988. Another good book to read to get the feel of JIT.

Hein, Leonard W., *The Quantitative Approach to Managerial Decisions*, Englewood Cliffs, NJ, Prentice-Hall, 1967. A good resource book if you want to explore the idea of decision making under uncertainty.

Hughes and Grawoig, *Statistics: A Foundation for Analysis*, Reading, MA, Addison-Wesley Publishing, 1971. A technically oriented text on statistical methods. Includes many simple statistical tests most introductory texts leave out.

Japan Management Association, *Kanban: Just-in-Time at Toyota*, Stamford, CT, Productivity Press, 1985. An in-depth examination of Kanban and its relationship to the just-in-time philosophy.

Juran and Gryna, *Quality Planning and Analysis*, New York, McGraw-Hill, 1980. The definitive book on quality assurance and its relationship to engineering and other manufacturing functions.

Mac Niece, E. H., *Production Forecasting, Planning and Control*, New York, John Wiley and Sons, 1961. A source book containing the fundamental methods of forecasting and planning.

Mason, Robert D., *Statistical Techniques in Business and Economics*, Homewood, IL, Richard D. Irwin, Inc., 1982. Possibly the best introductory text to statistics ever written. This book is highly recommended for anyone studying statistical methods for the first time.

Moffat, Donald W., *Handbook of Manufacturing & Production Management Formulas, Charts and Tables*, Englewood Cliffs, NJ, Prentice-Hall, 1987. Use this book to learn about the manufacturing calculations outside the scope of our text.

Rodgers, William P., *Introduction to Safety System Engineering*, New York, John Wiley and Sons, 1971. Discusses the science of ensuring the safety of a product.

Schlaifer, Robert, *Probability and Statistics for Business Decisions*, New York, McGraw-Hill, 1959. Another resource book about making decisions under uncertainty.

Schonberger, Richard J., *Japanese Manufacturing Techniques*, New York, Free Press, 1982. An overview of techniques that are now called world-class manufacturing.

Taguchi, Genichi, *Introduction to Quality Engineering*, Tokyo, Asian Productivity Organization, 1986. This is Dr. Taguchi's central work on experimentation. It is not easily read, but it does contain the elegant stories he is famous for on why a product must be robust.

Williamson, Karp, and Dalphin, *The Research Craft*, New York, Little, Brown and Co., 1977. An overview of surveying techniques.

Appendix

The following appendices were created on Lotus 1-2-3 spreadsheets and confirmed using *Elementary Statistical Tables* by Henry R. Neave. The data obtained is reproduced here with the kind permission of the publisher, George Allen & Unwin, Ltd., London.

Appendix A Area Under the Curve of the Normal Distribution
(multiply by 100 to obtain percentages)

Z-Score	0.00	0.01	0.02	0.03	0.04	0.05	0.06
0.00	0.0000	0.0040	0.0080	0.0120	0.0160	0.0199	0.0239
0.10	0.0398	0.0438	0.0478	0.0517	0.0557	0.0596	0.0636
0.20	0.0793	0.0832	0.0871	0.0910	0.0948	0.0987	0.1026
0.30	0.1179	0.1217	0.1255	0.1293	0.1331	0.1368	0.1406
0.40	0.1554	0.1591	0.1628	0.1664	0.1700	0.1736	0.1772
0.50	0.1915	0.1950	0.1985	0.2019	0.2054	0.2088	0.2123
0.60	0.2257	0.2291	0.2324	0.2357	0.2389	0.2422	0.2454
0.70	0.2580	0.2611	0.2642	0.2673	0.2704	0.2734	0.2764
0.80	0.2881	0.2910	0.2939	0.2967	0.2995	0.3023	0.3051
0.90	0.3159	0.3186	0.3212	0.3238	0.3264	0.3289	0.3315
1.00	0.3413	0.3438	0.3461	0.3485	0.3508	0.3531	0.3554
1.10	0.3643	0.3665	0.3686	0.3708	0.3729	0.3749	0.3770
1.20	0.3849	0.3869	0.3888	0.3907	0.3925	0.3944	0.3962
1.30	0.4023	0.4049	0.4066	0.4082	0.4099	0.4115	0.4131
1.40	0.4192	0.4207	0.4222	0.4236	0.4251	0.4265	0.4279
1.50	0.4332	0.4345	0.4357	0.4370	0.4382	0.4394	0.4406
1.60	0.4452	0.4463	0.4474	0.4484	0.4495	0.4505	0.4515
1.70	0.4554	0.4564	0.4573	0.4582	0.4591	0.4599	0.4608
1.80	0.4611	0.4649	0.4656	0.4664	0.4671	0.4678	0.4686
1.90	0.4713	0.4719	0.4726	0.4732	0.4738	0.4744	0.4750
2.00	0.4772	0.4778	0.4783	0.4788	0.4793	0.4798	0.4803
2.10	0.4821	0.4826	0.4830	0.4864	0.4868	0.4842	0.4846
2.20	0.4861	0.4864	0.4868	0.4871	0.4875	0.4878	0.4881
2.30	0.4893	0.4896	0.4898	0.4901	0.4904	0.4906	0.4909
2.40	0.4918	0.4920	0.4922	0.4925	0.4927	0.4929	0.4931
2.50	0.4938	0.4940	0.4941	0.4943	0.4945	0.4946	0.4948
2.60	0.4953	0.4955	0.4956	0.4957	0.4959	0.4960	0.4961
2.70	0.4965	0.4966	0.4967	0.4968	0.4969	0.4970	0.4971
2.80	0.4974	0.4975	0.4976	0.4977	0.4977	0.4978	0.4979
2.90	0.4981	0.4982	0.4982	0.4983	0.4984	0.4984	0.4985
3.00	0.49865	0.49869	0.49874	0.49878	0.49878	0.49882	0.49889
3.10	0.49903	0.49906	0.49910	0.49913	0.49916	0.49918	0.49921
3.20	0.49930						
3.30	0.49950						
3.40	0.49960						
3.50	0.49970						
3.60	0.49984						
3.70	0.49989						
3.80	0.49992						
3.90	0.49995						
4.00	0.49999						
5.00	0.49999						

Appendix A continued

Z-Score	0.07	0.08	0.09
0.00	0.0279	0.0319	0.0359
0.10	0.0675	0.0714	0.0753
0.20	0.1064	0.1103	0.1141
0.30	0.1443	0.1480	0.1517
0.40	0.1808	0.1844	0.1879
0.50	0.2157	0.2190	0.2224
0.60	0.2486	0.2517	0.2549
0.70	0.2794	0.2823	0.2852
0.80	0.3078	0.3106	0.3133
0.90	0.3340	0.3365	0.3389
1.00	0.3577	0.3599	0.3621
1.10	0.3790	0.3810	0.3830
1.20	0.3980	0.3997	0.4015
1.30	0.4147	0.4162	0.4177
1.40	0.4292	0.4306	0.4319
1.50	0.4418	0.4429	0.4441
1.60	0.4525	0.4535	0.4545
1.70	0.4616	0.4625	0.4633
1.80	0.4693	0.4699	0.4706
1.90	0.4756	0.4761	0.4767
2.00	0.4808	0.4812	0.4817
2.10	0.4850	0.4854	0.4857
2.20	0.4884	0.4887	0.4890
2.30	0.4911	0.4913	0.4916
2.40	0.4932	0.4934	0.4936
2.50	0.4949	0.4951	0.4952
2.60	0.4962	0.4963	0.4964
2.70	0.4972	0.4973	0.4974
2.80	0.4979	0.4980	0.4981
2.90	0.4985	0.4986	0.4986
3.00	0.49893	0.49897	0.49900
3.10	0.49924	0.49926	0.49929
3.20			
3.30			
3.40			
3.50			
3.60			
3.70			
3.80			
3.90			
4.00			
5.00			

Appendix B Critical *t*-values

		Percent Confidence	
One-Tail	95%	97.5%	99.5%
Two-Tail	90%	95%	99%
df 1	6.314	12.706	63.657
2	2.920	4.303	9.925
3	2.353	3.182	5.481
4	2.132	2.776	4.604
5	2.015	2.571	4.032
6	1.943	2.447	3.707
7	1.895	2.365	3.499
8	1.860	2.306	3.355
9	1.833	2.262	3.250
10	1.812	2.228	3.169
11	1.796	2.201	3.106
12	1.782	2.179	3.055
13	1.771	2.160	3.012
14	1.761	2.145	2.977
15	1.753	2.131	2.947
16	1.746	2.120	2.921
17	1.740	2.110	2.898
18	1.734	2.101	2.878
19	1.729	2.093	2.861
20	1.725	2.086	2.845
21	1.721	2.080	2.831
22	1.717	2.074	2.819
23	1.714	2.069	2.807
24	1.711	2.064	2.797
25	1.708	2.060	2.787
26	1.706	2.056	2.779
27	1.703	2.052	2.771
28	1.701	2.048	2.763
29	1.699	2.045	2.756
30	1.697	2.042	2.750
31	1.695	2.039	2.744
32	1.694	2.037	2.738
33	1.692	2.034	2.733
34	1.691	2.032	2.728
35	1.690	2.030	2.724
40	1.684	2.021	2.704
50	1.676	2.009	2.678
100	1.660	1.984	2.626
150	1.655	1.976	2.609

Appendix C Critical Chi-Square Values

Degrees of Freedom	0.5%	1%	Left Tail 2.5%	5%	10%
1	0.00004	0.00016	0.00098	0.00393	0.0158
2	0.010	0.020	0.051	0.103	0.211
3	0.072	0.115	0.216	0.352	0.584
4	0.207	0.297	0.484	0.711	1.064
5	0.412	0.554	0.831	1.145	1.610
6	0.676	0.872	1.240	1.640	2.200
7	0.989	1.240	1.690	2.170	2.830
8	1.34	1.65	2.18	2.73	3.49
9	1.74	2.09	2.70	3.32	4.17
10	2.16	2.56	3.25	3.94	4.86
11	2.60	3.05	3.82	4.58	5.58
12	3.07	3.57	4.40	5.23	6.30
13	3.56	4.11	5.01	5.89	7.04
14	4.07	4.66	5.63	6.57	7.79
15	4.60	5.23	6.26	7.26	8.55
16	5.14	5.81	6.91	7.96	9.31
17	5.70	6.41	7.56	8.67	10.08
18	6.26	7.01	8.23	9.39	10.86
19	6.84	7.63	8.91	10.12	11.65
20	7.43	8.26	9.59	10.85	12.44
21	8.03	8.90	10.28	11.59	13.24
22	8.64	9.54	10.98	12.34	14.04
23	9.26	10.20	11.69	13.09	14.85
24	9.89	10.86	12.40	13.85	15.66
25	10.52	11.52	13.12	14.61	16.47
26	11.16	12.20	13.84	15.38	17.29
27	11.81	12.88	14.57	16.15	18.11
28	12.46	13.56	15.31	16.93	18.94
29	13.12	14.26	16.05	17.71	19.77
30	13.79	14.95	16.79	18.49	20.60
50	27.99	29.71	32.36	34.76	37.69
100	67.33	70.06	74.22	77.93	82.36

Appendix C continued

90%	95%	Right Tail 97.5%	99%	99.5%
2.71	3.84	5.02	6.64	7.88
4.60	5.99	7.38	9.21	10.60
6.25	7.82	9.35	11.34	12.84
7.78	9.49	11.14	13.28	14.86
9.24	11.07	12.83	15.09	16.75
10.64	12.59	14.45	16.81	18.55
12.02	14.07	16.01	18.48	20.28
13.36	15.51	17.54	20.09	21.96
14.68	16.92	19.02	21.67	23.59
15.99	18.31	20.48	23.21	25.19
17.28	19.68	21.92	24.72	26.76
18.55	21.03	23.34	26.22	28.30
19.81	22.36	24.74	27.69	29.82
21.06	23.68	26.12	29.14	31.32
22.31	25.00	27.49	30.58	32.80
23.54	26.30	28.84	32.00	34.27
24.77	27.59	30.19	33.41	35.72
25.99	28.87	31.53	34.80	37.16
27.20	30.14	32.85	36.19	38.58
28.41	31.41	34.17	37.57	40.00
29.62	32.67	35.48	38.93	41.40
30.81	33.92	36.78	40.29	42.80
32.01	35.17	38.08	41.64	44.18
33.20	36.42	39.36	42.98	45.56
34.38	37.65	40.65	44.31	46.93
35.56	38.88	41.92	45.64	48.29
36.74	40.11	43.20	46.96	49.64
37.92	41.34	44.46	48.28	50.99
39.09	42.56	45.72	49.59	52.34
40.26	43.77	46.98	50.89	53.67
63.17	67.50	71.42	76.15	79.49
118.50	124.34	129.56	135.81	140.17

Appendix D Poisson Distribution (Cumulative)

c=	np	0.01	0.02	0.03	0.04	0.05	0.06	0.07
	0	0.9900	0.9802	0.9704	0.9608	0.9512	0.9418	0.9324
	1	0.9999	0.9998	0.9995	0.9992	0.9988	0.9983	0.9977
	2	1.0000	1.0000	1.0000	1.0000	1.0000	1.0000	1.0000
	3	1.0000	1.0000	1.0000	1.0000	1.0000	1.0000	1.0000
	4	1.0000	1.0000	1.0000	1.0000	1.0000	1.0000	1.0000
	5	1.0000	1.0000	1.0000	1.0000	1.0000	1.0000	1.0000
	6	1.0000	1.0000	1.0000	1.0000	1.0000	1.0000	1.0000
	7	1.0000	1.0000	1.0000	1.0000	1.0000	1.0000	1.0000
	8	1.0000	1.0000	1.0000	1.0000	1.0000	1.0000	1.0000

c=	np	0.08	0.09	0.1	0.11	0.12	0.13	0.14
	0	0.9231	0.9139	0.9048	0.8958	0.8869	0.8781	0.8694
	1	0.9969	0.9962	0.9953	0.9943	0.9933	0.9923	0.9911
	2	0.9999	0.9999	0.9998	0.9997	0.9997	0.9997	0.9996
	3	1.0000	1.0000	1.0000	1.0000	1.0000	1.0000	1.0000
	4	1.0000	1.0000	1.0000	1.0000	1.0000	1.0000	1.0000
	5	1.0000	1.0000	1.0000	1.0000	1.0000	1.0000	1.0000
	6	1.0000	1.0000	1.0000	1.0000	1.0000	1.0000	1.0000
	7	1.0000	1.0000	1.0000	1.0000	1.0000	1.0000	1.0000
	8	1.0000	1.0000	1.0000	1.0000	1.0000	1.0000	1.0000

c=	np	0.15	0.16	0.17	0.18	0.19	0.20	0.25
	0	0.8607	0.8521	0.8437	0.8353	0.8270	0.8187	0.7788
	1	0.9898	0.9884	0.9871	0.9856	0.9841	0.9824	0.9735
	2	0.9995	0.9993	0.9993	0.9991	0.9990	0.9988	0.9978
	3	1.0000	1.0000	1.0000	1.0000	0.9999	0.9999	0.9998
	4	1.0000	1.0000	1.0000	1.0000	1.0000	1.0000	1.0000
	5	1.0000	1.0000	1.0000	1.0000	1.0000	1.0000	1.0000
	6	1.0000	1.0000	1.0000	1.0000	1.0000	1.0000	1.0000
	7	1.0000	1.0000	1.0000	1.0000	1.0000	1.0000	1.0000
	8	1.0000	1.0000	1.0000	1.0000	1.0000	1.0000	1.0000

Appendix D continued

c=	np	0.30	0.35	0.40	0.45	0.50	0.55	0.60
	0	0.7408	0.7047	0.6703	0.6376	0.6065	0.5769	0.5488
	1	0.9630	0.9513	0.9384	0.9245	0.9098	0.8942	0.8781
	2	0.9963	0.9945	0.9920	0.9891	0.9856	0.9815	0.9769
	3	0.9996	0.9995	0.9992	0.9988	0.9982	0.9975	0.9967
	4	1.0000	1.0000	0.9999	0.9999	0.9998	0.9997	0.9997
	5	1.0000	1.0000	1.0000	1.0000	1.0000	1.0000	1.0000
	6	1.0000	1.0000	1.0000	1.0000	1.0000	1.0000	1.0000
	7	1.0000	1.0000	1.0000	1.0000	1.0000	1.0000	1.0000
	8	1.0000	1.0000	1.0000	1.0000	1.0000	1.0000	1.0000

c=	np	0.60	0.65	0.70	0.75	0.80	0.85	0.90
	0	0.5488	0.5220	0.4966	0.4724	0.4493	0.4274	0.4066
	1	0.8781	0.8613	0.8442	0.8267	0.8088	0.7907	0.7725
	2	0.9769	0.9716	0.9659	0.9596	0.9526	0.9451	0.9372
	3	0.9967	0.9955	0.9943	0.9928	0.9909	0.9888	0.9866
	4	0.9997	0.9994	0.9993	0.9990	0.9986	0.9981	0.9977
	5	1.0000	0.9999	0.9999	0.9999	0.9998	0.9997	0.9997
	6	1.0000	1.0000	1.0000	1.0000	1.0000	1.0000	1.0000
	7	1.0000	1.0000	1.0000	1.0000	1.0000	1.0000	1.0000
	8	1.0000	1.0000	1.0000	1.0000	1.0000	1.0000	1.0000

c=	np	0.95	1.00	1.05	1.10	1.15	1.20	1.25
	0	0.3867	0.3679	0.3499	0.3329	0.3166	0.3012	0.2865
	1	0.7541	0.7358	0.7173	0.6991	0.6807	0.6626	0.6446
	2	0.9286	0.9197	0.9102	0.9005	0.8901	0.8795	0.8684
	3	0.9839	0.9810	0.9777	0.9743	0.9704	0.9662	0.9617
	4	0.9970	0.9963	0.9954	0.9946	0.9935	0.9922	0.9908
	5	0.9995	0.9994	0.9991	0.9991	0.9988	0.9984	0.9981
	6	0.9999	0.9999	0.9998	0.9999	0.9998	0.9996	0.9996
	7	1.0000	1.0000	1.0000	1.0000	1.0000	0.9998	0.9999
	8	1.0000	1.0000	1.0000	1.0000	1.0000	1.0000	1.0000

Appendix D continued

np	1.30	1.35	1.40	1.45	1.50	1.55	1.60
c=							
0	0.2725	0.2592	0.2466	0.2346	0.2231	0.2122	0.2019
1	0.6268	0.6092	0.5918	0.5747	0.5578	0.5412	0.5249
2	0.8571	0.8454	0.8335	0.8213	0.8088	0.7962	0.7833
3	0.9569	0.9517	0.9463	0.9405	0.9343	0.9279	0.9211
4	0.9893	0.9876	0.9858	0.9837	0.9814	0.9789	0.9762
5	0.9977	0.9973	0.9969	0.9962	0.9955	0.9947	0.9938
6	0.9995	0.9995	0.9995	0.9992	0.9990	0.9988	0.9985
7	0.9998	0.9999	0.9999	0.9998	0.9998	0.9997	0.9996
8	0.9999	1.0000	1.0000	0.9999	0.9999	0.9999	0.9998

np	1.70	1.75	1.80	1.85	1.90	1.95	2.00
c=							
0	0.1827	0.1738	0.1653	0.1572	0.1496	0.1423	0.1353
1	0.4933	0.4779	0.4628	0.4481	0.4338	0.4197	0.4060
2	0.7573	0.7440	0.7306	0.7172	0.7038	0.6902	0.6767
3	0.9069	0.8992	0.8913	0.8831	0.8748	0.8660	0.8571
4	0.9705	0.9671	0.9636	0.9598	0.9560	0.9517	0.9473
5	0.9921	0.9909	0.9896	0.9882	0.9869	0.9851	0.9834
6	0.9982	0.9978	0.9974	0.9970	0.9967	0.9960	0.9954
7	0.9997	0.9995	0.9994	0.9993	0.9994	0.9990	0.9988
8	0.9999	0.9999	0.9999	0.9998	0.9999	0.9997	0.9997
9	1.0000	1.0000	1.0000	1.0000	1.0000	1.0000	1.0000
10	1.0000	1.0000	1.0000	1.0000	1.0000	1.0000	1.0000
11	1.0000	1.0000	1.0000	1.0000	1.0000	1.0000	1.0000
12	1.0000	1.0000	1.0000	1.0000	1.0000	1.0000	1.0000
13	1.0000	1.0000	1.0000	1.0000	1.0000	1.0000	1.0000
14	1.0000	1.0000	1.0000	1.0000	1.0000	1.0000	1.0000
15	1.0000	1.0000	1.0000	1.0000	1.0000	1.0000	1.0000

Appendix D continued

np	2.05	2.10	2.15	2.20	2.25	2.30	2.35
c=
0	0.1287	0.1225	0.1165	0.1108	0.1054	0.1003	0.0954
1	0.3926	0.3797	0.3669	0.3546	0.3425	0.3309	0.3195
2	0.6631	0.6497	0.6361	0.6227	0.6093	0.5961	0.5828
3	0.8479	0.8387	0.8290	0.8193	0.8094	0.7994	0.7891
4	0.9426	0.9379	0.9327	0.9275	0.9220	0.9163	0.9103
5	0.9814	0.9796	0.9773	0.9751	0.9726	0.9701	0.9673
6	0.9947	0.9942	0.9933	0.9925	0.9916	0.9907	0.9896
7	0.9986	0.9986	0.9982	0.9980	0.9977	0.9975	0.9971
8	0.9996	0.9997	0.9995	0.9995	0.9994	0.9994	0.9993
9	0.9998	0.9999	0.9998	0.9999	0.9998	0.9999	0.9999
10	1.0000	1.0000	1.0000	1.0000	1.0000	1.0000	1.0000
11	1.0000	1.0000	1.0000	1.0000	1.0000	1.0000	1.0000
12	1.0000	1.0000	1.0000	1.0000	1.0000	1.0000	1.0000
13	1.0000	1.0000	1.0000	1.0000	1.0000	1.0000	1.0000
14	1.0000	1.0000	1.0000	1.0000	1.0000	1.0000	1.0000
15	1.0000	1.0000	1.0000	1.0000	1.0000	1.0000	1.0000

np	2.40	2.45	2.50	2.60	2.70	2.75	2.80
c=
0	0.0907	0.0863	0.0821	0.0743	0.0672	0.0639	0.0608
1	0.3084	0.2977	0.2873	0.2674	0.2487	0.2397	0.2311
2	0.5697	0.5567	0.5438	0.5184	0.4937	0.4814	0.4695
3	0.7787	0.7682	0.7576	0.7360	0.7142	0.7030	0.6920
4	0.9041	0.8977	0.8912	0.8774	0.8630	0.8553	0.8477
5	0.9643	0.9612	0.9580	0.9509	0.9434	0.9391	0.9349
6	0.9884	0.9871	0.9858	0.9828	0.9796	0.9775	0.9756
7	0.9967	0.9962	0.9957	0.9946	0.9935	0.9926	0.9919
8	0.9992	0.9990	0.9988	0.9984	0.9982	0.9978	0.9976
9	0.9999	0.9998	0.9997	0.9995	0.9996	0.9994	0.9994
10	1.0000	1.0000	1.0000	0.9998	0.9999	0.9998	0.9999
11	1.0000	1.0000	1.0000	1.0000	1.0000	1.0000	1.0000
12	1.0000	1.0000	1.0000	1.0000	1.0000	1.0000	1.0000
13	1.0000	1.0000	1.0000	1.0000	1.0000	1.0000	1.0000
14	1.0000	1.0000	1.0000	1.0000	1.0000	1.0000	1.0000
15	1.0000	1.0000	1.0000	1.0000	1.0000	1.0000	1.0000

Appendix D continued

c=	np	2.90	3.00	3.10	3.20	3.30	3.40	3.50
	0	0.0550	0.0498	0.0450	0.0408	0.0369	0.0334	0.0302
	1	0.2146	0.1992	0.1847	0.1712	0.1586	0.1469	0.1359
	2	0.4460	0.4232	0.4012	0.3799	0.3594	0.3398	0.3209
	3	0.6697	0.6472	0.6249	0.6025	0.5803	0.5584	0.5367
	4	0.8319	0.8152	0.7982	0.7806	0.7626	0.7442	0.7255
	5	0.9259	0.9160	0.9057	0.8946	0.8829	0.8706	0.8577
	6	0.9714	0.9664	0.9612	0.9554	0.9491	0.9422	0.9348
	7	0.9902	0.9880	0.9858	0.9832	0.9803	0.9770	0.9733
	8	0.9970	0.9961	0.9953	0.9943	0.9932	0.9918	0.9902
	9	0.9992	0.9988	0.9986	0.9983	0.9979	0.9974	0.9968
	10	0.9998	0.9996	0.9996	0.9996	0.9995	0.9993	0.9991
	11	1.0000	0.9998	0.9999	0.9999	0.9999	0.9999	0.9998
	12	1.0000	1.0000	1.0000	1.0000	1.0000	1.0000	1.0000
	13	1.0000	1.0000	1.0000	1.0000	1.0000	1.0000	1.0000
	14	1.0000	1.0000	1.0000	1.0000	1.0000	1.0000	1.0000
	15	1.0000	1.0000	1.0000	1.0000	1.0000	1.0000	1.0000

c=	np	3.60	3.70	3.80	3.90	4.00	4.10	4.20
	0	0.0273	0.0247	0.0224	0.0202	0.0183	0.0166	0.0150
	1	0.1257	0.1162	0.1074	0.0991	0.0916	0.0845	0.0780
	2	0.3028	0.2854	0.2689	0.2530	0.2381	0.2238	0.2103
	3	0.5153	0.4941	0.4735	0.4531	0.4335	0.4142	0.3955
	4	0.7065	0.6872	0.6679	0.6482	0.6289	0.6093	0.5899
	5	0.8442	0.8301	0.8156	0.8004	0.7852	0.7693	0.7532
	6	0.9268	0.9182	0.9092	0.8993	0.8894	0.8786	0.8675
	7	0.9693	0.9648	0.9600	0.9544	0.9489	0.9426	0.9361
	8	0.9884	0.9863	0.9841	0.9813	0.9787	0.9754	0.9721
	9	0.9960	0.9952	0.9943	0.9929	0.9919	0.9904	0.9889
	10	0.9988	0.9985	0.9982	0.9974	0.9972	0.9965	0.9960
	11	0.9997	0.9996	0.9995	0.9990	0.9991	0.9988	0.9987
	12	0.9999	0.9999	0.9999	0.9995	0.9997	0.9996	0.9996
	13	1.0000	1.0000	1.0000	1.0000	0.9999	0.9998	0.9999
	14	1.0000	1.0000	1.0000	1.0000	1.0000	1.0000	1.0000
	15	1.0000	1.0000	1.0000	1.0000	1.0000	1.0000	1.0000

Appendix D continued

c=	np	4.30	4.40	4.50	4.60	4.70	4.80	4.90
	0	0.0136	0.0123	0.0111	0.0101	0.0091	0.0082	0.0074
	1	0.0719	0.0663	0.0611	0.0563	0.0518	0.0477	0.0439
	2	0.1973	0.1851	0.1736	0.1626	0.1523	0.1425	0.1333
	3	0.3771	0.3594	0.3423	0.3257	0.3097	0.2942	0.2793
	4	0.5704	0.5511	0.5321	0.5132	0.4946	0.4762	0.4582
	5	0.7366	0.7198	0.7029	0.6857	0.6684	0.6509	0.6335
	6	0.8557	0.8435	0.8310	0.8180	0.8046	0.7907	0.7767
	7	0.9289	0.9213	0.9134	0.9049	0.8960	0.8866	0.8769
	8	0.9682	0.9641	0.9597	0.9549	0.9497	0.9441	0.9383
	9	0.9870	0.9850	0.9829	0.9804	0.9778	0.9748	0.9717
	10	0.9951	0.9942	0.9933	0.9922	0.9910	0.9895	0.9881
	11	0.9983	0.9979	0.9976	0.9971	0.9966	0.9959	0.9954
	12	0.9994	0.9992	0.9992	0.9990	0.9988	0.9985	0.9984
	13	0.9998	0.9997	0.9998	0.9997	0.9996	0.9994	0.9995
	14	1.0000	1.0000	0.9999	0.9999	0.9999	0.9997	0.9999
	15	1.0000	1.0000	1.0000	1.0000	1.0000	1.0000	1.0000

c=	np	5.00	5.25	5.50	5.75	6.00	6.25	6.50
	0	0.0067	0.0052	0.0041	0.0032	0.0025	0.0019	0.0012
	1	0.0404	0.0327	0.0266	0.0215	0.0174	0.0140	0.0091
	2	0.1246	0.1050	0.0884	0.0741	0.0620	0.0517	0.0358
	3	0.2650	0.2316	0.2017	0.1749	0.1512	0.1303	0.0958
	4	0.4405	0.3977	0.3575	0.3199	0.2851	0.2530	0.1971
	5	0.6160	0.5721	0.5289	0.4866	0.4457	0.4064	0.3338
	6	0.7622	0.7247	0.6860	0.6464	0.6063	0.5662	0.4876
	7	0.8666	0.8392	0.8094	0.7776	0.7440	0.7089	0.6359
	8	0.9319	0.9143	0.8943	0.8719	0.8473	0.8204	0.7610
	9	0.9682	0.9581	0.9462	0.9322	0.9161	0.8978	0.8549
	10	0.9863	0.9811	0.9747	0.9669	0.9574	0.9462	0.9183
	11	0.9945	0.9921	0.9890	0.9850	0.9799	0.9737	0.9572
	12	0.9979	0.9969	0.9955	0.9937	0.9912	0.9880	0.9791
	13	0.9992	0.9988	0.9983	0.9975	0.9964	0.9949	0.9905
	14	0.9997	0.9995	0.9994	0.9991	0.9986	0.9980	0.9960
	15	0.9999	0.9998	0.9998	0.9997	0.9995	0.9993	0.9985
	16	1.0000	1.0000	1.0000	0.9999	0.9998	0.9998	0.9995

Appendix D continued

c=	np	7.00	7.25	7.50	7.75	8.00	8.50
	0	0.0009	0.0007	0.0006	0.0004	0.0003	0.0002
	1	0.0073	0.0058	0.0047	0.0037	0.0030	0.0019
	2	0.0296	0.0245	0.0203	0.0166	0.0137	0.0093
	3	0.0817	0.0696	0.0592	0.0500	0.0423	0.0301
	4	0.1729	0.1514	0.1321	0.1147	0.0996	0.0744
	5	0.3006	0.2699	0.2415	0.2151	0.1912	0.1496
	6	0.4496	0.4131	0.3782	0.3447	0.3133	0.2562
	7	0.5986	0.5615	0.5247	0.4882	0.4529	0.3856
	8	0.7290	0.6959	0.6620	0.6272	0.5925	0.5231
	9	0.8304	0.8042	0.7764	0.7469	0.7166	0.6530
	10	0.9014	0.8827	0.8622	0.8397	0.8159	0.7634
	11	0.9466	0.9345	0.9207	0.9051	0.8881	0.8487
	12	0.9729	0.9658	0.9573	0.9473	0.9362	0.9091
	13	0.9871	0.9832	0.9784	0.9725	0.9658	0.9486
	14	0.9942	0.9922	0.9897	0.9864	0.9827	0.9726
	15	0.9975	0.9966	0.9954	0.9936	0.9917	0.9862
	16	0.9989	0.9986	0.9980	0.9971	0.9962	0.9934
	17	0.9995	0.9994	0.9992	0.9987	0.9983	0.9970
	18	0.9997	0.9997	0.9997	0.9994	0.9992	0.9987
	19	1.0000	0.9998	0.9999	0.9997	0.9996	0.9995
	20	1.0000	1.0000	1.0000	1.0000	0.9998	0.9998
	21	1.0000	1.0000	1.0000	1.0000	1.0000	1.0000

Appendix E Critical *F*-values at 95% Confidence

df	1	2	3	4	5	6	7
1	161.40	199.50	215.70	224.60	230.20	234.00	236.80
2	18.51	19.00	19.16	19.25	19.30	19.33	19.35
3	10.13	9.55	9.28	9.12	9.01	8.94	8.89
4	7.71	6.94	6.59	6.39	6.26	6.16	6.09
5	6.61	5.79	5.41	5.19	5.05	4.95	4.88
6	5.99	5.14	4.76	4.53	4.39	4.28	4.21
7	5.59	4.74	4.35	4.12	3.97	3.87	3.79
8	5.32	4.46	4.07	3.84	3.69	3.58	3.50
9	5.12	4.26	3.86	3.63	3.48	3.37	3.29
10	4.96	4.10	3.71	3.48	3.33	3.22	3.13
11	4.84	3.98	3.59	3.36	3.20	3.09	3.01
12	4.75	3.88	3.49	3.26	3.11	3.00	2.91
13	4.67	3.81	3.41	3.18	3.02	2.91	2.83
14	4.60	3.74	3.34	3.11	2.96	2.85	2.76
15	4.54	3.68	3.29	3.06	2.90	2.79	2.71
16	4.49	3.63	3.24	3.01	2.85	2.74	2.66
17	4.45	3.59	3.20	2.96	2.81	2.70	2.61
18	4.41	3.56	3.16	2.93	2.77	2.66	2.58
19	4.38	3.52	3.13	2.89	2.74	2.63	2.54
20	4.35	3.49	3.10	2.87	2.71	2.60	2.51
21	4.32	3.47	3.07	2.84	2.68	2.57	2.49
22	4.30	3.44	3.05	2.82	2.66	2.55	2.46
23	4.28	3.42	3.03	2.80	2.64	2.53	2.44
24	4.26	3.40	3.01	2.78	2.62	2.51	2.42
25	4.24	3.38	2.99	2.76	2.60	2.49	2.40
30	4.17	3.32	2.92	2.69	2.53	2.42	2.33
35	4.12	3.27	2.87	2.64	2.48	2.37	2.28
40	4.08	3.23	2.84	2.61	2.45	2.34	2.25
50	4.03	3.18	2.79	2.56	2.40	2.29	2.20
75	3.97	3.12	2.73	2.49	2.34	2.22	2.13
100	3.94	3.09	2.70	2.46	2.30	2.19	2.10
150	3.90	3.06	2.66	2.43	2.27	2.16	2.07

Appendix E continued

8	9	10	12	15	20	25	30
238.90	240.50	241.90	243.90	245.90	248.00	249.30	250.10
19.37	19.38	19.40	19.41	19.43	19.45	19.46	19.46
8.84	8.81	8.79	8.74	8.70	8.66	8.63	8.62
6.04	6.00	5.96	5.91	5.86	5.80	5.77	5.75
4.82	4.77	4.74	4.68	4.62	4.56	4.52	4.50
4.15	4.10	4.06	4.00	3.94	3.87	3.84	3.81
3.73	3.68	3.64	3.58	3.51	3.44	3.40	3.38
3.44	3.39	3.35	3.28	3.22	3.15	3.11	3.08
3.23	3.18	3.14	3.07	3.01	2.94	2.89	2.86
3.07	3.02	2.98	2.91	2.84	2.77	2.73	2.70
2.95	2.90	2.85	2.79	2.72	2.65	2.60	2.57
2.85	2.80	2.75	2.69	2.62	2.54	2.50	2.47
2.77	2.71	2.67	2.60	2.53	2.46	2.41	2.38
2.70	2.65	2.60	2.53	2.46	2.39	2.34	2.31
2.64	2.59	2.54	2.48	2.40	2.33	2.28	2.25
2.59	2.54	2.49	2.42	2.35	2.28	2.23	2.19
2.55	2.49	2.45	2.38	2.31	2.23	2.18	2.14
2.51	2.46	2.41	2.34	2.27	2.19	2.14	2.11
2.48	2.42	2.38	2.31	2.23	2.16	2.11	2.07
2.45	2.39	2.35	2.28	2.20	2.12	2.07	2.04
2.42	2.37	2.32	2.25	2.18	2.10	2.04	2.01
2.40	2.34	2.30	2.23	2.15	2.07	2.02	1.98
2.38	2.32	2.28	2.20	2.13	2.05	2.00	1.96
2.36	2.30	2.26	2.18	2.11	2.03	1.98	1.94
2.34	2.28	2.24	2.16	2.09	2.01	1.96	1.92
2.27	2.21	2.16	2.09	2.02	1.93	1.88	1.84
2.22	2.16	2.11	2.04	1.96	1.88	1.82	1.79
2.18	2.12	2.08	2.00	1.92	1.84	1.78	1.74
2.13	2.07	2.03	1.95	1.87	1.78	1.73	1.69
2.06	2.01	1.96	1.88	1.80	1.71	1.65	1.61
2.03	1.98	1.93	1.85	1.77	1.68	1.62	1.57
2.00	1.94	1.89	1.82	1.73	1.64	1.58	1.54

Appendix E continued

50	75	100	150
251.80	252.60	253.00	253.50
19.48	19.48	19.49	19.49
8.58	8.56	8.55	8.54
5.70	5.68	5.66	5.65
4.44	4.42	4.40	4.39
3.75	3.73	3.71	3.70
3.32	3.29	3.28	3.26
3.02	2.99	2.98	2.96
2.80	2.77	2.76	2.74
2.64	2.60	2.59	2.57
2.51	2.47	2.46	2.44
2.40	2.37	2.35	2.33
2.31	2.28	2.26	2.24
2.24	2.20	2.19	2.17
2.18	2.14	2.12	2.10
2.12	2.09	2.07	2.05
2.08	2.04	2.02	2.00
2.04	2.00	1.98	1.96
2.00	1.96	1.94	1.92
1.97	1.93	1.91	1.89
1.94	1.90	1.88	1.86
1.91	1.87	1.85	1.83
1.88	1.84	1.82	1.80
1.86	1.82	1.80	1.78
1.84	1.80	1.78	1.76
1.76	1.72	1.70	1.67
1.70	1.66	1.64	1.61
1.66	1.61	1.59	1.56
1.60	1.55	1.52	1.50
1.52	1.47	1.44	1.41
1.48	1.42	1.39	1.36
1.44	1.38	1.34	1.31

Appendix F Critical Values for the Spearman Rank Correlation Coefficient

df	Percent of Confidence (One-Tail) 95%	Percent of Confidence (One-Tail) 99%
4	1.000	—
5	0.900	1.000
6	0.829	0.943
7	0.714	0.893
8	0.643	0.833
9	0.600	0.783
10	0.564	0.746
11	0.536	0.709
12	0.504	0.678
13	0.484	0.648
14	0.464	0.626
15	0.446	0.604
16	0.429	0.582
17	0.414	0.566
18	0.401	0.550
19	0.391	0.535
20	0.380	0.522
21	0.370	0.509
22	0.361	0.498
23	0.353	0.486
24	0.344	0.476
25	0.337	0.466
26	0.331	0.457
27	0.324	0.449
28	0.318	0.440
29	0.312	0.432
30	0.306	0.425
40	0.264	0.368
50	0.235	0.329
60	0.214	0.300
70	0.198	0.278
80	0.185	0.260
90	0.174	0.245
100	0.165	0.233

Index